MANDEVILLE STUDIES

ARCHIVES INTERNATIONALES D'HISTOIRE DES IDEES

INTERNATIONAL ARCHIVES OF THE HISTORY OF IDEAS

81

IRWIN PRIMER

MANDEVILLE STUDIES

NEW EXPLORATIONS IN THE ART AND THOUGHT OF

DR. BERNARD MANDEVILLE

(1670–1733)

Directors: P. Dibon (Paris) and R. Popkin (Washington Univ., St. Louis)
Comité de rédaction: J. Aubin (Paris); J. Collins (St. Louis Univ.); P. Costabel (Paris); A. Crombie (Oxford); I. Dambska (Cracovie); H. de la Fontaine-Verwey (Amsterdam); H. Gadamer (Heidelberg); H. Gouhier (Paris); T. Gregory (Rome); T. E. Jessop (Hull); P. O. Kristeller (Columbia Univ.); Elisabeth Labrousse (Paris); A. Lossky (Los Angeles); S. Lindroth (Upsala); J. Orcibal (Paris); I. S. Révah† (Paris); J. Roger (Paris); H. Rowen (Rutgers Univ., N.J.); C. B. Schmitt (Warburg Institute, London); G. Sebba (Emory Univ., Atlanta); R. Shackleton (Oxford); J. Tans (Groningue); G. Tonelli (Binghamton, N.Y.).

MANDEVILLE STUDIES

NEW EXPLORATIONS IN THE ART AND THOUGHT OF DR. BERNARD MANDEVILLE (1670–1733)

Edited by

IRWIN PRIMER
Rutgers University, Newark

MARTINUS NIJHOFF / THE HAGUE / 1975

ISBN 90 247 1686 1

PRINTED IN THE NETHERLANDS

TABLE OF CONTENTS

INTRODUCTION

For centuries readers have admired the writer who wields his pen like a sword – an Aristophanes, a Rabelais, a Montaigne, a Swift. Using ribaldry, satire and irony in varying proportions, such writers pierce the thick, comfortable hide of society and uncover, predictably, the corruption and hypocrisy that characterize the life of man in commercial society. Though a lesser talent than any of these literary giants, Bernard Mandeville is nevertheless a member of their class. The crucial year in the emergence of his reputation was 1723, the year in which he added his controversial *Essay on Charity and Charity-Schools* to his *Fable of the Bees*. From that point on he became one of the most reviled targets of the public guardians of morality and religion; for some he appeared to be truly the Devil incarnate, Mandevil, as Fielding and others spelled it. This reputation was attached to his name well into the nineteenth century. In a diary entry for June 1812 Henry Crabb Robinson recorded the following conversation with the elderly Mrs. Buller: "She received me with a smile, and allowed me to touch her hand. 'What are you reading, Mr. Robinson?' she said. 'The wickedest cleverest book in the English language, if you chance to know it.' – 'I have known the "Fable of the Bees" more than fifty years.' She was right in her guess." [1]

Only toward the end of the nineteenth century did scholars begin to realize how seminal an influence Mandeville's writings had exerted upon the European Enlightenment. In our century F. B. Kaye almost single-handedly revived Mandeville as one of the most important writers of the eighteenth century. Kaye concluded that "it is doubtful whether a dozen English works can be found in the entire eighteenth century of

---

[1] *Diary, Reminiscences, and Correspondence of Henry Crabb Robinson,* selected and edited by Thomas Sadler, 2 vols. (Boston: Field, Osgood & Co., 1870), I, 252.

such historical importance as *The Fable of the Bees*." [2] Notwithstanding Kaye's significant achievement in re-establishing Mandeville's importance, the "revival" of Mandeville has produced only a trickle of scholarly publications when measured against the explosion of articles and books on his famous contemporaries Swift, Pope and Defoe. There are many reasons for his subordinate position, but perhaps the two most obvious ones are, first, the lack of a tangible personality behind the writings, and second, the fact that Mandeville's major work does not attract the reading multitude in the way that they are captured by *Gulliver's Travels, The Rape of the Lock* or *Robinson Crusoe*.

One of the principles behind the popularity of these three works is simply that readers like and want a story. This Mandeville knew when, having published some translations he had made from the *Fables* of La Fontaine, he set to work on his own animal fable, *The Grumbling Hive* (1705). When he added explanatory prose "remarks" to certain of its lines of verse and renamed the entire work *The Fable of the Bees* (1714), the element of story or plot diminished considerably. Consequently, lacking the delicate wit and charm of Pope's elegant verse, the detailed fantasy of *Gulliver's Travels*, and the suspense and sustained realistic adventure of Crusoe's tale of human survival in a savage wilderness, *The Fable of the Bees* cannot compete with these works because it is a different kind of masterpiece. Though it began as a fable, it was ultimately the explanatory and digressive prose remarks that generated the power and reputation of this gradually-evolved miscellany. With *Gulliver* and *Rape of the Lock* it participates in the ancient traditions and forms of satire. Like *Gulliver, The Fable* has even been classified more specifically as Menippean satire, but such descriptions are exercises in scholarly precision – they are interesting but tell us little about the concrete appeal or the true power of any literary work.[3]

The novel as it happened was to emerge as the dominant instrument for literary expression in our century, a development that Mandeville could not have foreseen. If Menippean satire was indeed the intended form for Mandeville's *Fable*, a supposition which remains conjectural, his other preferred form was the philosophic dialogue. His elected forms for literary expression are thus more remote and strange to the contemporary non-specialist reader than are the forms of *Gulliver's Travels*

[2] F. B. Kaye, ed., *The Fable of the Bees* (Oxford University Press, 1924), I, cxlvi. Abbreviated below to "Kaye."
[3] See George Hind, "Mandeville's *Fable of the Bees* as Menippean Satire," *Genre*, I (1968), 307-15. Hind's interesting essay follows in the path of Northrop Frye's well-known association of *Gulliver's Travels* with Menippean satire.

and *Robinson Crusoe*. The form of *The Fable* is more difficult for the modern reader because it is neither a sustained narrative nor a continuous treatise on man and society. If we couple this with the paucity of biographical information about Dr. Mandeville, we can better understand what has prevented him from being as widely read and admired in later times as Swift, Pope and Defoe. All three had been close to political figures in government and left a trail of publications, private correspondence and other documents that have enabled us to plot the courses of their lives with great detail. All that we know of Mandeville in this regard is that after he had earned his M.D. at Leyden he emigrated to England before 1700 and liked it enough to marry and settle there. In addition to this medical practice (about which we are informed mainly by his *Treatise of the Hypochondriack and Hysterick Passions*, 1711), he also devoted his time to writing and publishing in verse and prose. By the second decade of the eighteenth century he had apparently cultivated the patronage of Sir Thomas Parker, first earl of Macclesfield. A surviving letter from Mandeville to the eminent physician and collector Sir Hans Sloane indicates that they were on friendly terms. The rest is a small collection of anecdotes, not a biography. It is clear that the Mandeville who wrote *Free Thoughts on Religion, the Church, and National Happiness* (1720) was a Whig, but, apart from his association with Lord Macclesfield, what other Whigs had he met and known? [4]

Unless a major body of new biographical evidence appears, it is only the works of Mandeville and not his life that we can hope to know. The biographical entry which was published by Dr. Birch in the 1738 volume of *A General Dictionary* five years after Mandeville's death supplies very few personal details. It is almost entirely a bibliographical record of Mandeville's literary career and of the heated controversy sparked by the 1723 edition of *The Fable of the Bees*.[5] F. B. Kaye did find more bio-

---

[4] Though Mandeville in his later career was clearly a Whig writer and took positions often similar to those of Trenchard and Gordon in *Cato's Letters* and in the *Independent Whig,* he apparently was not, for Professor Caroline Robbins, one of the eighteenth-century commonwealthmen. In her excellent study, *The Eighteenth Century Commonwealthman* (Harvard Univ. Press, 1959; Atheneum paperback, 1968), she cites him twice, in both places only incidentally. The dearth of information regarding his political activity and acquaintance may well have led Dr. Robbins to conclude that he was not sufficiently in the mainstream of English liberal thought. But in view of the evidence of his rather positive attitude toward Shaftesbury in his *Free Thoughts* (1720) and on the basis of his political outlook in that book, it seems to me that he deserved ampler attention in her comprehensive survey of a major stream of political thought.

[5] Thomas Birch, ed. and co-author, *A General Dictionary, Historical and Critical, in which a new and accurate translation of that of the celebrated Mr. Bayle . . . is included. . . .* (London, 1734-41; 10 vols.), VII, 388-95. Birch himself wrote the article on Mandeville.

graphical data, but nothing of a magnitude that would warrant a separate book-length life of Mandeville.[6] Through whatever intended or accidental causes, the *life* of Mandeville has been virtually obliterated from history. We miss both the practicing physician and the writer in his medical, literary and political milieu. The milieu is known in great detail but we cannot see clearly how Mandeville fits into the pattern.

As a result, Mandeville seems to stand alone, and his apparent separation from most other eminent Augustans is an important factor in his reputation (though Pope did include Mandeville as one of the targets of his *Dunciad*, that does not identify Mandeville as a member of a literary-political clique or group). It is difficult to say how much his Dutch background or his medical profession may have to do with his apparent isolation, but it is quite possible that our impression of his isolation results from the outspoken, radical element in his writings. For prudential reasons he generally withheld his name from the title pages of his non-medical English works. Hence the *Presentment of the Grand Jury of Middlesex* in 1723 against the evils allegedly propagated by *The Fable of the Bees* had to be directed not to the author but to his publishers.[7] It was legally impossible to implicate Mandeville, just as it was "impossible" to prove in a courtroom that Swift had written *A Tale of a Tub* or *The Drapier's Letters*. Swift, however, had his eighteenth-century apologists and defenders, including his friend Pope. Because Mandeville's defenders were few and barely visible in print, he gives the impression of maintaining a lonely, isolated position. Whether or not that was indeed Mandeville's lot during his literary career, the lack of published support did not affect the popularity of his *Fable of the Bees*, which was reprinted at intervals until 1806. Not only Dr. Johnson but Fielding, too, had studied him carefully.[8] Mandeville's major work was a book of strong ideas and pungent satire, and what kept it alive throughout the eighteenth century was mainly its status as a subversive document – a book of impiety and immorality. It had to be very superior in its kind to survive as well as it did. The serious thinkers who grappled with his paradoxes – Adam Smith, among others – came away often enough with an indelible impression of the Mandevillean framework of ideas that

[6] Kaye, I, xvii-xxxii.
[7] See Kaye, I, 383-86.
[8] In *Amelia* Fielding set up a weak parody of the Mandevillean view of man's nature in order to have the pleasure of shooting it down. On the other hand, Dr. Johnson, as Boswell reports, did not bear down as heavily on Mandeville as one might have expected but instead delivered a tempered assessment of him. See Boswell's *Life of Johnson* (Oxford Standard Authors edition), 948; the entry is for 15 April 1778.

would continue to influence their own thinking even after they had formally rejected the "errors" of Mandeville. A. O. Aldridge demonstrates below that this holds true for Voltaire, and one must add, it also holds for Montesquieu, Rousseau, Helvétius, d'Holbach and other leaders of the French Enlightenment. The decline of Mandeville's popularity in the nineteenth century, in which full reprints of his works basically halted after 1806, was just that: a decline, not an eclipse. We may attribute that decline more or less to the general devaluation of the Augustan writers known to have occurred in the nineteenth century, but Victorian prudery rather than shifts in literary taste was probably the main cause. Mandeville suffered more from neglect than from ill treatment at the hands of the Victorian pundits; a few serious readers of Mandeville, such as Sir Leslie Stephen, are the exceptions.

In dwelling upon the relationships between his changing reputation on the one hand and the problems of biography and literary form on the other, we ought to add that a special difficulty arises with respect to Mandeville's reputation, for in our time he really has not one reputation but many different ones. While this holds true for Swift and Defoe, they are primarily remembered as *literary* giants, masters in narrative and satire. Swift is also an Irish hero and, like Defoe, he wrote on economic subjects, on population and on women; in addition to Swift's sermons we have his political journalism. Swift's name will always appear in histories of Ireland and England, and Defoe's will predictably turn up in histories of economics and business and in social histories of Britain. Both authors figure also in histories of party journalism, but their highest distinction derives from their achievements in literary art. Though one might wish that this could as easily be predicated of Mandeville, it is obvious that most commentators have been so busy proposing one or another interpretation of his ideas that the question of his literary merit, if not totally ignored, has rarely proceeded beyond the textbook clichés.

Recently, Phillip Harth and other critics have deliberately focused on the literary values in Mandeville's writings, on technique as well as content, in order to rectify the one-sidedness or imbalance of the history-of-ideas approach in F. B. Kaye and some followers.[9] In this newer state of Mandeville criticism he is celebrated as a worthy rival of Swift and Pope, for he, too, is one of the greatest satirists in a great age of satire. Seen in the context of the recent efflorescence of "satire criticism," this latest path

---

[9] See Phillip Harth, "The Satiric Purpose of *The Fable of the Bees*," *Eighteenth*

in Mandeville studies is rather an expected than a surprising one, and the kind of literary encounter with Mandeville that it leads to will surely set a pattern for younger scholars in the next decade. But it is also likely that the study of Mandeville from a history-of-ideas point of view, an approach that is prevalent in most of the essays that follow, will continue to dominate this field.

Mandeville had and continues to have separate reputations: he will continue to mean one thing to the economists, another to the historians of government and political theory, a third to the philosophers and moralists, a fourth to the historians of religion. Though he was important as a theorist throughout the range of the social sciences, no particular social scientist conveys the full range and worth of his achievement. One of the most important presentations of Mandeville by a social scientist is F. A. Hayek's British Academy "Lecture on a Master Mind" (1966), in which Hayek reviews Mandeville's seminal contributions in social theory and concludes with measured praise. Hayek's praise of Mandeville is that he made possible Hume's philosophy of man and society – a weighty compliment in the light of Hayek's estimate of Hume "as perhaps the greatest of all modern students of mind and society. . . ." [10] Though Hayek's approach emphasizes Mandeville's contributions to European social philosophy, he does not altogether ignore Mandeville's role as a satirist but speaks laconically of ". . . that satire on the conceits of a rationalist age which was his initial aim." [11] The implication seems to be that Mandeville began as a satirist and then pursued social theorizing of a graver and more consequential nature. The literary scholars, on the other hand, tend to regard Mandeville as a satirist from the beginning to the end of his literary career. Apparently there will always be readers who are so strongly impressed by Mandeville's doctrines, regarding them either as shocking impieties or as brilliant anticipations of modern concepts, that they cannot or will not consider them in the context of the traditional aims and techniques of literary satire and paradox. On the whole, historians of economic thought have tended to concentrate on Mandeville's ideas in their field, paying little or no regard to his satiric intentions. This is evident in the masterly exposition of Mandeville's

Century Studies, 2 (1969), 321-40; his edition of The Fable of the Bees (Penguin Books, 1970); and the article by Hind, previously cited.

[10] F. A. Hayek, "Dr. Bernard Mandeville," Lecture on a Master Mind series, Proceedings of the British Academy, 52 (London: Oxford U. Press, 1966), 139.

[11] Hayek, 126. Though I have singled out Hayek's lecture here, another important contribution on Mandeville and the social sciences also deserves serious study: Louis Schneider, "Mandeville as Forerunner of Modern Sociology," Journal of the History of the Behavioral Sciences, 6 (1970), 219-30.

economic thought by Nathan Rosenberg and in a few other essays.[12] The most important exception, however, is the interpretation of Mandeville by the late distinguished economist and humanist, Jacob Viner. In his remarks on Mandeville published in 1953 Viner emphasized Mandeville's satire, taking the position that Mandeville's ethical rigorism was a mask employed by Mandeville to disguise his libertinism.[13]

The "reputations" of Mandeville will proceed apace in the different disciplines and keys to the true meaning of Mandeville will be forthcoming. The question of Mandeville's sincerity, broached by Kaye, is still a lively issue. The elucidation of Mandeville's satire will also continue to exercise critical talents, so that we shall eventually learn to recognize the weaknesses and limitations of the satirical way to the true meaning of Mandeville. Indeed, Philip Pinkus now challenges the commonplace assumption that *The Fable of the Bees* falls within the genre of satire. That the moral way to an understanding of Mandeville is not exhausted has been demonstrated by M. J. Scott-Taggart in a closely reasoned essay that regards Mandeville with a philosophic earnestness unrelieved by any recognition of the importance of the tones of paradox and satire in Mandeville's writing.[14] Hayek, interestingly, denounces the moral way as a hindrance: "... though a contribution to our understanding of the genesis of moral rules is part of [Mandeville's] achievement, it appears to me that the fact that he is regarded as primarily a moralist has been the chief obstacle to an appreciation of his main achievement." [15] It is this kind of basic disagreement upon the meaning and value of Mandeville, germane also to his various reputations, that signals the need for fresh assessments of this paradoxical and strangely elusive author.

The contributors to this volume affirm that Bernard Mandeville is "alive" and as paradoxical as ever, and that his stimulating writings are unfortunately still too little known and insufficiently studied. Hopefully the essays here offered will induce readers to return to Mandeville, for his central concerns, the nature of man and the manifold relationships between private morality and the public good or prosperity, are still problematic and even more crucial today than they were in his time.

[12] Nathan Rosenberg, "Mandeville and Laissez-Faire," *Journal of the History of Ideas*, 24 (1963), 183-96.
[13] Jacob Viner, "Introduction" to Mandeville's *A Letter to Dion (1732)*, Augustan Reprint Society, Publication 41 (Los Angeles, 1953), 4-5.
[14] M. J. Scott-Taggart, "Mandeville: Cynic or Fool?" *Philosophical Quarterly*, XVI, 64 (1966), 221-32.
[15] Hayek, 126.

But a band of scholars intent upon elucidating so complex an author as Mandeville cannot expect that as a direct result of their collective efforts Mandeville will shortly become a best-seller. It is sufficient that he was indisputably a best-seller in the eighteenth century. Now, as a confirmed classic, he challenges each generation to rediscover the power of his art and thought.

The occasion that first suggested the desirability of a collection of new essays on Mandeville was the tercentenary of his birth, 1970, but it soon became obvious that the wheels of communal scholarship proceed very slowly. An editor with a master plan for the revaluation of Mandeville's works, sources, influence and contemporary significance will also discover of necessity that such plans are bound to be modified by the whims of his scholars and the ravages of time. The present volume, therefore, has a rather looser organization than was originally intended, but each contributor, on the other hand, had the satisfaction of having a free hand in the execution of his task. By no means do these essays purport to represent a single school of thought or a unified approach to Mandeville. What is offered is a miscellany or a garland, and it takes into account the interests of more than one intellectual discipline. The learned reader who knows his Mandeville well and therefore deplores the gaps in our coverage is forewarned: these essays are perhaps the latest word on Mandeville, but surely not the last. Some of the essayists in this collection tend to be more comprehensive in their scale of inquiry, but all bring something new to the study of Mandeville or explore known territory more deeply.

IN MEMORIAM

We have already mentioned Jacob Viner as among the leading interpreters of Mandeville in our time. His death on September 12, 1970, at an early stage in the growth of this volume, prevented us from receiving his intended contribution, and his valuable guidance on this growing collection was no longer available. A few of the contributors who were fortunate enough to have met him acknowledge his contagious enthusiasm not only for Mandeville but for intellectual inquiry limited to no single author or historical movement. The others have known and admired Viner in his works. Because it is never too late to offer one's respects to the memory of such a man, it is hoped that this collection will stand among the many tributes to him, tributes that he so well deserved.

It is a sad task, also, to record the death of one of our contributors, Dr. John Robert Moore, on July 18, 1973. He had retired from Indiana University with the title Distinguished Service Professor Emeritus of English after having earned an international reputation as one of the foremost students of the life and writings of Defoe. His posthumous essay on Defoe and Mandeville, deceptively brief and modest, reveals how well he was able to draw upon his vast reserves of learning to illuminate a narrowly defined problem.

ON SOME OF MANDEVILLE'S MINOR WRITINGS

BERNARD MANDEVILLE'S *THE VIRGIN UNMASK'D*

GORDON S. VICHERT

Bernard Mandeville's fame rests firmly on *The Fable of the Bees*, largely because this book created such a scandal in the eighteenth century. F. B. Kaye's edition of *The Fable*, a masterpiece of scholarly editing, is readily available, and so *The Fable* remains the one work of Mandeville's that most students of the period have read, or at least glanced at. But much of Mandeville's work was not denounced from eighteenth-century pulpits, and so never acquired the fame of *The Fable of the Bees*. Thus, by an irony which the Augustan clergy would have deplored, we can now read the less offensive books only when we visit the great libraries. This is a pity, because Mandeville would certainly be more highly regarded in histories of literature if his works were better known.

My purpose in this paper is to do a little missionary work for Mandeville by describing his earliest prose work in English, *The Virgin Unmask'd*, a book of two hundred pages, published in 1709 and reprinted once only, in 1724, presumably to capitalize on the notoriety of *The Fable of the Bees*. It is a moral dialogue devoted largely to a defense of feminism, but by an initial Mandevillean irony the unsuspecting male book-buyer is tricked into anticipating a work of pornography.

In the first place, the dialogues are between an elderly woman and a young virgin, her niece. This was a standard convention; as D. F. Foxon reminds us, in speaking of that archetypal work of pornography, the *Ragionamenti* of Aretino, "the form they take – a dialogue between an older and a younger woman – is one which remained the norm for at least 150 years." [1] More immediately in everyone's mind than Aretino was doubtless Nicolas Chorier's *Satyra Sotadica*, first published in 1660, which has some claim to being the most obscene product of the seven-

---

[1] "Libertine Literature in England, 1660-1745," Part II, *The Book Collector,* XII, ii (Summer, 1963), p. 165.

teenth-century pornographic tradition, if only because of the diversity of sexual activity it describes, and the frankness of its appeal to the salacious. The first English translation, according to Professor Foxon, was *A Dialogue between a Married Lady and a Maid*, in 1688, which was followed by another, *The School of Love containing severall dialogues between Tullia and Octavia*, published in 1707, just two years before *The Virgin Unmask'd*. The notoriety of *The School of Love* was guaranteed by the prosecution of its publisher, John Marshall.

The reader of *The School of Love* would be instantly attracted by Mandeville's title-page: "The Virgin Unmask'd: or, Female Dialogues Betwixt an Elderly Maiden Lady, and her Niece, On several Diverting Discourses on Love, Marriage, Memoirs, and Morals, &c. of the Times." Any browser caught by this title-page who turned to the text would find a highly promising beginning:

> *Lucinda.* Here, Niece, take my Handkerchief, prithee now, if you can find nothing else to cover your Nakedness; if you knew what a Fulsome Sight it was, I am sure you would not go so bare: I cann't abide your Naked Breasts heaving up and down; it makes me Sick to see it.[2]

But alas for the salaciously-minded; Mandeville frustrates his expectations completely. The first dialogue of *The Virgin Unmask'd* is devoted to a bitter argument between Lucinda and Antonia, her niece, over the extent to which Antonia should follow current fashions in exposing her bosom. The discussion is perfectly frank – Mandeville is never guilty of euphemisms – but no more licentious than the first paragraph. With the second dialogue even the slight titillation caused by Antonia's bosom is abandoned, and the succeeding conversations are devoted to perfectly serious, though often witty discussions of a wide range of topics, chiefly concerned with marriage and the role of women in society.

The Virgin Unmask'd is part of a large body of controversial writing about the role of women. Throughout the Restoration women in literature tended to be treated cynically, as sources of pleasure but also of trouble. The designing, money-grubbing, hypocritical female is a stock figure. Francis Osborne's *Advice to a Son*, one of the most popular books of the time, presents the archetype:

> Our Beldame *Eve*, to save her longing, sold us all for an Apple; and still as we fall into the same desires, *apprehending Felicities in things we never tryed*, we are carried away by her peevish *Daughters*, the true *Syrens* wise

---

[2] *The Virgin Unmask'd*, 2nd edition (London, 1724), p. 1.

Ulysses stopt his Ears against, who under Pretence of Pleasure and Love, lead us into Dens and obscure Holes of the Rocks, where we consume our pretious Time and bury our Parts.[3]

The many translations of *Les Quinze Joyes de Mariage*, which describes fifteen ways in which wives make their husbands miserable, also exploited the popular cynicism about women. Restoration comedy, of course, was not behindhand in using the same theme. This cynicism may not have run very deep, but the actual content of these attacks hardly mattered. It is the attitude which is significant, an attitude which finds nothing interesting in women themselves, except as they affect men. The analysis of feminine nature which we find in *Moll Flanders*, and later in *Pamela*, was still years away.

The defenders of women were little better; they willingly accepted feminine subservience. Nahum Tate, for example, imagined that he was being an ardent feminist when he said that "there is generally such a Sincerity conspicuous in the Female, as appears to be the natural Result of their Temper: They are formed to Cherish and Relieve, and while they are dispensing Benefits, they seem but auspicious Planets acting in their proper Sphere." [4] As the Marquis of Halifax smugly told his daughter: "We are made of differing *Tempers*, that our Defects may the better be mutually supplied: Your *Sex* wanteth our *Reason* for your *Conduct*, and our *Strength* for your *Protection*: Ours wanteth your *Gentleness* to soften, and to entertain us." [5] Even Mary Astell, vehement though she was in defence of her sex, saw no alternative for the married woman but total subservience to her husband: "She then who Marrys ought to lay it down for an indisputable Maxim, that her Husband must govern absolutely and intirely, and that she has nothing else to do but to Please and Obey." [6] When Mandeville discusses the role of women in *The Virgin Unmask'd*, therefore, he is embarking on a subject fraught with preconceived notions. The common sense and perceptiveness of his observations is thus all the more remarkable.

Mandeville makes the spinster aunt, Lucinda, one who mortally detests all men, while her niece, Antonia, cannot conceal "that there is something in my Heart, that pleads for Man in general." [7] Lucinda's is the rational, philosophic mind; she insists that "I always was so un-

---

[3] *The Works*, 9th edition (London, 1689), p. 34.
[4] *A Present for the Ladies*, 2nd edition (London, 1693), p. 22.
[5] [George Savile, Marquis of Halifax], *The Lady's New-Year's Gift: or, Advice to a Daughter*, 5th edition (London, 1696), p. 27.
[6] *Reflections upon Marriage*, 3rd edition (London, 1706), p. 56.
[7] *Virgin Unmask'd*, p. 29.

natural, as to deny my Appetite what my Reason told me would hurt me, tho' my Inclination was never so strong," [8] and thus she provides the epitome of Mandevillean virtue in contrast to Antonia's passion.

Despite Lucinda's admiration for reason, however, she admits that women cannot match wits with men, and that as soon as a man is allowed to use rational arguments, he can overcome any woman. This is not because of any intrinsically feminine defect, however; women are in this unfortunate position because of man's skilful management. As Lucinda says:

No, Niece, she that listens to them, is ruined, and her Liberty is lost. In Reasoning, Women can never cope with Men, They have a Thousand Advantages beyond us; our Wit may be equal with theirs, but in every Thing else they exceed us, as well as in Strength of Body; it is thought sufficient, if a Woman can but Read and Write, we receive no other Education, as to Learning: But where we leave off, they set out; they are not trusted to manage their own Affairs, before they are sent to Schools, and Universities, to have their Intellectuals mended and sharpen'd: not by one Master, or by ordinary Men, but by several, that are picked and culled out of Thousands, for excelling every one in his own Profession; here they have the Quintessence of Arts and Sciences, Politicks, and Worldly Cunning infused into them; and for Seven or Eight Years, all manner of Knowledge, as it were, beat into their Brain, with all the Application imaginable, whilst we are pricking a Clout.[9]

According to Lucinda, and Mandeville, therefore, women have no intrinsic inferiority to men; their practical inferiority is only the result of poor education.

It is Lucinda's contention that only education can make women equal, and by that she does not mean the kind of education women were traditionally supposed to receive. As she says of a typical boarding school education for girls, "there they may be taught to Sing and Dance, to Work and Dress, and if you will, receive good Instructions for a Genteel Carriage, and how to be Mannerly; but these Things chiefly concern the Body, the Mind remains uninstructed." [10] Lucinda has great contempt for the traditional womanly crafts, and would replace them with studies hitherto strictly the monopoly of men:

I have read several Books of Physick, and abundance of things, that Women seldom trouble their Heads with; but I always was of Opinion, that in knowing the World, was comprehended the understanding of one's self;

[8] *Virgin Unmask'd*, p. 113.
[9] *Virgin Unmask'd*, p. 27.
[10] *Virgin Unmask'd*, p. 48.

and think, that the Study of *Anatomy*, and the inward Government of our Bodies, is as diverting and fully of as much use, as the contriving, and making the best order'd, and most exact Piece of Fillegrew Work, that ever was seen; and I'm sure, what I know of the first, has not cost me half the Time, that I have known People, when I was young, bestow upon the latter.[11]

Self-knowledge, the understanding of the true sources of one's actions: this is the ideal towards which Mandeville is constantly urging us to aspire, not only in *The Virgin Unmask'd*, but in *The Fable of the Bees* and indeed in all his writings. Self-knowledge is the only truly liberating form of knowledge; as he reminds us in *An Essay on Charity and Charity-Schools*, this knowledge must be denied to those whom we wish to keep in a subservient position. If women are to escape this position they must become educated enough to acquire insight.

And yet Mandeville knows that very few women will ever be rational enough to escape the slavery of marriage, with its enforced subservience to the husband. As he makes Antonia exclaim to her aunt, "It is a wonder, that since you have been so curious, in examining all these things that belongs [sic] to Men and Women, it never came into your Head, to confirm your Knowledge by Experience." Lucinda's reply, considering her former plea for knowledge, is weak: "I hate Experiments that are dangerous, and would rather be ignorant in some things, than run mad for knowing too much." [12] Mandeville makes Antonia hit unwittingly upon a degree of self-knowledge denied even to the philosophical Lucinda. Antonia can admit all Lucinda's arguments, and yet be aware that she must try the experiment; in the end her passion will overcome her reason. Self-knowledge, Mandeville implies, is most truly liberating when it makes us understand clearly the power of our passions. Dr. Johnson's philosopher in *Rasselas*, confronted by the death of his daughter, says, "What comfort . . . can truth and reason afford me? Of what effect are they now, but to tell me that my daughter will not be restored?" Lucinda, like the philosopher, can be cool and rational until faced with the real feelings of Antonia, but then philosophy is no longer enough. Mandeville always gives Lucinda the best of the argument, and yet he makes it perfectly plain that with Antonia she can never prevail. The moral is obvious; we must all see ourselves as clearly and logically as we can, but must not expect such insight to make any real difference in our behaviour. The most we can hope for is to be freed of our illusions.

[11] *Virgin Unmask'd*, p. 111.
[12] *Virgin Unmask'd*, p. 111.

The common illusions of contemporary popular fiction are those which *The Virgin Unmask'd* sets about most vigorously to destroy. The novel of the time was almost always concerned with a love intrigue, and usually with one of two kinds. The first kind of plot is one in which the pure love of the hero and heroine is frustrated by a series of obstacles, often financial, until finally all difficulties are overcome and they are able to marry, thus presumably entering upon a state of bliss unconfined. This type of story exists in the exotic and improbable romances which were still extremely popular, but it had also been domesticated in familiar novels which often had a certain psychological penetration. In Congreve's contribution to this genre, *Incognita*, he makes the distinction between the older romance and the more modern novel:

Novels are of a more familiar nature; Come near us, and represent to us Intrigues in practice, delight us with Accidents and odd Events, but not such as are wholly unusual or unpresidented, [sic] such which not being so distant from our Belief bring also the pleasure nearer us. Romances give more of Wonder, Novels more Delight.[13]

Both romances and novels, however, were concerned with "Intrigues in practice" and were thus restricted by fairly rigid conventions. Mandeville's rebellion against the psychological falsity of these artificial conventions is expressed by Lucinda as she relates one of the tales in *The Virgin Unmask'd*:

Had I been telling you a Romance, I would have made use of Art; I know as well as you, Niece, what should have been done according to their Rules. . . . But in a true Story, we must relate things as they happen.[14]

The obstacle-strewn love intrigue which culminates in marriage was, however, only one of two main themes in Augustan fiction. The other was in a direct descent from medieval romance, but by the Restoration had become anti-romantic and cynical in tone. This was the tale of illicit love, usually of a married woman and her lover. The themes of deception and intrigue predominated, with the cuckolded husband usually treated as a figure of fun, or else as the epitome of all mankind caught in the toils of sinful Eve. The remote lady of ravishing beauty and her pining knightly lover rarely appear; the atmosphere is much more that of the *fabliau* than of the heroic romance. Rarely is there any attempt at psy-

---

[13] *Incognita or Love and Duty Reconcil'd*, ed. H. F. B. Brett-Smith (Oxford, 1922), p. 5.
[14] *Virgin Unmask'd*, p. 79.

chological realism; the sinning wife is usually pictured simply as a woman who enjoys participating in what is essentially a game of deception, or else as a harlot who receives the retribution due to her.

Mandeville gives Lucinda two lengthy stories to tell in *The Virgin Unmask'd*, one of each of these types. In each case he tries to show what the implications of such behaviour in real life would be, particularly for the woman.

The first story compresses the courtship of Aurelia and Dorante, the obstacles placed in their way by Aurelia's parents, and their elopement to Chester all into just three pages. This is the point at which most romances would end, but Mandeville goes on for fifty-six pages more to trace the consequences in marital life of such a tempestuous romance. Because Aurelia conforms to the romantic convention of love at first sight, she has no opportunity of acquiring any real knowledge of Dorante. Because she disobeys her parents, again in best romantic fashion, she is left with nowhere to go when Dorante begins to treat her cruelly. In "an Age in which nothing went down but Pastime and Pleasure, and few Vertues were allowed of, but Valour and Good Humour," [15] Dorante is a typical rake, interested only in Aurelia's money. When the money is not forthcoming, Dorante first tries to prostitute Aurelia, and then, when this scheme fails, forces her to live with his mother in a servitude little better than that of a housemaid. Dorante is increasingly brutal to Aurelia, and finally his cruelty causes the death of their son, which in turn, because it deprives Dorante of an heir, causes Aurelia to be even more harshly treated. Only Dorante's death in a duel finally releases her to begin life again.

Mandeville tells this story with great attention to Aurelia's feelings, but without sentimentalising her. She could easily have become a kind of patient Griselda, but Mandeville refuses to allow her any particular virtue. As Lucinda says, "All is not Gold that glisters; many things are done daily, for which People are extoll'd to the Skies, that at the same time, tho' the Actions are good, would be blamed as highly, if the Principle from which they acted, and the Motive that first induc'd them, were throughly [sic] known." [16] Aurelia's suffering is the consequence of "her Superlative Love to *Dorante*: He was Quality, Riches, Honour, he was every thing to her; she doated upon him so excessively, that she thought there was no Bliss without him." [17] Lucinda reminds us that.

---

[15] *Virgin Unmask'd*, p. 45.
[16] *Virgin Unmask'd*, p. 66.
[17] *Virgin Unmask'd*, p. 67.

If it had been a Principle of Virtue she acted by, she would have let him
know, that she dislik'd the horrid Doctrine which he Preach'd to her; but
she never so much as shewed herself of another Opinion: All what came
from him was diverting and pleasing to her, without ever consulting the
Morality or Immorality of what he said or did, if he appear'd but Gay and
Good Humour'd.[18]

Mandeville is concerned to show the extravagance of Aurelia's love
for Dorante, a love which survives months of cruelty and only ceases
completely after the death of her son. This love is the source of her
suffering; Mandeville never suggests that Aurelia is punished for her
love, but neither will he admit that her suffering is morally commendable. Dorante is an obvious villain, and Aurelia's passion for him brings
her to grief. Both husband and wife are the victims of their passions;
Mandeville sees tragedy here, but no virtue. Even if Dorante had been
entirely admirable, Aurelia's love for him would not have been a virtue.
In a foreshadowing of the ethical ideas which he later developed more
explicitly in *The Fable of the Bees*, Mandeville argues that gratification
of one's passions can be harmless, and even sometimes beneficial, but
never virtuous.

The second story starts with an account of the love between Leonora
and Cleander, a love which is frustrated by Cleander's father, who exiles
Cleander and then starts a rumour that he is dead. When Leonora hears
this she marries for security, only to be discovered by Cleander, back
from exile, shortly after her marriage. Her virtue, however, is so great
that she sends Cleander away. Meanwhile her husband, Alcandor, whom
she does not love, brings a boarder, Mincio, to the house. Mincio is intent
upon seducing Leonora, but he feigns total indifference towards her for
a long period, during which time he wins her affection by his kindnesses.
Then he fakes an illness, and when he seems near death he admits to
Leonora that only she can cure his illness. She is on the point of yielding
to him when the story breaks off.

It is at this point that *The Virgin Unmask'd* ends as well. The final
words are Lucinda's to Antonia, "Consult your Pillow upon it, and to
Morrow you shall know all." This promise of things to come represented
Mandeville's intention as well; in the first edition he remarked in his
preface, "By leaving the Story of *Leonora* unfinished, you may expect I
intend to go on." In later editions he was more explicit: "By leaving the
Story of *Leonora* unfinished, it might have been expected these Dialogues
should have been continued, as 'tis hoped they will, when the Story of

18 *Virgin Unmask'd*, p. 67.

Leonora will be compleated, and the Character of *Mincio* will be added."
There is no record, however, of any steps by Mandeville to fulfil his
intention.

The significance of these two stories, however, is clear enough. In the
story of Aurelia Mandeville shows the kind of suffering that can result
from a conventionally romantic courtship, and demonstrates also that the
easy black and white categories of virtue and evil in most romances are
highly misleading. In the story of Leonora he reveals the kind of mental
suffering that a conventional seduction plot can cause to a virtuous
woman. Paradoxically, the faithful wife Aurelia is shown to be not really
virtuous, while Leonora, who is left on the verge of cuckolding her husband, has far more of what Mandeville would define as virtue.

The moral judgment in these two stories remains somewhat tentative;
Mandeville is still some distance from the straight moralising of *The
Fable of the Bees*. Nevertheless, his desire to show the facts of marriage
from a woman's point of view emerges clearly. Various male attitudes
are suggested and compared with the truth. Against the romantic notion
of courtship is put the suffering of Aurelia, a suffering which is the more
genuine because it is complicated by conflicting emotions. Against the
wiles of Mincio, which in most stories would have been used to demonstrate his masculine ingenuity is put the real mental distress of Leonora.
The conversations of Lucinda and Antonia as well, with their conflict of
age and youth, rationalism and impetuosity, suggest some of the emotion-
al conflict which must face all women contemplating marriage. But
perhaps the greatest blow to conventional male thinking lies in the tantal-
izing title-page. The reader is invited to think that he is getting one more
account of women purely as machines for sensual pleasure, until by a
supreme Mandevillean irony he finds himself linked with Dorante and
Mincio as the cause of genuine suffering to real women.

Mandeville's desire to destroy male illusions about the life women
really lead is perhaps best shown by his detailed description of pregnancy.
In all contemporary fiction conception and pregnancy, provided they
are legitimate, are treated as happening automatically and blissfully.
Children are born, sometimes mothers die in childbirth, but otherwise
the nine months before birth are passed over in silence. Mandeville, the
physician, refuses to allow the real suffering of women to be ignored. He
makes Lucinda describe at length the pains and miseries of pregnancy,
and then suggest some of the long-range effects:

I have not spoke of the Faintings, Cramps, the intollerable Headachs, and
violent Cholicks, that are so familiar to them: I have not told ye what Multi-

tudes, tho' they survive, are made miserable, nor mention'd the Unskilfulness and Neglect of Midwifes, or the lingring Distempers and lesser Ailments, that attend some Women as long as they live: But if this they escape, the Skin will be wrinkled, the little Capillary Veins, that are so ornamental to it, must be broke in many Places; the Flesh be loosen'd, the Ligaments relax'd, the Joynts be stiffen'd, and made unactive: This perhaps you may slight, but be assured, that the Bearing, as well as Bringing forth of Children, wastes Women, wears 'em, shakes, spoils, and destroys the very Frame and Constitution of them.[19]

It is this anxiety to give the truth, to show what the condition of women is really like, in contrast to the various popular representations of them, that remains the most important aspect of *The Virgin Unmask'd*. To reveal this truth, Mandeville describes four women, Lucinda, Antonia, Aurelia, and Leonora, with a psychological insight that makes them far more credible than most of their contemporary fictional counterparts. Ian Watt, in trying to define the novel, says that it "is surely distinguished from other genres and from previous forms of fiction by the amount of attention it habitually accords both to the individualisation of its characters and to the detailed presentation of their environment." [20] Mandeville spends no time on environment, but by deliberately breaking down fictional stereotypes he creates four highly individualised women and thus anticipates the techniques of novelists to come. Historians of the novel would do well to pay some attention to *The Virgin Unmask'd*.

---

[19] *Virgin Unmask'd*, p. 110.
[20] *The Rise of the Novel* (London, 1957), p. 17.

MANDEVILLE AND EUROPE: MEDICINE AND PHILOSOPHY

G. S. Rousseau

Bernard Mandeville, who was born about 1670 in Holland and died in 1733 in London, remains one of the lesser known among the figures of European intellectual history. Virtually nothing of substance is known about his life except that he studied medicine in Leyden in the 1680's, and later settled for unknown reasons in London where he never acquired a practice or a reputation (save as an habitué of drinking places). A lack of extant documents and the further unlikelihood that any will ever come to light, cast a permanent shadow on the possibility of knowing the man firsthand.[1] Whatever renown he thus far possesses rests upon a single iconoclastic work, *The Fable of the Bees*, published in 1714, a large Hobbesian tome attempting to prove systematically that 'private vice is public good' and that the whole social order rests upon this rudimentary but quintessential principle. Fourteen other published works are attributed to Mandeville, all relatively brief and inconsequential except one, *A Treatise of Hypochondriack and Hysterick Passions*, first published in 1711.[2] This work of 280 quarto pages has gone unnoticed and unappreci-

[1] The available sources are very few; there are less than a dozen letters revealing almost nothing, no diaries, journals, or commonplace books, and no biography other than the brief life in the *DNB* and in F. B. Kaye's introduction to his scholarly edition of *The Fable of the Bees* (Oxford: The Clarendon Press, 1924, 2 vols.). The legend that Mandeville's commonplace book is extant and housed in the library of the Earl of Macclesfield in Oxfordshire has now been disproved by G. S. Rousseau in "Bernard Mandeville and the First Earl of Macclesfield," *Notes and Queries,* Vol. 18 n.s. (1971), p. 335. If Mandeville's biographical statements in the *Treatise* are true, this adds considerably to our meagre knowledge about him. See below, n. 6.

[2] In London by Dryden Leach, "in Elliot's Court, in the Little-Old-Baily, and W. Taylor, at the Ship in Pater-Noster-Row." Although Dryden Leach was a well-known London printer (see Plomer, *Dictionary of the Printers and Booksellers... in England 1726-1775,* Oxford: Oxford University Press, 1932, p. 151), nothing is known about the circumstances of publication of Mandeville's *Treatise*. According to records in the Stationers' Hall it was entered against the name of "B. de Mandeville Feb. 27 1710/11," his only work listed there.

ated for two and a half centuries but for a brief word of praise from Dr. Johnson,[3] and while its contents are not nearly so radical as those of *The Fable*, its obscurity among medical historians remains somewhat perplexing.[4] No one of any import, it seems, has actually deemed it worth reading.

The *Treatise* is cast in the form of three dialogues between a physician Philopirio and his patient Misomedon; Misomedon's wife Polytheca, their daughter, and a druggist named Pharmaenio also enter into the dialogue as minor figures, but the first two, physician and patient, are the main characters. Misomedon, as well as his wife and daughter, suffers from the hyp,[5] but he is also manic-depressive and undergoing male menopause; Philopirio, the model of a competent physician and Mandeville's mouthpiece,[6] attempts to cure all three conditions. In the dénouement of this doctor-patient plot, Philopirio has prescribed such an extensive program of remedies that Misomedon, having promised to abide by his advice, is kept too busy doing so to contemplate his aches and pains. Philopirio doubtlessly espouses Mandeville's own beliefs. However, since absolutely nothing is known about Mandeville as a physician,

[3] James Boswell, *The Life of Samuel Johnson, LL. D.* (London, 1791), 2 vols., II, p. 107.

[4] Both in conventional medical histories and works solely devoted to the history of hypochondriasis. Here one could compile a long list of important secondary works that omit it.

[5] Abbreviated form of hypochondriasis used in the eighteenth century in common parlance and throughout this paper.

[6] No reason exists to disbelieve Mandeville's statement in the preface, p. xi: "In these Dialogues, I have done the same as *Seneca* did in his *Octavia,* and brought my self upon the Stage; with this difference, that he kept his own Name, and I changed mine for that of Philopirio, a Lover of Experience, which I shall always profess to be; Wherefore I desire my Reader to take whatever is spoke by the Person I name last, as said by my self." Even the author's vigorous irony and calculated rhetoric of understatement should not lead us to distrust this important remark. Nor should his disclosures about his father's medical practice in Holland and the social standing of his family be discredited, a significant utterance because so little is known about Mandeville's family background: "The two Populous Cities there meant, are *Amsterdam* and *Rotterdam*; in the latter of which, the Physician mention'd in the same Place, lived in Repute above Thirty Years, and for the greatest part of that time in Request among the better sort of People than any other; as no body can be ignorant of, that lived there before the Year 92, and knew any thing at all" (p. xii). If Mandeville's statement about his own career as a physician is true, then we perhaps ought to revise our conception of his medical practice: "Mine [my thesis] was *de Chylosi vitiata,* which I defended at Leyden in the Year 1691, Dr. *William Senguerdus,* Professor of the Aristotelian Philosophy, being then *Rector Magnificus.* My reason of telling you this, which otherwise might seem impertinent, is because I have often thought it very remarkable, that I always had a particular Eye upon, and have been led, as it were, by instinct to what afterwards appear'd to be the cause of the Hysteric and Hypochondriack Passions, even at a time, when I had no thought of singling out these Distempers for my particular Study, and was only design'd for general Practice, as other Physicians are" (p. 121).

it is futile to pursue this approach as a strategy for explication and interpretation. The Misomedon family, on the other hand, are *hypochondriaci*, all suffering from the conventional symptoms: fits, flutters, flushes, indigestion, heart pain, headaches, sore eyes, and of course wild flights of imagination and bizarre dreams.

Thus far nothing indicates that the *Treatise* deserves more attention than dozens of other similar works written throughout the seventeenth and eighteenth centuries in England and on the Continent; and even Mandeville's flair for language, his quick wit and biting satire, cannot compensate, one may well argue, for a lack of new material on the matter. After all, both hypochondriasis and hysteria were prevalent, popular diseases and by 1700 enough ink had flowed about both to render still another book on the subject gratuitous – *liber non grata*. Ever since the Renaissance and probably before then, physicians, surgeons, barbers, apothecaries, empirics, quacks, nurses, and even handmaidens had prescribed for this curiously nebulous ailment which few understood and even fewer could cure; by 1700 one became afflicted with it almost as readily as one contracts a cold upon exposure to wintry rains and slush – with the foreknowledge that both are unpleasant and that do what one may they will again return. At least from the time of Burton's prescriptions in the *Anatomy* to the giant moneymaking cures of the eighteenth century, every pill and potion, powder and water, had failed.[7] Why then, one might ask, concern oneself with a single treatise about the hyp? Merely because it was written by the heterodox Mandeville? Surely this answer will not suffice as a valid reason for considering the work important or even of mild interest to the history of medicine.

Nonetheless other reasons exist, not all of them immediately apparent on a first reading. For example, from the Renaissance to the nineteenth century the literature of hyponchondria, especially in England, is an impoverished literature.[8] Few, if any, works contain the substance of Burton's and most are like Sir John Hill's treatise of 1766, a paltry and hastily written handbook of sixty pages professing to be a *vade mecum*

---

[7] In the sense that only incidental, fortuitous cure was obtained; obviously the problem is somewhat circular: one can't cure a condition that one knows little about.

[8] On several counts: (1) as well-written literature; (2) insofar as it deals with its ostensible subject of discourse; (3) regarding originality and the relationship of intuition and execution of such intuition; (4) in the degree to which it plundered and plagiarised from other authors; and most important, (5) in taking itself far too seriously to permit truly spontaneous flashes. Some sense of this literature may be found in Ilza Vieth, *Hysteria, The History of a Disease* (Chicago: University of Chicago Press, 1964); John Sena's recent bibliographical survey of works on melancholy 1600-1800; and Lawrence Babb, *The Elizabethan Malady: A Study in Melancholia in English Literature from 1580 to 1642* (East Lansing, Michigan State College, 1951).

for the patient but in fact a parade of the author's own penchant for spleenwort, root of valerian, bardana, and other ineffective herbs he was then growing in his lucrative garden at Bayswater.[9] Mandeville's treatise rises far above such works by taking its subject more seriously and by investigating the relation of melancholy to non-medical aspects of culture generally. In both areas Mandeville was ahead of his time, and if his argument is not propounded with the same brilliant originality one discovers in *The Fable*, also a dialogue, this can be held against him only to a degree since he was politically radical and medically conservative. For the purposes of clarity and brevity I have summed up his achievement, at least as it appears to me, in ten distinct categories: [10]

1. Definition

Mandeville believes that the *condition*, hardly a single disease, encompasses so many different symptoms and courses of treatment that it is meta-definitional. He therefore indicates at considerable length why hypochondria or hysteria cannot be reduced to a *single* disease, and he never hazards definitions that would be inordinately simple-minded and clinically reductionistic to knowledgeable men; but unlike most other writers, he is nevertheless acutely sensitive to the definitional problem, one not altogether dissimilar from that attached to neurosis in this century.[11] So many medical authors of his period adhered to the old conception of hyp as a *single* ailment, pasteurized, homogenized, and packaged, as it were, into one entity that Mandeville's treatise stands out like a solitary tower. Precisely why the hyp evolved into the English malady *par excellence* is another matter; [12] what counts here is Mandeville's

---

[9] See G. S. Rousseau, *Sir John Hill: The Life of a London Literary Quack,* 1975 forthcoming, chap. vi, "Hill's Herbal Remedies."

[10] Obviously there are others, for example Mandeville's indebtedness to other writers, but extensive revision of these sections has persuaded me that these categories are the most important.

[11] Every psychiatrist or historian of twentieth-century psychological jargon will agree with this observation, that a distinction must be drawn. The term neurotic poses vast definitional problems as soon as it is brought, as it were, into the realm of society: for example, society considers it "neurotic" to be a "neurotic compulsive worker," yet the question is begged whether that so-called neurotic condition is any more neurotic than equally irrational modes of mass behaviour, such as the cigarette smoking condoned by much of society. How then does one adequately define neurotic? Similar difficulties exist for the term hypochondriacal or melancholic at the turn of the eighteenth century, a term which by then had become so various in its meanings that Mandeville saw the urgent need for a discrimination of "hyps," or barring that, the meaninglessness of the term altogether. See *Treatise*, p. 210 ff.

[12] Some reasons have been offered by Cecil A. Moore in *Backgrounds of English Literature, 1700-1760* (Minneapolis, University of Minnesota Press, 1953).

grasp of it as a complex system of behavioural conditions arising from a large number of different sources, not merely the usual ones, such as solitude, a sedentary life, excessive reading, and so forth.

2. Curability versus Incurability

Something of a paradox exists here: the titlepage advertises the *Treatise* as one "in which the Symptoms, Causes, and Cures of those [hypochondriacal] Diseases are set forth after a Method intirely new," as if to suggest that cure exists, and yet Philopirio makes it perfectly clear that no real cure exists at all.[13] Whatever the name given to the cluster of conditions or variety of ailments designated by the term hypochondriasis, Mandeville believes that most, if not all, cases are virtually hopeless. The term 'incurable' is actually used (p. 200) and there can be no doubt about Mandeville's connotation; although Philopirio prescribes extensive lists of drugs and activities, especially exercise, for his melancholic patients and is optimistic to the extent of feigning cheerfulness, he does so with a knowledge of their incurability. This inner sense of inevitable incurability is rare in seventeenth and eighteenth-century treatises and anticipates later theory.[14] Mandeville sees some hope for partial cure through strengthening of the doctor-patient relationship, an attachment not often commented upon in medical treatises at the turn of the eighteenth century.[15] At this point there seems to crop up the complicated process called 'transference' in modern psychiatry, a subtle and elusive concept that theoreticians today are just beginning to comprehend, especially in the realm of child psychology.

3. A Priori and A Posteriori Reasoning

Observation and empiricism are the only worthy guides in the treatment of disease, according to Mandeville, and for this reason Philopirio must

[13] See his final program of remedies beginning on p. 255 of the *Treatise*. Misomedon is to be kept so busy taking purges and vomits that he will literally not have the time to realize he has not been cured.

[14] This intuitive sense of the incurability of major diseases is almost non-existent among Mandeville's contemporaries. While numerous medical authors admit to having no certain remedy for a particular disease, almost all express the certainty of being on the verge of the discovery of one; and it was precisely this certainty in cure that caused physicians of the mid and late eighteenth century to criticize earlier doctors. Mandeville's extraordinary trust in "experience" over "reason" taught him that the hyp frequently cannot be cured at all, and engendered in him a type of medical skepticism about cure in general.

[15] Many passages make this point perfectly clear, as, for example, *Treatise*, preface, p. iv.

evaluate each hypochondriacal case on its own terms as a medically unique phenomenon. Mandeville entertains no pre-conceived notion whatsoever about the form a particular case may take, his wisdom deriving largely from definitional sophistication but also from experience in treating patients for several decades. While there is nothing unusual about the presence of *a posteriori* reasoning in medical treatises of the eighteenth century, it is a rare work that espouses it at the beginning of the period over a *priori* reasoning *both in theory and in practice*. In a survey of medical treatises written in England from 1700 to 1800, I discovered that the former type of reasoning overtakes the latter in both realms, theory and practice, after 1740 and does not really establish itself until the 1770's.[16]

4. *Necessary and Adequate Conditions*

Mandeville disqualifies *necessary* conditions on definitional grounds and replaces them with *adequate* conditions; in other words four or five symptoms are sufficient to indicate the presence of the condition but no specific four or five are necessary.[17] The distinction among these conditions is subtle and not commonly found in the literature of melancholy until the mid-nineteenth century, certainly not as a guiding methodological principle.

5. *The 'Procatarctic Cause'*

Mandeville believes that the hyp, unlike most other diseases, is not occasioned by bodily disturbances but by external, non-bodily conditions; thus his insistence of the physician's discovery of a procatarctic, or external, cause. Stated in less antiquated terms, Mandeville would consider

---

[16] See G. S. Rousseau, " 'Sowing the Wind and Reaping the Rain:' Rationalism and Empiricism in Eighteenth-Century Medicine," in *Studies in Change and Revolution*, ed. P. J. Korshin (London: Scolar Press, 1972), pp. 229-59. The matter is of course more complicated than this and involves the whole history of critical thinking in medicine, not merely the somewhat artificial division into 'reason' and 'experience;' and because Mandeville favoured experience over reason, his hero, as stated in the preface (pp. iv-v), is Baglivi. Like Baglivi, he, too, distinguished sharply between theory and practice, diminishing greatly the value of reason in practice, as seen throughout Philopirio's prescriptions. In the realm of theory, Philopirio's briefest and clearest statement is made on p. 269 of the *Treatise*: "The reason you [Misomedon] give may be good for ought I know: Being made *à Posteriori*, it cannot mislead us, yet it is far from being satisfactory to me." Throughout the study of the role of reason and experience in medical writing, I have benefitted from the work of Dr. Lester King.

[17] See, e.g. p. 80. Here, again, experience alone is a worthy guide.

it unlikely that a young or middle-aged woman who manifested all the typical signs of hypochondria could be dying of hypoglycemia; her hypoglycemia could be the bodily manifestation of an external procatarctic agent, usually some disturbance in her environment, but the origin of the entire condition could not be hypoglycemia. In distinguishing internal and external agents and, beyond that, secondary bodily manifestations, Mandeville's work is important in the history of the psychosomatic theory of medicine. Nowhere in the writings of Cheyne, Robinson, or Highmore, for example, is a 'procatarctic cause' so clearly delineated nor does it determine so clearly the author's argument.[18]

6. Relation of the 'Procatarctic Cause' and the Physiological Aspects of Hypochondriasis

Although the condition usually originates from external sources, it naturally manifests itself later in the body, and Mandeville spends much time demolishing theories that incorrectly account for the role of the stomach, spleen, brain, and animal spirits in its mechanical phases. Space here does not permit a detailed analysis of Mandeville's grasp of the functions of these organs, but while he is not truly original he distinguishes well between superior and inferior anatomists and relies on the best ones for his purposes. For example, he recognizes the valuable contribution that Willis' brain theory makes in the diagnosis and treatment of the hyp and he discards lesser theorists whom time has proved inconsequential. Furthermore, he believes, unlike his contemporaries, that once the condition has taken root, the animal spirits play a smaller role, and the brain a larger role – as if to suggest that throughout its course the illness is more psychological than physiological.[19]

---

[18] To prove this rigorously one would naturally have to read many treatises about a single disease and then show the absence of a procatarctic cause; this I have undertaken for the hyp and find Mandeville's work fairly singular. See my introduction to the Augustan Reprint Society Edition of John Hill's *Hypochondriasis: A Practical Treatise 1766* (Los Angeles, California, 1969), pp. i-xiii. Also influencing Mandeville's theory of a procatarctic cause is his intuitive sense of the hyp as forming part of a realm of non-physiological conditions having somatic consequences. While he does not carry his ideas very far, he does intimate time and again that medicine must explore this nebulous region of illness. Mandeville, in any case, is not a systematic thinker in medicine (in the sense that Linnaeus was in botany) but he does have a considerable 'medical intuition' that guides him well.

[19] See, for example, *Treatise,* p. 277, in which Philopirio forbids the use of redundant medicines "in all Distempers, but more especially those [like the hyp], in which the Fancy has so great a share, and the least trifle is of moment." These and other similar remarks reveal the large role of 'Fancy' in the aetiology of the condition.

7. The Treatise as a Document in the History of Medicine

Obviously it is most difficult to rate documents with any yardstick other than extremely concrete ones. However some works are clearly more important than others for a great variety of reasons including direct and indirect influence. While Mandeville's *Treatise* was not influential either as a direct source or an indirect system of medical thinking it is one of the lengthiest treatments ever given to the hyp; and if it cannot hope to assume the importance of Burton's *Anatomy of Melancholy* or Cheyne's *English Malady,* it will nevertheless fascinate students of Mandeville's views as well as historians of psychiatry. But most of all it should engross medical historians with a broad spectrum of interests because of the variety of subjects it treats: rationalism and empiricism, estimates of seventeenth-century medicine in the eyes of a practicing eighteenth-century physician, the quarrel of the Ancients and the Moderns, the decline of Galenism, the role of book learning in actual treatment, theories of venereal disease, the relative merits of the medical schools of Europe, controversies over the chemical nature and mechanical operations of the animal spirits, the anatomical function of the stomach in digestion and of the brain in thinking, and many others – these will arrest at least the passing interest of medical historians. Moreover, this work represents philosophical medicine at its best,[20] always centered on its avowed topic but perpetually aware of the larger implications, historically and medically, of its subject matter.

8. The Treatise as a Literary Document

Literary critics are beginning to appreciate Mandeville's satirical gifts, especially his penchant for irony and rhetorical inversion.[21] These talents abound in the *Treatise*, itself a satire of bad doctors, bad patients, and false medical reasoning, addressed primarily to an audience of patients rather than doctors; in addition it is logically organized and well written. Too little, however, has been written about the dialogue tradition in English literature to assign it an unequivocal role,[22] but one can fairly say

[20] A type of medical writing that did not really get under way until the 1760's and which flourishes in the writings of Drs. Robert Whytt, William Cullen, and John Brown.

[21] See Martin Price, *To the Palace of Wisdom: Studies in Order and Energy from Dryden to Blake* (New York: Doubleday, 1962), pp. 122-137; and Robert Hopkins, "The Cant of Social Compromise: Some Observations on Mandeville's Satire," below.

[22] Standard works say little about the eighteenth century altogether, leaving out such important works as Hume's *Dialogues of Natural Religion* and Mandeville's

that dialogue here admirably serves the author's purposes: through Philopirio Mandeville is able to speak autobiographically (a liberty he does not take even in *The Fable*), while other characters allow him to demonstrate important varieties of the hyp and such qualities as Misomedon's pedantic learning in, though amateur knowledge of, medicine. Because the treatise is ostensibly medical in content it cannot hope to interest such a wide audience as does *The Fable*; but if literary historians can somehow modify their prejudice that the history of medicine is entirely a technical and specialized subject remote from the domain of literature, they would discover here a document every bit as polished and tightly organized, especially in its well-wrought preface, as *The Fable*.

9. The Treatise as a Sociological Document

Expressed statistically, at least half the *Treatise* is devoted to subjects other than hypochondriasis, namely the quarrel between physicians and apothecaries, the true duties of different types of medical men, the role of hypotheses in medical theory, and such seemingly remote topics – remote, that is, from the hyp – as diet and exercise. In considering all these subjects Mandeville demonstrates more than a usual grasp of the social dimensions of illness, a deep sense that medicine, even in its most abstract theories about the aetiology and pathology of disease, remains closely affiliated to social processes – to economics, politics, education, and even to language. Among all these diverse social topics Mandeville concentrates mostly on two, the quarrels between the physicians and the apothecaries, and the role of the physician in society-at-large.

Regarding the first, Mandeville sums up the arguments on both sides and maintains throughout an objective, almost dispassionate, stance; while he himself probably continued to practice medicine as a physician throughout his life, he understands the grievances of the apothecaries.[23] Here it is not an adjudication in favor of one side or the other that matters but rather Mandeville's acute understanding that the dispute had greater social ramifications than his contemporaries imagined – that it was the symptom of a deep malaise, *au fond* economic but also signifying

---

Fable of the Bees. In the case of the *Treatise*, the dialogue form draws attention to the doctor-patient relationship, which Mandeville considers therapeutic and beneficial to cure, if incorporating a strong sense of trust.

[23] See *Treatise*, pp. 215-220, 260 ff. The quarrel had flared up during the 1690's and again at the turn of the eighteenth century, but Mandeville's lengthy descriptions do more than state the case for each side: they present the strengths and weaknesses with detached, almost dispassionate understanding.

the emergence of professional groups within a single vocation.[24] By devoting so much attention to the dispute he underscored its social relevance, especially the role of pride within a professional group and the psychological way in which group jealousies manifest themselves professionally.

Regarding the second, the physician's role, I have discovered no other work written in English in the eighteenth century, with the exception of Smollett's inimitable satires,[25] which grasps so well as Mandeville's the overarching role of a physician, his strengths and weaknesses, frailties and foibles, potentials and limitations. It is indeed no exaggeration to say that Mandeville, writing almost 300 years ago, has prophetically anticipated the medical problems facing such a nation as the U.S.A., for example, in which present-day discussions about socialized medicine evolve around the physician's conception of himself as an economic creature, a social creature, an ethical and, of course, a professional creature diagnosing and curing illness.[26] Mandeville's originality on this subject includes the notion that a doctor is nothing more than the sum of what his society imagines him to be; if he is imagined as the godhead, omniscient and infallible, he, the physician, will attempt to fulfill this conceived posture even though he knows that such a stance engages him in pretension and outright dishonesty. For precisely this reason Misomedon is made to conceive of Philopirio in impossibly grandiose terms missing no opportunity to display his own learning to medicine; and also for this reason Philopirio is portrayed as humbler and less dishonest than many practicing specialists in the hyp of his time. Eighteenth-century medical writers adhered, wittingly or otherwise, to a typology of the physician, and Mande-

[24] The organization of various medical groups with different professional aims at the turn of the eighteenth century has not received attention except in passing. See, for example, Sir George N. Clarke's *A History of the Royal College of Physicians* (Oxford: The Clarendon Press, 1964-1966, 2 vols.). A sociology of medicine, taking account of these professional developments, is urgently needed.

[25] Especially in *Humphry Clinker* and *Peregrine Pickle*. Smollett's vision is essentially negative, concentrating the thrust of its energetic attack on all those abominable qualities physicians seemed to have acquired since the Restoration: pride, smugness, pretence, obsession with lucre, heartless disconcern whether they cured or killed. In some deep ways Mandeville and Smollett are not so far apart: they were both physicians, both practiced, and both were intuitively aware of the foibles of medical men.

[26] Here, again, Mandeville's medical intuition, as I have been calling it, has proved right. At a meeting in April 1972 in Washington, D.C. in the USA, young doctors were told by senior medical officers of the medical profession that they should make all the money they expected to make in the next seven or eight years, for by 1980 American doctors would be earning just about the same as other workers – i.e. because of socialized medicine. This is, of course, not the case at present, when doctors are probably the very highest paid members of any profession.

ville stands on the side of those who would melodramatically diminish his profits, radically alter his role, and therefore hopefully expand his true medical calling within the community.[27]

10. Medicine, a Science or an Art?

Finally, the treatise must be viewed as one more link in the long chain of seventeenth- and eighteenth-century debates about the status of medicine as a science or an art.[28] Mandeville's unequivocal insistence on experience as the essential attribute of every good physician leaves no doubt about his opinion of the matter: if book learning and school training are worthwhile, experience alone teaches the doctor to cure, i.e. to fathom the secrets of Nature. Medical treatment therefore requires more skill than knowledge, and is at bottom an art. Here, again, the prophetic Mandeville anticipates a future debate, one that hardly died in his own epoch but that continued to gather momentum in the next two centuries, in fact one that remains far from a satisfactory solution in 1972.

[27] The typology is complex and changed from decade to decade; for example, the "pedantic Canting Physician," as one medical author calls it, remained a stock image throughout the century, while the "lucre-seeking mongrels," described by another, faded in and out. I have attempted to survey the typology of doctors throughout the century in *Doctors and Medicine in the Novels of Tobias Smollett* (Princeton University Ph.D. Dissertation, 1966), chap. i.

[28] The standard histories of medicine (Garrison, Castiglione, Singer, etc.) say very little about this debate; to find anything substantial about it the student must look in periodical literature, articles. In any case, almost nothing to my knowledge has been written about the debate in the eighteenth century; and while it is not usually of prime concern to that century, say to the extent that whole works are devoted to the question, it does play a role as a *topos* in a great deal of medical writing.

"THE GREAT LEVIATHAN OF LEACHERY": MANDEVILLE'S *MODEST DEFENCE OF PUBLICK STEWS* (1724)

Richard I. Cook

As early as 1714 (in "Remark H" of the *Fable of the Bees*) Bernard Mandeville wrote:

I am far from encouraging Vice, and think it would be an unspeakable Felicity to a State, if the Sin of Uncleanness could be utterly Banish'd from it; but I am afraid it is impossible: The Passions of some People are too violent to be curb'd by any Law or Precept; and it is Wisdom in all Governments to bear with lesser Inconveniences to prevent greater. If Courtezans and Strumpets were to be prosecuted with as much Rigour as some silly People would have it, what Locks or Bars would be sufficient to preserve the Honour of our Wives and Daughters? . . . some Men would grow outrageous, and Ravishing would become a common Crime. Where six or seven Thousand Sailors arrive at once, as it often happens at *Amsterdam*, that have seen none but their own Sex for many Months together, how is it to be suppos'd that honest Women should walk the Streets unmolested, if there were no Harlots to be had at reasonable Prices? For which Reason, the Wise Rulers of that well-ordered City always tolerate an uncertain number of Houses in which Women are hired as publickly as Horses at a Livery-Stable.[1]

Such complacent acceptance of both the inevitability and social utility of prostitution did not sit well with the Grand Jury of Middlesex, and in its formal presentment declaring the *Fable of the Bees* a public nuisance the Grand Jury complained (among other things) that in Mandeville's work "the very *Stews* themselves have had strained Apologies and forced Encomiums made in their Favour and produced in Print, with Design, we conceive, to debauch the Nation." [2] In the *London Journal* for August 10, 1723, Mandeville undertook to defend himself, asserting that:

The Encomiums upon Stews complained of in the Presentment are no where in the Book. . . . I am sorry the Grand-Jury should conceive that I published

---

[1] *Fable of the Bees,* ed. by F. B. Kaye (Oxford, 1957), I, 95-96.
[2] *Ibid.,* I, 385.

this with a Design to debauch the Nation, without considering that in the first Place, there is not a Sentence nor a Syllable that can either offend the chastest Ear, or sully the Imagination of the most vicious; or in the second, that the Matter complained of is manifestly addressed to Magistrates and Politicians, or at least the more serious and thinking Part of Mankind.[3]

It was one year after this exchange that Mandeville – as if further to provoke those who had responded so prudishly to his earlier opinions on the subject – amplified and significantly extended those opinions in the *Modest Defence of Publick Stews: Or, an Essay upon Whoring, As it is now practis'd in these Kingdoms*.[4] In the majority of his writings as a social philosopher, Mandeville's approach is that of a diagnostician whose primary concern is with description and analysis, rather than with practical reform, and though the direction of his social and economic sympathies is sufficiently apparent, he rarely embarks on any extended argument in behalf of specific programs of action. In the *Modest Defence*, however, Mandeville offers not merely his observations on the delicate social and moral problem of prostitution, but he goes on to advocate an impressively detailed plan for dealing with it.

In brief, Mandeville's line of argument in the tract is as follows: despite the efforts of religious reformers, whoring – with its attendant evils of disease, murder of bastard infants, and destruction of moral character – has been greatly on the rise. Restrictive legislation (mostly directed against the shabbier sort of street-walker) has always been ineffective, since the passion for illicit sex is much too strong ever to be suppressed by mere laws. But if whoring cannot be eliminated, it can at least be controlled and its social disruptions minimized, and these ends can be best accomplished by the establishment – under parliamentary license

---

[3] *Ibid.,* I, 405-06.

[4] J. H. Harder, in "The Authorship of *A Modest Defence of Public Stews* Etc." (*Neophilologus,* XVIII, 1933, 200-203), questions F. B. Kaye's ascription of this work to Mandeville. Harder – who was evidently unaware that Kaye had fully and convincingly argued the ascription in "The Writings of Bernard Mandeville: A Bibliographical Survey" (cited below) – claims that Kaye "gives no motives" for assigning the work to Mandeville. It is Harder's dubious contention that Mandeville, having already signed his name or initials to such presumably scandalous works as the *Virgin Unmask'd* and *Wishes to a Godson,* would not have hesitated to acknowledge the "immoral" *Modest Defence* had it been his. Harder's own candidate for the tract's authorship is "Lawrence Le Fever," whose name he found assigned to the work in an entry (for which Harder gives no year) in the registry at Stationer's Hall. Since Harder admits that his investigation was "somewhat hasty" and that "Further research in the Lib. Brit. Mus. for more information about this writer has, up to the present, had no results," it is rather hard to accept his case. "Lawrence Le Fever," in any event, sounds suspiciously like another of the punning pseudonyms ("Luke Ogle, Esq." is another) which were attached to the *Modest Defence* in its subsequent editions. For a rebuttal of Harder's article, see R. S. Crane, *Philological Quarterly,* 13 (1934), 122-123.

and support – of a series of government-operated brothels. Under such an arrangement, no competition from street-walkers or independent brothels would be allowed: all prostitutes who either refused or could not qualify to enter a government house would be obliged to give up their profession or face transportation. By such means, "publick whoring" would be kept within orderly confines and its socially noxious side effects sharply curtailed. By the same token, "private whoring" (i.e., rape, seduction, and adultery without exchange of money) would be drastically reduced, since few men would be willing to expend time and effort on such activities if they could avail themselves of the cheap, safe, and convenient services of a government-approved prostitute. To so practical and demonstrably desirable a proposal, Mandeville concludes, there can be no serious objection, though it is perhaps possible that some over-scrupulous persons might object that the plan employs immoral means to serve its worthy end. To such, Mandeville answers that although an individual may rightly be condemned for doing certain evil to produce uncertain good, a legislature cannot be so judged. The actions of the government – whose overriding concern must be for the welfare of society as a whole – can be assessed only by their results, and if these are bene-ficial, the act itself must by definition be good. Others may object that by instituting public stews the government will be encouraging vice and hence endangering immortal souls. To this Mandeville replies:

> . . . it is universally allow'd as one of the greatest Perfections of the Christian Religion, that its Precepts are calculated to promote the Happiness of Man-kind in this World as well as the next; if so, then it is a direct Arraignment of the Lawgivers infinite Wisdom, *i.e.* a Contradiction to assert, that, in Matters of Law and Government, the Publick Breach of any Gospel Precept can possibly be for the temporal Good of any *Society* whatever: And there-fore we may with Confidence affirm, that no sinful Laws can be beneficial, and *vice versa*, that no beneficial Laws can be sinful.[5]

In this overt expression of a utilitarian morality the *Modest Defence* is all but unique among Mandeville's work. Although the thrust of Mandeville's social, moral, and political thought nearly always *implies* an unstated utilitarian standard, in the rest of his work he typically chooses to adopt a surface argument wherein morals and religion, rigor-ously interpreted, are pictured as being inevitably at odds with the de-mands of worldly society. Yet (as Mandeville's opponents among the

---

[5] *Modest Defence of Publick Stews* (1724), intro. by Richard Cook, Augustan Reprint Society Publication 162 (Los Angeles, 1973), 69. All quotations (hereafter identified by page number in the text) are from this edition.

pious were quick to see) one way of resolving the paradox that private vices can sometimes lead to public benefits is to revise our ideas of what constitutes vice. By ostensibly embracing the most ascetic ideas of morality, all the while demonstrating how economically disastrous such ideas would be in actual practice, Mandeville in effect offers a tacit argument in favor of a more workable (which is to say, a more latitudinarian) concept of morality. In the *Modest Defence*, however, Mandeville prefers to assume openly the position he elsewhere pretends to deny – namely, that no genuinely beneficial social act can ever be considered contrary to religion or morality.

To account for Mandeville's uncharacteristically direct statement of his position in the *Modest Defence,* F. B. Kaye cites the special requirements of Mandeville's new role as a projector:

> In the *Modest Defence* the author is considering a *practical* matter. He is arguing in favor of a definite program, and not simply theorizing. Therefore, had he added to his argument the tag that, however desirable he made his program, it was nevertheless wicked – as Mandeville does in the *Fable* – he would have had no chance of gaining his point. . . . therefore, though he might employ this paradox in a non-propagandistic work such as the *Fable*, where it would be ineffectual to contradict his real desires, [he] would never use it in a book like the *Modest Defence* where it *would* negate them.[6]

Kaye is undoubtedly correct in his assumption that the *Modest Defence's* plan for government-run prostitution reflects Mandeville's "real desires." As a logical (if not necessarily feasible) answer to a genuine social problem, the proposal bears an authentically Mandevillean stamp. I would suggest, however, that Mandeville was far too realistic ever to suppose that his scheme stood much chance of being adopted, and that accordingly, in the *Modest Defence* he is less interested in convincing his readers of the virtues of his plan than he is in using the occasion for a series of ironical asides on the related topics of puritanism, sexual economics, and moral reformers.

Had Mandeville entertained any real intentions of winning acceptance for his proposal, he would hardly have presented it in a manner so well-calculated to antagonize the general readers whose support he claims to be soliciting. Government *sponsorship* of brothels (as opposed to mere toleration) is the sort of emotionally-charged issue which requires of its advocates a good deal of earnest sobriety and discrete euphemism, assuming that popular persuasion is the desired goal. Mandeville, on the

---

[6] F. B. Kaye, "The Writings of Bernard Mandeville: A Bibliographical Survey," *Journal of English and Germanic Philology*, 20 (1921), 456.

other hand, takes an obvious relish in the humorous possibilities of his subject, and though his argument remains quite serious in its basic intent, the comic detail with which he surrounds it more clearly suggests the satirist than the propagandist. The very title-page gives the reader a fair warning of what to expect, for the ambiguous promise of a "modest" defense of so immodest a subject is at once belied by the punning inscription "Written by a Layman." And this is only the first, and perhaps the least scabrous, of the numerous puns which enliven the text – e.g. (after a clinically exact discussion of feminine anatomy), "We may conclude . . . that Female Chastity is, in its own Nature, built upon a very *ticklish* Foundation" (p. 49).

Mandeville introduces his tract with a mock-dedication to the gentlemen of the Societies for the Reformation of Manners. These were private religious associations whose purpose was the discovery and prosecution of fornicators, blasphemers, sabbath-breakers, and similar moral offenders. So zealous were the members in their activities that in 1735 the London and Westminster societies could boast a forty-year record of no fewer than 99,380 prosecutions for debauchery and profane behavior.[7] As hostile critics pointed out, however, the purity of motive behind such reform was open to some question, since in many cases informants could legally demand as reward a portion of the offender's fine. Swift – himself a vigorous proponent of moral reform – was reporting a widespread opinion when he remarked in his *Project for the Advancement of Religion* (1708): "Religious Societies, although begun with excellent Intention, and by Persons of true Piety, are said, I know not whether truly or no, to have dwindled into factious Clubs, and grown a Trade to enrich little knavish Informers of the meanest Rank, such as common Constables, and broken Shop-keepers." [8]

It is not so much for their hypocrisy as for their ineffectuality that Mandeville twits the Societies in his dedication. Unfortunately, the pious harassment of "strolling Damsels" has failed to diminish public lewdness: instead, it has merely served to redirect that lewdness toward more respectable targets. For, as he ruefully comments, "what better could we expect from Your Carting of Bawds, than that the Great Leviathan of Leachery, for Want of these Tubs to play with, should, with one Whisk of his Tail, overset the *Vessel* of Modesty?" (pp. ii-iii). Characteristic of Mandeville's tone in the dedication are his remarks on the Societies'

---

[7] For an account of the Societies for the Reformation of Manners, see W. E. H. Lecky, *A History of England in the Eighteenth Century* (London, 1883), II, 546-548.
[8] Jonathan Swift. *Prose Works,* ed. by Herbert Davis (Oxford, 1937-1968), II, 57.

"present Method of Conversion, especially in the Article of Whipping."
As one reformer to another, Mandeville helpfully explains:

It is very possible, indeed, that leaving a Poor Girl Penny-less, may put her in
a Way of living Honestly, tho' the want of Money was the only Reason of
her living otherwise; and the Stripping of her Naked, may, for aught I know,
contribute to Her Modesty, and put Her in a State of Innocence, but surely,
Gentlemen, You must all know, that Flogging has a quite contrary Effect
(pp. x-xi).

To the self-righteous puritans of the Societies for Reformation of Manners, it must have seemed altogether appropriate that Mandeville should
sign his dedication with the name "Phil-Porney," which is to say, "Lover
of Whores."

After a short preface (in which the author assures his audience of the
lofty altruism which is his sole motive in writing), the tract itself opens
with a seemingly forthright renunciation of any further levity.

There is nothing more idle, or shows a greater Affectation of Wit, than the
modern Custom of treating the most grave Subjects with Burlesque and
Ridicule. The present Subject of *Whoring,* was I dispos'd, would furnish me
sufficiently in this kind, and might possibly, if so handled, excite Mirth in
those who are only capable of such low Impressions. But, as the chief Design
of this Treatise is to promote the general Welfare and Happiness of Mankind, I hope to be excus'd, if I make no farther Attempts to please, than are
consistent with that Design (p. 1).

As if to re-enforce this promise of high seriousness, Mandeville sets about
his argument in an orderly, almost legalistic, fashion, compiling methodical lists of current conditions, the virtues of his scheme, answers to
possible objections, and so on. The very thoroughness of his approach,
however, creates an emphasis which at crucial moments becomes palpably
destructive of his announced intention to avoid frivolity. For though he
professes to base his advocacy on the principle that *"of two Evils, we
ought to chuse the least"* (p. 67), the *real* momentum of his argument is
toward proving that government-sponsored brothels will be a *positive
good,* and in support of this theme he periodically introduces comically
extravagant descriptions of the social and sexual benefits his plan will
produce.

Among other happy effects, for example, Mandeville pictures the full
and satisfying life that government prostitutes will live. Relieved of the
economic and physical anxieties of the free-lancer, such courtezans, he
predicts, will discover a new sense of pride and fulfillment in their status

as respectable civil servants. No longer social outcasts, they will vie with each other to raise professional standards.

It is natural for Mankind to regard chiefly the good Opinion of those with whom they converse, and to neglect that of Strangers; now in this Community [*i.e.*, the state-run brothel], Lewdness not being esteem'd a Reproach, but rather a Commendation, they will set a Value on their good Name, and stand as much upon the Puncto of Honour, as the rest of Mankind; being mov'd by the same commendable Emulation . . . (pp. 18-19).

As for the patrons, not only will they be spared the now prevalent risks of disease and robbery, but they will be able to satisfy their needs inexpensively and without undue neglect of their more important concerns:

. . . if a Man should be overtaken with a sudden Gust of Lechery, it will be no Hindrance to him even in the greatest Hurry of Business, for a ready and willing Mistress will ease him in the twinkling of an Eye, and he may prosecute his Affairs with more Attention than ever, by having his Mind entirely freed and disengag'd from those troublesome Ideas which always accompany a wanton Disposition of the Body (pp. 25-26).

Under the circumstances, it is no wonder that the only possible problem Mandeville can anticipate is that public stews might attract more trade than they can efficiently handle, in which case, he says, Parliament might find it desirable to pass an "Act *for encouraging the Importation of foreign Women*." The benefits of such legislation would be manifold:

. . . besides the Honour of our Females, which would be preserv'd by such an Act, it might bring this farther Advantage; That whereas most of our estated Youth spend a great Part of their Time and Fortunes in travelling Abroad, for no other End, as it seems by most of them, but to be inform'd in the *French* and *Italian* Gallantry; they would then have an Opportunity of satisfying their Curiosity in foreign Amours, without stirring out of *London* (pp. 65-66).

Whatever real advantages his scheme might have (and these are quite plausibly argued elsewhere in the tract) Mandeville's mock-enthusiastic vision of happy whores and contented customers is meant as a parody of the kind of glowing predictions with which his fellow projectors were apt to recommend their programs.

However, it is not merely the naively optimistic reformer who is parodied in the *Modest Defence*; more specifically, Mandeville here employs for satiric purposes the manner and apparatus of the mercantilist school of economic philosophers – a school of which he himself in his other

mercantilism

writings is a conspicuous example. As applied today to early eighteenth-century England, the term "mercantilist" covers a bewilderingly wide range of authors on economic theory. But despite their differences on points of doctrine, the authors so designated share certain fundamental assumptions, and among these is the belief that the economic good of the state overshadows the welfare of the individual. In arguing in support of this principle and the many proposed policies they derived from it, mercantilist authors often assumed a dispassionately analytical manner that was equally offensive to the churchman and to the humanitarian. For in a system of values which measures men and institutions primarily in terms of their economic utility, there is very little room left for such commercially unproductive considerations as religious morality or even human compassion. Instead, the mercantilists cultivated a cool scientific detachment in which people in general and the laboring poor in particular became mere commodities to be dealt with as unsentimentally as any other economic resource. Though Mandeville's wit goes a long way toward softening the harsher implications of the mercantilist ideas which inform most of his economic writings, he can on occasion be brutally direct, as in his "Essay on Charity and Charity Schools" (1723), where he maintains that:

`. . . in a free Nation where Slaves are not allow'd of, the surest Wealth consists in a Multitude of laborious Poor. . . . To make the Society happy and People easy under the meanest Circumstances, it is requisite that great Numbers of them should be Ignorant as well as Poor. . . . The more a Shepherd, a Plowman or any other Peasant knows of the World, and the things that are Foreign to his Labour or Employment, the less fit he'll be to go through the Fatigues and Hardships of it with Chearfulness and Content.[9]

Among other things, it is the callous indifference to human suffering behind such an attitude that Jonathan Swift so pointedly satirizes in his *Modest Proposal for Preventing the Children of Poor People in Ireland from being a Burthen to their Parents or Country* (1729).

In making satiric use of a mercantilist approach in the *Modest Defence*, Mandeville is not, of course, trying to discredit that approach, as was Swift in his tract. The purely utilitarian resolution of social problems might bruise the religious and moral sensibilities of some, but what they saw as amorality, Mandeville no doubt thought of as hard-headed realism. Thus, on one level (and that the most important), Mandeville is perfectly serious in his mercantilist contention that the government ought

---

[9] *Fable of the Bees*, (Kaye), I, 287-288.

to set itself up in the brothel business. But serious though he may be, Mandeville is also perfectly aware of the comic potentialities of writing about a subject like prostitution from within a framework of such typically mercantilist preoccupations as quality controls, cost estimates, and product distribution. In a happy mercantilist utopia where utility and logic ruled supreme, presumably there would be nothing intrinsically comic or shocking about applying such sensible business criteria to the problems of commercial sex. But until that utopia is achieved, most readers will find such an approach either scandalous or laughable, and Mandeville is at pains to elicit both types of response. Obviously, Mandeville's pretended obliviousness to the incongruity of his treatment involves a degree of self-parody, and in that respect the *Modest Defence* contains an oblique attack upon the humorlessness of some mercantilists. Yet amused as he is at the narrow scientism of his fellow projectors, Mandeville is rather more amused by the predictable nervous laughter and moral outrage (equally squeamish from his point of view) with which he knows much of his audience will react to a briskly rational treatment of a subject society has usually preferred to view emotionally.

Very early in the tract Mandeville, in effect, announces his philosophical position by citing in support of his proposal a maxim that had been a favorite of mercantilists since the second half of the seventeenth century: namely, that people are the riches of a nation. According to this doctrine (which Mandeville had soberly endorsed a year earlier in the "Essay on Charity Schools"), increase of population is everywhere and at all times desirable, since a large labor force means that wages can be held to a minimum and manufacturing processes kept cheap. As Defoe expressed it in 1704: "... the glory, the strength, the riches, the trade, and all that is valuable in a nation as to its figure in the world, depends upon the number of its people, be they never so mean and poor...." [10] In the *Modest Defence* Mandeville introduces the subject by pointing out that one of the worst evils of unregulated whoring is that it leads to the murder of bastard children by mothers who are either unwilling to endure the disgrace or loathe to accept the inconvenience of such offspring. With commendable indignation, Mandeville asserts that "a Mind capable of divesting itself so intirely of Humanity, is not fit to live in a civiliz'd Nation." But the reader who applauds this sentiment,

[10] Daniel Defoe, *Giving Alms No Charity*, as quoted by Louis A. Landa, "*A Modest Proposal* and Populousness," *Modern Philology*, XL (1942), 163. For a further survey of mercantilist ideas in the early eighteenth century, see also George Wittkowsky, "Swift's *Modest Proposal*: The Biography of an Early Georgian Pamphlet," *Journal of the History of Ideas*, 4 (1943), 75-104.

may find it disconcerting to realize a few lines later that Mandeville is less appalled by the cruelty of infanticide than by its shocking economic wastefulness. This practice, as he points out, "tends very much to dispeople the Country. And since the Prosperity of any Country is allow'd to depend, in a great measure, on the Number of its Inhabitants, the *Government* ought, if it were possible, to prevent any Whoring at all, as it evidently hinders the Propagation of the Species" (pp. 4-5). The projector in Swift's *Modest Proposal*, it will be recalled, was likewise one who was distressed by the commercial improvidence of murdering unwanted children. But whereas Swift's irony is meant to expose his projector's moral blindness, Mandeville's intrusive elevation of pragmatic concerns over those of mere morality – here and elsewhere in the tract – is primarily intended to bait the tender-hearted reader.

To this end he assumes a crisp, business-like manner, especially in those portions of his pamphlet where he explicates the working details of his proposed brothels. As a man who has obviously given the matter a great deal of thought, he is prepared to give a painstaking rundown of such matters as organizational policy, operating procedure, and personnel management. After modestly conceding that Parliament, "being compos'd of *Spirituals* as well as *Temporals*" (p. 12), will no doubt wish to add its own embellishments, he spells out the mechanics of his proposal. London, he estimates, will require at least one hundred houses, each containing twenty prostitutes and a resident matron "of Abilities and Experience." Conveniently nearby will be an infirmary staffed by two physicians and four surgeons, and supervising all will be three royal commissioners whose job will be "to hear and redress Complaints, and to see that each House punctually observes such Rules and Orders as shall be thought Necessary for the good Government of this Community" (p. 13). By way of encouraging trade, "each House must be allow'd a certain Quantity of all sorts of Liquor, Custom and Excise free; by which Means they will be enabled to accommodate Gentlemen handsomely, without that Imposition so frequently met with in such Houses" (p. 13).

Building enthusiasm as he gets down to crucial money matters, Mandeville explains that:

For the better Entertainment of all Ranks and Degrees of Gentlemen, we shall divide the twenty Women of each House into four Classes, who for their Beauty, or other Qualifications, may justly challenge different Prices.

The first Class is to consist of eight, who may legally demand from each Visitant Half a Crown. The second Class to consist of six, whose fix'd Price may be a Crown. The third Class of four, at half a Guinea each. The remaining two make up the fourth Class, and are design'd for Persons of the first Rank, who can afford to Pay a Guinea for the Elegancy of their Taste (pp. 13-14).

Further employing the sort of statistical computations and "political arithmetic" so favored by mercantilist writers, Mandeville goes on to point out that:

To defray the Charges of this Establishment, will require but a very moderate Tax: For if the first Class pays but forty Shillings Yearly, and the rest in Proportion, it will amount to above ten thousand Pounds a Year, which will not only pay the Commissioners Salaries, Surgeons Chests, and other Contingencies, but likewise establish a good Fund for the Maintenance of Bastard-Orphans and superannuated Courtezans (p. 14).

Discipline will be strictly enforced, with each matron empowered to see to it that no girl leaves without permission and that disorderly or drunken patrons are refused admission. Recruitment or working staff, Mandeville says, will present no problems, other than perhaps at first an embarrassment of riches, for "the vast Choice and Variety... of these Women, will give us an Opportunity of making a very beautiful Collection" (pp. 63-64). But if ever the day should come when "Supplies should not prove Sufficient to answer the greatness of the Demand," the worst that can happen is that frustrated customers will go back to seducing virgins, which practice, Mandeville triumphantly points out, will in time produce a whole new crop of potential employees for the public stews.

As befits a physician, Mandeville is particularly concerned that hygenic standards be maintained:

For the *Society's* Security in Point of Health, it must be order'd, That if any Gentleman complains of receiving an Injury, and the Woman, upon Search, be found tainted, without having discover'd it to the Mistress, she shall be stripp'd and cashier'd. But if a Woman discovers her Misfortune before any Complaint is made against her, she shall be sent to the *Infirmary*, and cured at the Publick Charge. No Woman that has been twice pox'd shall ever be re-admitted (pp. 14-15).

With a nice sense of distinction, Mandeville adds to these medical regulations the explanatory comment: "*Note*, That three Claps shall be reckon'd equivalent to one Pox" (p. 15).

In the preface to his tract Mandeville had told his readers:

I am in some pain for the Event of this Scheme, *hoping the* Wicked *will find it too Grave, and fearing the* Godly *will scarce venture beyond the Title-*

*Page: And should they even, I know they'll object, 'tis here and there inter-
woven with too ludicrous Expressions, not considering that a dry Argument
has occasion for the larding of Gaiety to make it the better relish and go
down* (p. xiv).

Not all the *Modest Defence of Publick Stews* is written with a "*larding
of Gaiety,*" but, as I have tried to show, even in his most sober passages
Mandeville has a way of moving from earnest advocacy over to a sly
parody of such advocacy. Knowing, as he did, that the "Godly" ad-
herents of the Societies for the Reformation of Manners were likely to
find his proposal offensive even without its satiric trimmings, Mandeville
shrewdly concluded that he had nothing to lose by couching his basically
serious argument in terms that would enable him to share his amusement
at what he saw as the irrationality and hypocrisy of society's attitude
toward sex in general and prostitution in particular.

RELIGION AND ETHICS IN MANDEVILLE

M. R. JACK

At the beginning of his full-length work on religion entitled *Free Thoughts on Religion, the Church, and National Happiness,* Mandeville defines religion as "an Acknowledgment of an Immortal Power." [1] He later says that "Men of Sense, and good Logicians" have vainly wasted their time arguing about and discussing the subject since time immemorial, for knowledge of God is something "which no Language can give them the least Idea of." [2] God is ineffable, religion is mysterious, and "no Man therefore ought to be too dogmatical in Matters of Faith." [3] Mandeville has thus ruled out the possibility of religion on epistemological grounds: being a matter outside human comprehension, nothing can be known about God and nothing worthwhile can be said on this subject. He thus leaves himself free to concentrate on what really interests him in the rest of the book, namely, a general review of religious phenomena as an aspect of human behavior, an exposé of the corrupt practices of the clergy through the ages and a plea for toleration if not permissiveness.[4]

It will be my contention in this essay that it is essential to understand this point, clearly evidenced in Mandeville's works, before any meaningful discussion of his treatment of religion and ethics can take place. For in taking the position outlined above, Mandeville has declared his lack of interest in religion for its own sake. He has announced that he will not indulge in what has been called "the grand subterfuge" of the seventeenth century, that is, the fear of examining "religious emotion nakedly as

---

[1] London, 1720, p. 1; all future references to his work are to this edition, the first.
[2] *Ibid.,* 67.
[3] *Ibid.,* 68.
[4] Mandeville's anticlericalism is quite marked. He believed that since it was against their own interest, the clergy would not encourage compromise or reasonable behavior. It was also an aspect of his notion that the professions live off the vices and deficiencies of men.

an aspect of human nature." [5] At the same time there can be no doubt about his interest in the phenomenon of moral behavior, but it is an interest that is altogether divorced from the otherworldly. This divorce, I believe, can be interpreted in the light of his Calvinist background, but it has to be emphasized that Mandeville has taken the Baylian severance of religion and ethics to its extreme, so that any interpretation relying heavily on assuming a theological basis to his thinking on ethical matters is bound to be misleading. It may help us to understand the origin of the kind of distinction Mandeville makes between religion and ethics to consider the matter in terms of the Calvinist distinction between grace and nature, but it obscures his intentions as a psychologist interested in giving a naturalistic account of ethical phenomena.

My contention is, therefore, that Mandeville must be read as primarily one who is uninterested in religion for its own sake and one who is concerned with giving a naturalistic account of ethical behavior. This account is naturalistic both in the sense of its being unrelated to any transcendent theological position and in the sense of its being an explanation of morality in terms of human nature. I shall argue that most modern critical studies of these aspects of Mandeville's thought, by concentrating on elucidating his views in the light of some theological framework such as Calvinism, miss his main intention and interest. As much of this modern discussion has arisen within the framework sketched by F. B. Kaye in what is the standard modern edition of *The Fable of the Bees*, I will begin by considering this account.

ii

Kaye's exposition of Mandeville's ethics depends upon accepting that there are two different standards applied by Mandeville in his assessment of the morality of actions: the first is "rigoristic" (ascetic and rational) and is applied as a criterion for judging the motives of individuals' behavior; the second is "empirical" or "utilitarian" and is applied as a criterion for judging the social consequences of such behavior. Thus for an action to be judged virtuous under the first condition, it must be disinterestedly motivated; that is, the individual must be attempting to deny his own inclination and further he must be doing this because he believes such denial to be good.[6] For an action to be judged virtuous

---

[5] Frank E. Manuel, *The Eighteenth Century Confronts the Gods* (Harvard Univ. Press, 1959), 21.

[6] Thus he says virtue is applicable to "every Performance, by which Man, contrary to the impulse of Nature, should endeavor the Benefit of others, or the Conquest of

under the second condition, it is necessary to judge the results which it
led to, or, in other words, whether it was publicly beneficial. By holding
to both these standards at the same time, Kaye asserts, Mandeville arrived
at his paradox that public benefits arose from private vices. However,
Kaye then says that in fact Mandeville's adoption of the first condition
of "rigorism" was indeed disingenuous and that by insisting upon it at
the same time as he insisted upon the utilitarian condition, he was achiev-
ing a *reductio ad absurdum* of rigorism. And this was entirely understandable since, according to Kaye, Mandeville's rigorism was in any
case an entirely artificial addition to his thought.[7]

The confusion of Kaye's treatment of Mandeville's ethics has been
clearly shown up in an important article by M. J. Scott-Taggart, entitled
"Mandeville: Cynic or Fool?" [8] Scott-Taggart is concerned with rejecting
both the traditional view that Mandeville's *Fable* was a testimonial for
vice and Kaye's view that the adoption of two standards led Mandeville
to paradox and to a *reductio ad absurdum* of rigorism. In dealing with
Kaye's interpretation, Scott-Taggart holds that there may be no inconsistency in holding to the two standards as Kaye has understood them.
"In a footnote," writes Scott-Taggart, "Kaye explains that he is using the
terms 'rigorism' and 'utilitarianism' loosely, and intends his use of the
latter term to mark 'an opposition to the insistence of "rigoristic" ethics
that not results but motivation by right principle determines virtuous-
ness." [9] Where Kaye wrote that "The paradox that private vices are
public benefits is merely a statement of the paradoxical mixing of moral
criteria which runs through the book," [10] Scott-Taggart would substitute
the following revision: " 'The paradox that private vices are public benefits is merely a statement of the paradoxical mixing of appraisal of conduct in terms of motive and appraisal of conduct in terms of consequences.' But," adds Scott-Taggart, "there is nothing paradoxical about
this mixing as such. We might analogously be interested both in the
dexterity and effectiveness of an action, and discover that, although
connected, the two were not exactly correlated with one another. To

his own Passions out of a Rational Ambition of being good." *The Fable of the Bees*,
ed. F. B. Kaye (Oxford Univ. Press, 1924), I, 48-9.
  [7] See Kaye, I, lii-lvi. This is also the view taken by J. Viner who regarded "the
advocacy, real or pretended, of unqualified rigorism in morals" as "an essential element of Mandeville's system of thought." Viner supported Kaye's view in saying that
Mandeville achieved a *reductio ad absurdum* of rigorism, though unlike Kaye he
insisted that this is a deliberate part of Mandeville's intention. See J. Viner, *The
Long View and the Short* (Glencoe, Ill., 1958), 334.
  [8] In *Philosophical Quarterly*, v. 16, no. 64 (July, 1966).
  [9] Scott-Taggart, 228.
  [10] *Loc. cit.*

infer from this that one of them must be dropped as in some way impossible would be absurd: we select between them according to the purposes we want served." [11] In short, Mandeville offers to the world two competing varieties of moral principle, without overtly recommending that we adopt the one or the other.[12]

Kaye's interpretation of Mandeville as defending a substantially utilitarian ethic which defines the morality of actions in terms of their social consequences is thus confused and misleading. Mandeville was not concerned with advancing a substantive moral view when he advanced his paradox, "private vices, public benefits"; rather he was concerned with exposing the inconsistency and hypocrisy of those who in his own society did try to retain an ascetic and utilitarian ethic simultaneously. His argument showed, in a characteristically pungent manner, the absurdities which resulted from such combinations. Although we may be tempted to ascertain his own commitment to one ethic or another, such a commitment cannot be deduced from his paradox. Moreover, a concentration on this aspect of his thought – i.e., his satirical intentions – obscures a more interesting and ambitious attempt of Mandeville's, namely, his attempt to derive an explanation of moral motivation from the psychological facts about human nature, to wit, his naturalism.

Mandeville's naturalism can be clearly seen if we examine the context of his initial definition of vice and virtue in *An Enquiry into the Origin of Moral Virtue*. As the title suggests, Mandeville in this work is examining the origins of morality or trying to give an account of the way in which man became a moral being. He does this by saying that "Lawgivers and other wise Men, that have laboured for the Establishment of Society," having thoroughly examined human nature, agreed upon the need for a "myth" which represented men as either angelic (if they were rational and disinterested) or brutish (if they were "passionate" and selfish).[13] This mythical division of men into those who by their behavior benefitted society at large and those who benefitted none but themselves, was the first distinction made between virtue and vice, for the former men's actions were characterized as virtuous while the latter's were characterized as vicious. According to this myth, the lawgivers relied upon the natural instinct of man to seek the esteem of his fellows to lead men to try to emulate the virtuous. Although in the second part of *The Fable* Mandeville shows that social norms evolved over vast epochs (that

---

[11] *Loc. cit.* J. C. Maxwell also takes this view in his essay "Ethics and Politics in Mandeville," *Philosophy*, **XXVI** (1951), 242-52.
[12] Scott-Taggart, 228.
[13] Kaye, I, 42.

in fact the literal "invention" of morality by particular men was to be read as an allegory), the basic understanding of moral behavior as a reaction to the opinion of other men remained Mandeville's basic tenet.

Scott-Taggart explains the way in which Mandeville thereby moves from "you ought" to "I ought" as follows: "The fact that *other people* have an interest in my being moral entails that *I* have an interest in being moral, not merely to the extent that other people are able to punish me physically for not being moral, but also to the further extent that other people are able to back up their interest with approval or disapproval." [14] In the social context as a whole, Mandeville sees this motivation as making for stability; each individual, in pursuing his need for the approbation of his fellows (ultimately deriving from what Mandeville calls "self-liking"), contributes to the welfare of society as a whole. This is thus his view of the harmony of interests. Whenever there is a threat to this naturally smooth-running order of things, it is the responsibility of political leaders to suppress or control this potential disturbance.

To continue this line of discussion would be to enlarge upon Mandeville's social theory, whereas my intention has been only to establish the naturalistic basis of his ethics. It is therefore to consider his religion that I now turn.

iii

To support my contention that a naturalistic interpretation also gives us a clearer idea of the place of religion in Mandeville's thought, I propose to consider his *Free Thoughts on Religion, the Church, and National Happiness*. Although this work, as its title implies, is concerned with religion, the Church and questions of faith and happiness, it is also, as soon becomes apparent to the reader, a plea for toleration and an end to sectarian schism. However, what might be called the political intention of the book – the strict control of the clergy in the public interest – covers up yet another aspect of the author's interest, namely, his obsession with "anatomizing" human nature.[15] Although an understanding of the theological background to his plea for toleration helps us to understand one part of the *Free Thoughts*, it does little to shed light on this really important intention – the exploration of the motives and behavior of men in religious matters.

---

[14] Scott-Taggart, 230-31.
[15] Thus Mandeville speaks of "The curious, that are skill'd in anatomizing the invisible Part of Man. . . ." Kaye, I, 145.

One of the most striking features about the *Free Thoughts* is Mandeville's tendency to avoid religious controversy altogether. He does this on the grounds that the traditional controversies are too complicated for him or any man to solve. Thus it is his view that men have wasted their time in trying to solve the problem of how God can be both one and three persons at the same time. They have vainly wrestled with the complex problems of free-will and predestination, mysteries which were beyond the competence even of St. Paul to elucidate. They have taken to arguing about such matters as the symbolic function of the cross and various other rites and ceremonies of the Christian religion. Mandeville's attitude in these matters has, of course, been seen as part of what I have called the political intention of the book, that is, the aim of getting the Church entirely under the control of the state. This aim has been interpreted in the light of events and ideas in seventeenth-century Holland (which Mandeville knew well), as well as in the context of Augustan England. Thus G. S. Vichert traces the growth of toleration in Holland after the bitter sectarian struggle between the Calvinists and the Arminian Remonstrants and remarks that these events were followed closely in England.[16] In addition, Englishmen themselves had seen religious disputes cause major disruptions in their own country and were therefore well-disposed towards latitudinarianism.

While this type of explanation helps to make clear the likely considerations which gave rise to Mandeville's plea for tolerance, it does not convey the sense in which his avoidance of theological discussion is inextricably linked to his desire to pursue the subject from the point of view of a psychologist examining human actions and responses. Thus in the examples I have referred to, when discussing the problem of the trinity, Mandeville is more interested in the way men come to accept ideas contrary to their senses and to reason, than in the theological merits of the various views on this subject. He anticipates the modern school of behaviorist psychology when he speculates upon the manipulation of religious belief: ". . . were Men to be taught from their Infancy that it was a Mystery, that on a certain occasion Two and Two made Seven, with an addition to be believ'd on pain of Damnation, I am perswaded, that at least Seven in Ten would swallow the shameful Paradox. . . ." [17] In a similar manner his consideration of the question of free will and determinism is largely taken up with an analysis of human behavior only

[16] G. S. Vichert, *A Critical Study of the English Works of Bernard Mandeville (1670-1733)*, Ph.D. Thesis, U. of London, 1964, 166-67.
[17] *Free Thoughts*, 80.

tenuously connected with the theological problem itself. He asserts that everyone "can wish what he pleases," but not will what he pleases, for,

was the one as Arbitrary as the other, there would be more Virtue, and not half the Misery, and what are call'd Misfortunes in the World, of what we now see Men labour under. There is hardly a Person so debauch'd, but what has often wish'd, tho' but for his Health's or Fortune's sake, that it was in his Power to lead a more regular Life: What is it hinders him, but his Appetites and Inclinations, that influence and seduce his Will, and do him the same Prejudice he could receive from a fatal and unavoidable Necessity of Sinning? [18]

Not only does such a passage reveal that Mandeville is back to his favorite pastime of scrutinizing human motives, but it confirms his treatment of moral behavior as being comprehensible in psychological terms. The other example mentioned above, that of the symbolic role of the cross in Christianity, is also discussed in the context of a psychological examination, this time into the role of rites and their impact on the human psyche.

If Mandeville's concern in the *Free Thoughts* is with a pathology of the religious instinct in man and a psychological account of religious behavior, this concern remains active in his other works on religion. The title of his last work, *An Enquiry into the Origin of Honour and the Usefulness of Christianity in War*, suggests that he is again investigating how men reconcile their religious beliefs with their behavior. Once again this interest can be understood in terms of a Calvinist background, but an extended treatment of his thought in terms of a doctrinal position is liable to obscure rather than clarify what he is doing. For example, Vichert observes that "Bayle's view of man is darker and sterner than Mandeville's, but the difference is only of degree. Immediately behind both of them stand the words of the Heidelberg catechism." [19] Such an approach surely obscures the fact that in Mandeville's hands the doctrine has become entirely secularized: not only has he abandoned redemption for corrupted man, but he concentrates his attention on considering in detail the behavior of fallen man. When his views come closest to Calvinism, he is being satirical or expressing cynicism. M. M. Goldsmith succinctly elucidates this point as follows:

Rigorous Calvinism or Augustinianism can produce a condemnation of human beings so thorough that it caricatures itself. If all men sin all the

---

[18] *Ibid.*, 89-90.
[19] Vichert, 165-66.

time, if no man can be righteous, the distinction between good and evil seems meaningless. If men are damned for helping others because they do it as a result of their natural desire to win the approval of other men (approbativeness, a form of pride) and damned for gratifying themselves and ignoring others, damned if they do and if they don't, then, says the cynic, why not do as you please? [20]

It is the entire inability of such versions as E. Chiasson's to account for this secular, not to say wordly, tone of Mandeville's which make them so unconvincing.[21] Not only does such a strictly "doctrinal" account

---

[20] M. M. Goldsmith, Introduction to *An Enquiry into the Origin of Honour and the Usefulness of Christianity in War* (London, 1971), xvii.

[21] See E. J. Chiasson, "Bernard Mandeville: A Reappraisal," *Philological Quarterly,* XLIX, 4 (October 1970), 489-519. Chiasson is concerned with refuting the view that Mandeville is to be read as an exponent of "segregation," i.e., a complete division between grace and nature. He maintains that Mandeville must be seen in the "massive but flexible" tradition of Christian humanism, as a successor to Hooker in asserting the need for grace and regeneration. Moreover, he observes, "the supposition that Mandeville could seriously propose embracing *either* the world *or* religion is a serious misunderstanding of what he means by both terms. For just as he recognizes in his philosophy of man that grace is given to nature to regenerate it, so he recognizes, in his social philosophy, that the purely secular state is a truncated version of what the state might be if grace and revelation were permitted to perform their illuminating function" (p. 515).
There seems to be little evidence from the texts to support Chiasson's main argument and where he does quote from Mandeville to support his position, his references often seem to ignore entirely the contexts from which they are removed. Thus his reference to Mandeville's acknowledgement of the possibility of knowledge of an infinite and eternal being (Kaye, II, 208) appears in the context of Mandeville's explanation of savage man; prompted by fear, the savage begins to entertain "some glimmering Notions of an invisible Power" (Kaye, II, 207). In this passage Mandeville explores the psychological origins of the religious impulse – a factor ignored by Chiasson.
Later on, quoting from Mandeville to show his awareness of man's obligation to God, Chiasson neglects to point out that this remark is to be found in a passage dealing with the development of the religious instinct in man, once man had advanced beyond paying "his Respects to the Tree, he gathers Nuts from" (Kaye, II, 211). The type of analysis Mandeville pursues in this part of *The Fable* seems to be entirely ignored by Chiasson. Mandeville's concern here is to relate the religious impulse in men to the passions and to trace the development of the ideas man had of the supernatural as society advanced. Thus he clearly says, "Another Reason, why Fear is an elder Motive to Religion, than Gratitude, is, that an untaught Man would never suspect; that the same Cause, which he receiv'd Good from, would ever do him Hurt; and Evil, without doubt, would always gain his Attention first" (Kaye, II, 212).
When he deals with Mandeville's attitude to reason, Chiasson again seems to miss the point, for rather than reason guiding the passions, the reverse is Mandeville's stated view. According to Mandeville, ". . . we are ever pushing our Reason which way soever we feel Passion to draw it, and Self-love pleads to all human Creatures for their different Views, still furnishing every individual with Arguments to justify their Inclinations" (Kaye, I, 333). At least part of Mandeville's satire rests upon ridiculing those who pretend that this is not the case. In the end, Chiasson seems to provide his own refutation by alluding (p. 504n.) to Mandeville's "patience with the immoralities of men resulting from his tendency to look at these matters *as a sociologist* rather than a moralist . . ." [my italics] for he thereby casts doubt on the idea which he began with,

render his satire unintelligible, but it greatly obscures his real interests which are in the psychology of religion rather than in theology or dogma.

iv

I have argued in this paper that Mandeville's religion and ethics are best understood as naturalistic. By this I mean that they are a reflection of his worldly, as opposed to otherworldly, interests and that they derive from his psychology. The approaches taken by Kaye, Vichert, Chiasson and others to an understanding of Mandeville's ethics and religion err to the extent that each attributes to Mandeville a kind of religious concern or involvement, more or less, which results from a misreading of the general drift of his writings. Their misreadings in this area result from an unwillingness to accept the fact that his discussions of religion do not proceed upon any assumptions of the value of piety and do not aspire to advance the cause of any specific sect. This is not to say, however, that Kaye and Vichert show no appreciation of the importance of the empirical side of Mandeville; they seem not to emphasize sufficiently how committed Mandeville was to his naturalistic outlook. Religion, for Mandeville, presents social and political problems. He is not concerned with worship, redemption and so forth; he *is* concerned with keeping the different sects "tractable" or manageable from a political point of view. As for ethics, he is far more interested in analyzing the hidden springs of human behavior than in prescribing cures for the behavioral problems in society.

These were closer to his central interests. As M. M. Goldsmith put it, "By showing that prosperity and power were based on luxury and pride, Mandeville confronted the eighteenth century with a set of problems that stimulated others to attempt solutions." [22] These problems Goldsmith broadly considers as problems of moral theory, of economics and of history or evolution. They are problems of social science rather than of theology or substantive ethics. Thus Mandeville is concerned above all with a psychological theory about how men actually behave; he says little about how they ought to behave, making only a limited satirical plea for consistency. Temperamentally Mandeville is worldly, and he makes no effort to have us believe otherwise. With Walpole he would happily have joined in saying he was no saint, no Spartan, no reformer.

that of regarding Mandeville as a Christian moralist.
[22] M. M. Goldsmith, xvii.

FAITH, SINCERITY AND MORALITY:
MANDEVILLE AND BAYLE

E. D. Jᴀᴍᴇꜱ

Mandeville's debt to the moralists of seventeenth-century France is generally admitted, and it is sometimes argued that, if his reputation as a thinker is lower than it might be, this is due to his belonging to an alien tradition. In particular, the Augustinian rigorism much in evidence in his thought seems out of character with the more indulgent temper of the English mind at the time. Other reasons, however, suggest themselves for the uncertain reputation of Mandeville. There is diffuseness and digression in his work and some lack of definiteness of view, although the

Note

In the body of the article references are made to the two volumes of *The Fable of the Bees,* ed. Kaye (Oxford, 1924) in the form "Kaye I" or "Kaye II" followed by page numbers. Otherwise page references are given to original editions and two modern photographic reprints: *A Letter to Dion,* ed. J. Viner (Augustan Reprint Society, Ann Arbor, 1953) and *An Enquiry into the Origin of Honour,* ed. Maurice Goldsmith (London, 1971).

My references to Bayle's *Historical and Critical Dictionary* (1710) give the name of the article followed by the letter denoting the Remark. References to the *Miscellaneous Reflections on the Comet* (1708) give the number of the section.

The excellent short monograph of H. Deckelmann, *Untersuchungen zur Bienenfabel* (Hamburg, 1933) also deals at some length with the ideas of Bayle. Since Deckelmann's time our understanding of Bayle has become fuller. The standard work on Bayle's thought is now É. Labrousse, *Pierre Bayle.* Tome II. *Hétérodoxie et rigorisme* (La Haye, 1964). English language readers may safely refer to Walter Rex, *Essays on Pierre Bayle and Religious Controversy* (The Hague, 1965) and Craig B. Brush, *Montaigne and Bayle* (The Hague, 1966).

On French Augustinian ideas, there are A. Levi, *French Moralists. The Theory of the Passions 1585 to 1649* (Oxford, 1964) Ch. 8; G. Chinard, *En lisant Pascal* (Lille/ Genève, 1948); R. Taveneaux, *Jansénisme et politique* (Paris, 1965). Apart from a very occasional echo of Pascal in his writings there is no evidence that Mandeville knew the work of the Jansenists at first hand.

Of the articles on Mandeville, the most incisive is that of J. C. Maxwell, "Ethics and Politics in Mandeville," *Philosophy,* 26 (1951). Also valuable is A. K. Rogers, "The Ethics of Mandeville," *The International Journal of Ethics,* 36 (1925). Elias J. Chiasson's "Bernard Mandeville: A Reappraisal," *Philological Quarterly,* 49 (1970) learnedly situates Mandeville in the "massive but flexible tradition" of Christian humanism, but plays down the dark side of Mandeville – his denunciation of, yet connivance at, man's depravity.

latter feature is attributable not so much to lack of penetration as to a feeling for the complexity of human motives and relations. It so happens that these same remarks could be made with equal justice of Pierre Bayle, the erudite French Protestant philosopher and historian to whom Mandeville is much indebted.

Bayle was professor at Rotterdam while Mandeville was at the Erasmian school there, but we do not know whether they met. It seems in any case unlikely that Mandeville could have gained more from meeting Bayle or attending his lectures than he gained or was to gain from reading his major works in French or in English translation. Bayle's *Pensées diverses sur la comète* (1683) were published when Mandeville was in his early teens. The publication of the *Dictionnaire historique et critique* (1697, 1702) was roughly contemporary with Mandeville's earliest years in England. The *Pensées diverses* were translated into English under the title *Miscellaneous Reflections* and published in 1708. The *Historical and Critical Dictionary* was translated and published in 1710. Mandeville quotes almost wholly from the English, but the *Dictionary* seems to have been known to him in French and it is possible that he also read the *Continuation des pensées diverses* (1704) which explicitly propounds the principle of the utility of luxury.

Bayle occupies an anomalous position in the history of religious thought around the turn of the century. If theologians in France and England commonly rejected a thorough-going religious rationalism, they nevertheless insisted on the reasonableness of Christianity. Even a Pascal, who wrote some decades earlier, seeks, while maintaining the necessity and reality of Revelation, to present the Christian religion as in some sense the religion of reasonable man. Mandeville takes a similar line. But, as has often been pointed out, the combination of belief in revealed mysteries with an emphasis on the reasonableness of so believing is somewhat precarious. The distinctive feature of Baylian apologetics, on the other hand, is its insistence on the *un*reasonableness of Christianity. While it may be true in a metaphysical sense of reason, a sense known to God, that the Christian mysteries are above the reason but not contrary to the reason, the mysteries are contrary to the reason in the ordinary sense of the word. To argue for the reasonableness of Christianity is to argue feebly, and to produce feeble arguments for religious belief is to give aid to its enemies. Against rationalist theologians in the Huguenot community in the Netherlands, Bayle argues that traditional Calvinism emphasized the mysteriousness of the mysteries and did not consider that they were truly believed by those who claimed to believe them on rational grounds.

Those, Bayle argues, who seek to make Christianity reasonable do not know their religion (*Dict. Éclaircissement sur les manichéens*). Scholarly opinion inclines on the whole to the view that Bayle was sincere in his fideism. Nevertheless, his anti-rationalism can seem utterly to remove any justification for belief. Apologists for religion did not follow him along his dangerous path. He had, however, combined his intransigent fideism with a deeply felt advocacy of religious tolerance. Personal experience of persecution and the death of his elder brother in Catholic France influenced him in this, but his advocacy of tolerance was consistent with his conviction that there were no perfectly clear objective marks of religious truth. In his plea for tolerance he is followed by Mandeville.

The plea for tolerance is central to the *Free Thoughts on Religion, the Church and National Happiness* (1720), a work of the middle period of Mandeville's literary career, published over the initials B.M. and expressing Whiggish views characteristic of him. While displaying a relentless hostility to Papists and priestcraft, the work aims at promoting tolerance between the National Church and the Dissenters. This is to be achieved by allowing latitude in doctrine and practice. Mandeville's extensive references to the history of Church and doctrine are taken quite straightforwardly and almost entirely from Bayle's *Dictionary*. And in discussing crucial theological issues he makes use of unmistakably Baylian arguments. Apart from one or two direct references he recognises his debt to Bayle only in general terms, but does not seek to disguise its extent.[1] Mandeville's criteria for determining whether a man is or is not a Christian are more elastic than Bayle's, and he cannot be described as a rigorist in this respect. A Christian is required to believe "the misterious as well as the historical Truths of the Gospel, and, by the Assistance of God's Spirit, to live up to the Rules of it," but, "whoever allows of the Old and New Testament, how differently soever from others he may construe some passages of either, so he but believes the Whole to be the Word of God, ought to be call'd a Christian, even before he is baptiz'd" (pp. 2-3). Mandeville's fourth chapter, *Of Mysteries*, begins with the observation that a rigid doctrinal requirement as to belief in the mysteries, and the exclusion from the ranks of the Reformed Church of those not in perfect accord with its interpretation of Scripture, would leave it without an answer to Rome's condemnation of Protestantism for rejecting the doctrine of Transubstantiation. Mandeville's use of Roman

---

[1] This is not the place for a detailed account of Mandeville's borrowings from Bayle. However, with the aid of Professor Primer I have identified in the *Free Thoughts* allusions to some seventy articles in Bayle's *Historical and Critical Dictionary*.

doctrine in order to raise questions about Protestant doctrine imitates Bayle's technique in the famous Remark B to his *Dictionary* article *Pyrrho*. The aim in both thinkers seems to be to bring men of their own faith to consider its grounds dispassionately by way of an examination of the analogous doctrines of a confession not their own. But whereas Bayle seeks to show that the mysteries are contrary to the reason and must be believed as such, Mandeville argues that an interpretation of the mysteries as contrary to the reason puts them beyond belief, and unlike Bayle he makes a distinction between what is above the reason and what is contrary to the reason in the ordinary sense of reason.

Writing of what we can know of God independently of Revelation, Mandeville observes: "In the Idea we can form of the Supreme Being, the first Attributes we are convinc'd of, are his Power and Wisdom, though in a degree of Perfection vastly beyond our Capacity to conceive; and if we continue in that Contemplation, we shall find, that the Unity of a GOD must be equally necessary with his Existence." But if, independently of Revelation, we conceive of God as a unity, the Scriptures reveal to us "something that surpasses, if not shocks our Understanding, which is the Divinity of JESUS CHRIST, and that of the HOLY GHOST." That the Scriptures reveal precisely this is clear to all but the "very blind or very obstinate." Mandeville will not admit that either the divine unity or the divine trinity may be denied and advises us to "look upon the whole as a mysterious Truth, which GOD has not been pleased to reveal to us in a more intelligible manner" (p. 66). What causes mischief is the attempts of theologians to give it a clear explanation. The doctrine is best left in the simplicity of the words of the Scripture and, in a Church which does not claim infallibility, every man must understand it as best he can. Jeremy Taylor's *Liberty of Prophesying* is quoted to the effect that the divine mysteries in the Scriptures "seem to have been left as Tryals of our Industry, and as Occasions and Opportunities for the exercise of mutual Charity and Tolleration, rather than as the Repositories of Faith and Furniture of Creeds" (p. 68).

So far, then, Mandeville has argued against adopting any precise theological formulation of the triune nature of God, and his subsequent discussion of the history of the doctrine of the Trinity betrays dissatisfaction with the formulations of the Council of Nicaea following upon the Arian controversy. Mandeville's detailed account of the controversy derives from Bayle's *Dictionary* article *Arius*. The Arian heresy was a topical issue in the eighteenth century. The careers of several men, including those of Samuel Clarke and, more recently, of William Whiston, had suffered as a result of their inclination to Arianism, and the debate continued among Dissenters after Mandeville's death. Mandeville points to the uncertainty of the doctrine of the Church before the Council of Nicaea and the wavering attitude of the Emperor Constantine towards Arius and his accusers. He also notes the way in which charges of heresy were made on both sides in a dispute in which the issues were very unclear, and asserts that some disputants were moved more by private grudges than by the love of truth. Mandeville voices the Baylian complaint that in theological battles the clergy are both judges and parties and intent on crushing their adversaries (*Dict.*, Modrevius B). He observes that the Arians were ready to submit to a form of words proposed to them but that the orthodox Bishops reformulated the doctrine lest the Arians should interpret it to their own advantage. In fact, more than one abortive attempt was made to concede something to the Arian belief that Christ is not consubstantial with God the Father. Significantly, Mandeville accuses the orthodox Bishops of imposing a formula which turned the doctrine of the Trinity from "an incomprehensible Mystery" into "a plain and intelligible contradiction." And he quotes disapprovingly a passage from the (*Petite*) *Perpétuité de la foi catholique* of the Jansenist Pierre Nicole which insists on the contra-rational character of the doctrine (p. 75). Mandeville had found the quotation from Nicole's rare and little known work in Bayle's *Dictionary* (Xenophanes L). His disapproval contrasts markedly with the glee with which Bayle pounced on such passages from Catholic authors because they supported his own fideism.

The chapter on mysteries ends with Mandeville setting forth "in two easy Instances the difference there is, between Things that are above Reason, and surpass our Capacity, and such as are against Reason, and contradict Demonstration." The examples are one of a man "who could see through an oaken Plank two inches thick, every where solid and entire," and the other of a man who "knows that Two and Two makes Four, and yet asserts, that he believes that Two and Two on a certain occasion may make Seven." The distinction between the two instances is indeed clear, for the first is of a natural or physical impossibility and the second of a logical impossibility. Mandeville is right in saying that what is naturally impossible may nevertheless be logically possible. But of a man who claims to believe what is logically impossible, he remarks: "if he be sincere it is evident, that he either knows not what he says, or at least understands not what to believe signifies. For after all, tho' a Man may believe a thing to be true, which he apprehends not at all [and such is the case with the example of vision through an oaken plank], it is impossible he should believe the contrary of what he plainly apprehends to be true." We may believe, then, what is incomprehensible so long as we do not see it to be self-contradictory. But Mandeville has claimed that the doctrine of the Trinity as strictly formulated involves "a plain and intelligible contradiction," and this reminds us of his instance of the contradictory belief that two and two make seven. It is difficult to see how Mandeville can suppose himself to have an adequately orthodox view of the doctrine of the Trinity. Although in chapter seven of the *Free Thoughts* he dismisses Arianism as a heresy, he may well be unconsciously influenced by it.

Whereas Bayle seeks sharply to define doctrine and doctrinal differences while yet concluding with a plea for tolerance given the impossibility of perfect demonstration, Mandeville, in a much more English manner, seeks to promote tolerance by the blurring of differences. When, in the second part of the *Fable of the Bees* (1729), he says of his spokesman Clcomenes that "He had a strong Aversion to Rigorists of all sorts" (Preface, p. 18), it is those who demand rigour in creeds that he has particularly in mind. But if, in the *Free Thoughts*, he rejects what he considers unintelligible formulae, Mandeville nevertheless rebukes the rationalists.

The proud Naturalists and Mathematicians, who should endeavour to disswade me from my Belief, I would lead into a Contemplation of the immensity, and the order of the Creation, the union between Soul and Body, and other wonders of the Universe, that are most obvious; and having made them sensible of the pitiful stock of real knowledge they are possess'd of, I would ask them: What it was, He could not make, that had made Heaven and Earth (p. 86).

The subject of the fifth chapter of the *Free Thoughts* is the insoluble problem of free will and predestination, on which Mandeville has no personal view. Predestination he sees as a plainly revealed doctrine whose interpretation is supremely difficult. In the end he contents himself with putting before us the example of Calvin and Melanchthon. Differing in their doctrines, the one defending absolute predestination, the other human freedom, both nevertheless aim at the same thing, the greatest glory of God. The chapter displays the same irenic purpose as the earlier one, and it is for this purpose that Mandeville uses Bayle's forceful exposition in his *Dictionary* of the merits of Manichaean doctrines [Manichaeans B; Paulicians F; Zoroaster F] – not, as Bayle the fideist chiefly does, in order to demonstrate the contra-rationality of orthodox doctrine on divine omnipotence, human freedom and the problem of evil, but purely to urge tolerance in matters which transcend the powers of human reason. The point is made simply and directly in the second part of the *Fable*. Horatio, the layman, argues that "the Fall of man was determin'd and predestinated," but the Christian Cleomenes replies: "Foreknown it was: nothing could be hid from Omniscience: that is certain; but that it was predestinated so as to have prejudic'd or in any ways influenced the Free-will of *Adam* I utterly deny. But that word *predestinated* has made so much noise in the World, and the thing itself has been the Cause of so many fatal Quarrels, and is so inexplicable, that I am resolved never to engage in any Dispute concerning it" (Kaye II, 236).

With the doctrines which are mysteries in a strict sense belongs another which for Bayle and, in effect, for Mandeville is also a mystery, namely the immortality of the soul. Mandeville does not deal formally with this in his *Free Thoughts* and we must look largely at earlier and later works for his views. There are no clear signs that he was influenced by Bayle's views on this head. In his early philosophical dissertation *de Brutorum operationibus* (1689), Mandeville defends a Cartesian view. Beasts do not think, and to attribute thought to them would be to attribute a rational soul also, and hence immortality. Kaye has argued that Mandeville was perhaps deferring to the opinion of an intransigent Cartesian teacher, but there is no actual evidence which could lead us to doubt Mandeville's sincerity here. Kaye also remarks that in the *Treatise of the Hypochondriack and Hysterick Passions* (1711) Mandeville raises doubts about the immortality of the soul. More correctly, Mandeville refers to the difficulty of explaining how the soul can be immortal when it appears so dependent upon the body. The reality of the soul is not disputed, but we are told that we must "consider the Soul as the skill of an Artificer, whilst the Organs of the Body are her Tools . . . the Soul cannot exert herself without the Assistance of the Organick Body more than the Artificer's Skill can be put in execution without the Tools" (pp. 128-9). A similar conception is found in the second part of the *Fable*, and the soul is thought of as acting mechanically on the body (Kaye II, 164). This is not incompatible with one at least of Descartes' accounts of the relation between mind and body. In the *Treatise of the Hypochondriack and Hysterick Passions* the Cartesian conception of the soul is reaffirmed in an objection which is raised: "How then can the Soul whose Essence consists in Thinking continue after she shall be separated from the Body?" Mandeville's spokesman Philopirio replies: "This I confess is very misterious, and whatever the subtilty of some acute Philosophers

may pretend to, it is utterly incomprehensible, and would be contradictory to human Reason, that when the Body is dead Thought should
remain, if from Principles of Religion we were not assured of the Soul's
immortality" (p. 129). The terminology here does not appear to be the
same as that of the *Free Thoughts*, published nine years later. In the
Treatise of the Hypochondriack and Hysterick Passions, Mandeville
appears to be saying that the doctrine of immortality, although incomprehensible and seemingly contradictory, is revealed to be true. It may be
noted that later in the *Treatise* Mandeville remarks of women that "their
immortal substance is without doubt the same with ours" (p. 174). Kaye
also draws attention, however, to the concluding paragraph of Remark P
to the *Fable of the Bees*, where Mandeville affirms his belief that animals
feel, and rejects the philosophy of "that vain Reasoner" Descartes. If this
means, as Kaye argues, that Mandeville has become a disciple of Gassendi, it should nevertheless be remembered that Gassendi attributed to
human beings an immortal rational soul or aspect of the soul distinct
from the material aspect. In the second part of the *Fable,* Horatio, the
man of the world, remarks: "The main Spring in us is the Soul, which is
immaterial and immortal: But what is that to other Creatures that have a
Brain like ours, and no such immortal Substance distinct from Body?
Don't you believe that Dogs and Horses think?" Cleomenes replies: "I
believe they do, though in a Degree of Perfection far inferior to us"
(Kaye II, 166). Cleomenes expresses Gassendi's view. Both interlocutors
presuppose the immortality of the soul.

A passage which might with greater reason appear suspect, and certainly appeared so to the acute mind of William Law, is to be found in
the controversial Remark T to the *Fable*. It is just such an ambiguous-
sounding aside as puzzles or divides the commentators on Pierre Bayle,
though it does not derive from him. "We are all so desperately in love
with Flattery," Mandeville writes, "that we can never relish a Truth that
is mortifying, and I don't believe that the Immortality of the Soul, a
Truth broach'd long before Christianity, would have ever found such a
general reception in human Capacities as it has, had it not been a pleasing
one, that extoll'd and was a Compliment to the whole Species, the
Meanest and most Miserable not excepted" (Kaye I, 230). Law's interpretation rests, rather surprisingly for that luminous mind, on a logical
fallacy. From Mandeville's assertion that we can never relish a mortifying truth, he infers that for Mandeville what is not mortifying, i.e. the

doctrine of immortality, cannot be a truth.[2] Clearly this does not follow, and Mandeville in any case speaks of the truth of immortality. Mandeville's introduction into the argument at this point of a remark on this dogma is nevertheless curious. He probably has in mind that the doctrine finds no support in experience and so would not have been believed in the absence of Revelation unless there had been some psychological advantage in believing it. This setting up of a natural explanation of a phenomenon as a complement to the supernatural explanation is a familiar feature of Mandevillian thought, and very much in accord with Bayle's.

Finally, doubts have been raised as to the sincerity of Mandeville's belief in divine providence. Kaye reads with a systematic scepticism the remarks on this topic in the second part of the *Fable*. The two interlocutors in that work are not radically opposed, and Kaye argues that Mandeville's views are sometimes expressed by Horatio, the man of the world (Kaye II, 21-2 note). Cleomenes the Christian says he himself was once such a man. Since Cleomenes undoubtedly expresses certain views which are characteristically Mandeville's, we should have, on Kaye's argument, to suppose that Mandeville speaks now through the mouth of Cleomenes, now through the mouth of Horatio with whom he is in dispute. On this basis, the interpretation of the dialogues becomes a highly delicate matter and liable to subjectivity. In fact there appears to be no compelling evidence to make us doubt Mandeville's assertion that his own views are expressed by Cleomenes and not by Horatio.

Challenged at one point (Kaye II, 237) to explain how the first men were not destroyed by wild beasts, Cleomenes replies: "Providence." Asked to explain this concept, he does so in natural terms without reference to miracles. Thus, Kaye argues, Cleomenes yields to Horatio's naturalistic mode of thinking, which is Mandeville's. In another exchange (Kaye II, 320), Horatio asks what it is "that raises opulent Cities and powerful Nations from the smallest Beginnings." Cleomenes again answers: "Providence," and Horatio observes: "But Providence makes use of Means that are visible; I want to know what Engines it is perform'd with." Both agree that providence works through natural means, but this hardly shows that Mandeville disbelieves in providence; it shows, rather, what his conception of providence is, and it is a conception very much in accord with the spirit of the age, so much concerned with per-

---

[2] William Law, *Remarks upon a Late Book entituled "The Fable of the Bees"* (1724) § IV, 3rd edition (1726) pp. 72 ff.

ceptible order and regularity. Mandeville is following an earlier Male-branchian and semi-deistic view of Bayle's rejecting as unworthy the idea of a divine providence which should infringe the laws of nature that God himself had established (Kaye II, 256; *Misc. Refl.*, § 231).

In general, Mandeville is more inclined to the naturalistic mode of thought than to the fideistic. It is of course not fideistic to believe the mysteries of the faith, otherwise all Christians would be fideists, but there is some incongruity between Mandeville's unworried belief in the myster-ies and his naturalistic leanings. This incongruity does not compare, however, with the tension between Baylian fideism and Baylian natural-ism. The sense of strain and paradox is deliberately cultivated by Bayle himself in order to bring out the supra-naturalism, the contra-rationality of Christian belief. Mandeville's religious views are really very much more conventional and anodyne than Bayle's. They display neither Bayle's dialectical bent nor his provocativeness.

Nothing is more characteristic of Mandeville, as the titles of several of his writings suggest, than his concern to search into the natural origins of things. Not that he intends to displace or reject the supernatural, but rather to supplement it. The supernatural is the source of perfect truth and goodness, which are hard to find. Man lives largely in the world of the ersatz. Yet the natural contrives to stimulate the supernatural very successfully, a state of affairs which is to be attributed, apparently, to the workings of providence.

Mandeville, like Bayle, sees man as dominated by his passional and instinctual impulses (Kaye I, 39). He believes, indeed, that it is here that we must seek the *natural* origin of religion. The true religion, the Judaeo-Christian, is divinely revealed; all other religion is superstitious or idola-trous. Mandeville has the same contempt for idolatry and superstition as Bayle, though he rejects Bayle's view that idolatry is a greater insult to God than atheism (*Origin of Honour*, pp. 154-5; *Misc. Refl.*, § 118). But whether religion be true or false, the source of the concept of the divine is to be traced to fear of an invisible power. Men come, or may come, to "the certain knowledge of an infinite and eternal Being" as their faculty of reflection develops, but adequate knowledge of God re-quires a more than natural power (Kaye II, 207-8).

Similar considerations apply to virtue. Mandeville's arguments in the *Enquiry into the Origin of Moral Virtue* (Kaye I, 49-51) and in *A Letter to Dion* (pp. 55-6) rejecting Christian and heathen origins for con-ventional virtue are adapted from Bayle's *Miscellaneous Reflections* (e.g. § 146). Virtue requires the conquering of natural impulse or appetite. The practice of supernatural virtue requires the assistance of divine grace. What is normally called virtue, as also its specious substitutes, honour and polite manners, is the product of controlled or manipulated pride or self-interest. Mandeville's discussions of human egoism echo the French Augustinians' analysis of the workings of what by them is called *amour-propre*. Two terms, "self-love" and "self-liking," are employed by Mandeville, and the need for the second term is explained by his spokesman Cleomenes in the second part of the *Fable*: "As no Creature can love what it dislikes, it is necessary, moreover, that every one should have a real liking to its own Being, superior to what they have to any other" (Kaye II, 129). Self-liking in human beings is assimilated to the tendency to self-display found in birds and other animals. Self-love and self-liking are means to self-preservation, and the "instinct" of self-liking "by which every Individual values itself above its real Worth" is given by Nature in order to "encrease the Care in Creatures to preserve themselves" (Kaye II, 130). The distinction is illustrated in a curious, and as Mandeville recognises, highly paradoxical account of the motivation of suicide. When we cease to like ourselves, self-love, out of kindness, impels us to kill ourselves (Kaye II, 136). Perhaps we can conclude that the distinction between self-love and self-liking is roughly that between self-protective and self-assertive tendencies.

Mandeville's distinction seems to be an adaptation of a traditional distinction between *amour de nous-mêmes* and *amour-propre*, between a due concern for our own welfare and the corrupt selfishness that expresses itself in pride and vanity. The association of both tendencies with self-preservation appears to be peculiar to Mandeville, although there is a Hobbesian flavour to the conception. It looks as if Mandeville is now seeking to avoid the pitfall into which he falls elsewhere of representing basic and inescapable human needs as reprehensible. Where, if anywhere, he came upon the distinction between *amour-propre* and *amour de nous-mêmes*, which we are told St François de Sales thought was already being lost in the early seventeenth century,[3] is not clear. Possibly he reinvented it. At all events it seems certain, despite Kaye's assertions, that he did not get it from the celebrated analysis in Bishop Butler's eleventh sermon, which Kaye quotes. Far from fitting "so pat to Butler's objections," as Kaye puts it (Kaye II, 130n), Mandeville's dis-

---

[3] Cf. H. Bremond, *Histoire littéraire du sentiment religieux* (Paris, 1916 ff.) T. I, p. 121 note; and *L'Esprit de S. François de Sales*, extrait des divers écrits de M. J.-P. Camus par M. P. Collet (Paris, 1727, several reprints) 13e partie, Ch. III.

tinction of self-liking from self-love remains wide open to Butler's incisive criticism. Like Hobbes or La Rochefoucauld, Mandeville attributes certain actions, which by all normal standards are disinterested, to selfish motives – to self-liking as he calls it. Butler's objection is to the use of a single blanket term – and self-liking is such a term – to apply to actions which are determined by totally different principles, for example "an action, proceeding from cool consideration that it will be to my own advantage; and an action, suppose of revenge, or of friendship, by which a man runs upon certain ruin, to do evil or good to another." Butler concludes: "It is manifest the principles of these actions are totally different, and so want different words to be distinguished by." Butler's distinction is not the one Mandeville makes.

For Mandeville, as for Bayle, it is pride and honour, not a disinterested concern for the good, which are the sources of most human conduct. But Bayle is concerned only to argue that the mere existence of a morally based social order is no proof of the moral excellence of its members, and wishes simply to distinguish a society inspired by Christian charity from one inspired by self-interest. Mandeville, on the other hand, also makes qualitative distinctions within the category of self-interested acts – a fact which suggests that Butler was right in claiming that blanket terms blur morally significant distinctions. A good example of Mandeville's distinctions is his irreverent comparison of the concept of honour among the ancients – "like their Armours very massy and heavy," with its modern counterpart – "very easy and portable to what it was" (Kaye I, 218). The superiority of ancient honour to modern was due, however paradoxical it may seem in the context of an egoistic theory of morality, to the quantity of disinterestedness it incorporated. Modern honour incorporates less, but is not wholly lacking in disinterested content. The view has something in common with La Rochefoucauld's preference for nobler and more controlled forms of pride and honour over cruder and lazier manifestations of self-regard.[4] Horatio in the second part of the *Fable* affirms that "that high Value which Men of Honour set upon themselves as such, and which is no more than what is due to the Dignity

<hr/>

[4] For a balanced account of La Rochefoucauld's ideas, see the Introduction to La Rochefoucauld, *Maximes,* ed. J. Truchet (Garnier, Paris, 1967). Mandeville quite possibly read La Rochefoucauld in English. In one place (Kaye I, 230) he exceptionally attributes a maxim of La Rochefoucauld to "a worthy Divine," which suggests that he may have confused La Rochefoucauld with his ex-Oratorian associate Jacques Esprit. Esprit's *La Fausseté des vertus humaines* (1677-8) was published in English translation in 1706 under the title *Discourses on the Deceitfulness of Humane Virtues* together with a translation of La Rochefoucauld's *Moral Reflections and Maxims.* Mandeville quotes La Rochefoucauld twice but his English versions do not correspond exactly to those in the translation of 1706.

of our Nature, when well cultivated, is the Foundation of their Character, and a Support to them in all Difficulties, that is of great use to the Society. The Desire likewise of being thought well of, and the Love of Praise and even of Glory are commendable Qualities, that are beneficial to the Publick." The pious Cleomenes scarcely objects. He requires only that "that high Value, that Desire and that Love are kept within the Bounds of Reason" (Kaye II, 89-90). Particularly interesting is the assertion that honour is a later and greater human achievement than virtue, though both have the same psychological origin. Mandeville had claimed in the *Enquiry into the Origin of Moral Virtue* that "the Moral Virtues are the Political Offspring which Flattery begot upon Pride" (Kaye I, 51). Finally, in the *Origin of Honour*, Cleomenes argues that the invention of honour "was an Improvement in the Art of Flattery, by which the Excellency of our Species is raised to such a Height, that it becomes the Object of our own Adoration, and Man is taught in good Earnest to worship himself." Honour is a greater achievement than virtue because it is "more skilfully adapted to our inward Make. Men are better paid for their Adherence to Honour, than they are for their Adherence to Virtue. The First requires less Self-Denial; and the Rewards they receive for that Little are not imaginary but real and palpable" (pp. 42-3).

But Mandeville's feeling for the benefits conferred on society by the principle of honour is balanced by his insistence on the self-regard which is its source. He sometimes undermines where even La Rochefoucauld approves or praises. The kind of bravery without witnesses which La Rochefoucauld represents as perfect valour (max. 216), reveals, in Mandeville's view, "no small symptoms of pride" (Kaye I, 57). The general whose calm serenity amid the noise of battle La Rochefoucauld would admire (max. 217) figures very clearly for Mandeville among those driven by vanity and a concern for fame (Kaye I, 213). The two moralists come together, however, in their concern to attack the fashionable and hypocritical outward shows of merit or virtue. In *A Letter to Dion*, Mandeville was to explain: "what I call Vices are the Fashionable Ways of Living, the Manners of the Age, that are often practis'd and preach'd against by the same people" (p. 31). In Remark Q to the *Fable* he had already written: "To be at once well-bred and sincere, is no less than a Contradiction; and therefore whilst Man advances in Knowledge, and his manners are polish'd, we must expect to see at the same time his Desires enlarg'd, his Appetites refin'd and his Vices encreas'd" (Kaye I, 185). La Rochefoucauld himself remarks that the education given to young men adds to their self-regard (max. 261) and mentions – admittedly very rarely – that humility is the true test of Christian virtue (max. 358, 537). Much stronger for humility and against vanity is the Cleomenes of the second part of the *Fable*, whom Mandeville introduces thus: "Cleomenes was of Opinion, that of all religious Virtues, nothing was more scarce, or more difficult to acquire, than Christian humility; and that to destroy the Possibility of ever attaining to it, nothing was so effectual as what is call'd a Gentleman's Education; and that the more dextrous, by this means, Men grew in concealing the outward Signs, and every Symptom of Pride, the more entirely they became enslaved by it within" (Kaye II, 17). And yet, Mandeville in Remark R to the *Fable* (1714) and Cleomenes in the *Enquiry into the Origin of Honour* (1732) – texts which straddle the second part of the *Fable* in time – affirm mildly that the *only* thing they have against honour is that it is contrary to the principle of Christian humility (Kaye I, 221; *Origin*, p. 92).

All in all, it must be said that Mandeville's attitude towards self-regard is markedly more ambivalent than La Rochefoucauld's. For La Rochefoucauld, human egoism is indeed regrettable, but he does not grieve over it. Rather does he seek to make something elegant and honourable out of what he only half believes a defect. He has all but escaped from the other-worldly Catholic Augustinianism which was the matrix of his thought. Mandeville, on the other hand, although far more worldly than his fellow-Protestant Pierre Bayle, is still pricked by a conscience which will not let him rest easy in a worldly morality.

For Mandeville virtue, whatever its source, requires resistance to the promptings of passion. There is no virtue without self-denial (Kaye I, 156; II, 108-9). The principle may be called Calvinist provided it is remembered that for Calvin himself self-denial meant particularly denial of the reason, and in this respect Bayle is nearer Calvin than is Mandeville. The view that virtue consists in conquering one's desires is also found in Bayle, whose dismissal of Loyola's claim to virtue on account of a continence which required no such conquest (*Dict.*, Loyola M) is alluded to by Mandeville in his *Free Thoughts* (p. 194). That virtue consists in self-denial is in any case a natural corollary of the seventeenth-century French Augustinian emphasis on the corruption of the will and the passions.

Mandeville is very much aware of the difficulty of practising self-denial, and aware also that much ingenious hypocrisy is put into attempting to evade the difficulty. His satire is properly understood only if it is seen as directed against the hypocritical pretensions of those who are un-

willing to make the sacrifices that virtue requires. Professor Harth, however, who has opportunely drawn attention in a recent article to "The
Satiric Purpose of the *Fable of the Bees*," [5] has questioned Mandeville's
sincerity in demanding self-denial as a proof of virtue. He argues that
Mandeville's observations on the Stoics show that he considers rigorism
to be an unreal doctrine. And indeed Mandeville accuses himself, through
the mouth of an imaginary Epicurean, of making virtue unattainable in
order to discredit it; but he rejects the accusation as hypocritical (Kaye I,
233-4). In support of his interpretation of Mandeville, Professor Harth
adduces an important but truncated passage from Remark O to the
Fable. In that passage Mandeville speaks of the Stoics as claiming to
have reached the height of self-denial. He then refers to other moralists
(clearly belonging to an Augustinian tradition which, in seventeenth-
century France, included the Jansenists, La Rochefoucauld and Bayle)
who argued that such self-denial was above human capacities and consequently that the Stoics were guilty of arrogance. Harth fails to notice
what Mandeville goes on to say, namely that the generality of wise men
since the Stoics nevertheless agree with them in their chief points, which
are the need to deny ourselves and to put what is spiritual before what is
sensual (Kaye I, 151). So that when Mandeville writes later in the same
Remark that "the Divines and Moralists of every Nation [will] tell you
with the *Stoicks* that there can be no true Felicity in Things Mundane
and Corruptible" (Kaye I, 166), he does not, as Harth maintains, re-
affirm ironically what he has previously refuted. Certainly he mocks
divines and moralists, but for not trying to live up to their principles. The
French Augustinians who attacked Stoicism did not argue that the highest
self-denial was wholly impossible, but rather that it was impossible without the aid of divine grace. Such is also Mandeville's view. Both he and
the French Augustinians would agree that some self-denial or something
like self-denial is possible without grace. The question was how far such
self-denial could be thought meritorious.

It seems that Mandeville's satirical manner obscures the sincerity of
his principles. True, he finds the most prominent advocates of self-denial
to be hypocrites, but it does not follow that he is mocking the concept of
self-denial. His sharpest satire is directed against pious hypocrisy, not
against true virtue which he finds so rare. A Whig himself, he finds Tory
Churchmen devout in words but determined by self-interest in their
desire to restore the ancient power and dominance of the Church by
political means and to create a submissive bigoted populace by social

5 See *Eighteenth-Century Studies*, Vol. 2, No. 4 (1969).

action. In the latter part of Remark T to the *Fable*, Mandeville ironically offers a programme for the achievement of a frugal and innocent society. It is an obscurantist, reactionary, economically retrograde programme favouring a self-indulgent hypocritical clergy who seek to inspire passivity and conformity in the populace for their own ends. Mandeville ridicules the unreal notion of a return to a primitive economy, but above all questions the motives of those who would favour the change. That he is not intending in this Remark to mock the principle of self-denial is apparent from the satirical portrait of the Epicure which follows. The Epicure paints an initially reasonable picture of a virtuous society which becomes suspect when he argues that "to be frugal and saving is a Duty incumbent only on those whose Circumstances require it, but that a man of a good Estate does his Country a Service by living up to the Income of it." His profession of Shaftesburyan benevolism is at once seen to be a cloak for self-indulgence, and indeed Mandeville goes on to say so in terms of the strongest possible condemnation.

It would seem that both the benevolist Epicurean and the professed rigorist are being satirised for failing in self-denial. But Professor Harth argues on the contrary that rigorist and benevolist are satirised for shutting their eyes to the ineradicable selfishness of human nature. On this view self-denial is an impossible doctrine. Harth quotes a telling passage from Remark O to the *Fable*, in which, after noting that the clergy look after their sensual needs and live in comfort, Mandeville comments: "All this I have nothing against," and asks only why any one should claim merit for not taking more than a reasonable share of worldly pleasures and for abstaining from palpable vice (Kaye I, 156). Evidently Mandeville is not an unbending rigorist, but it does not follow that he is in no sense a rigorist or that he does not have a rigorist conception of virtue. He may accept self-indulgence as a fact of life, but that is not to say that he wishes to cast doubt on the reality and desirability of virtue considered as self-denial. And in particular it is not to say that he considers it undesirable because unreal to ask for self-denial from the clergy. The opposite seems to be the case. In the splendid parable of the small beer (*Fable*, Remark T) it is the failings of the Church and of the leaders of society that are satirised, not the principle of self-denial. The clergy confess in Church that they have followed the devices and desires of their own hearts; they admit their craving for self-indulgence; they argue that moderate indulgence is inevitable but excess wicked. Yet they indulge themselves generously while not admitting they do so. They petition and then thank God for the plenty which they condemn as pernicious. Mandeville confesses himself puzzled, and perhaps not wholly ironically. He seems sincere when at the end of Remark O to the *Fable* he agrees with Bayle that there is a contradiction in the frame of man which makes him act contrary to his principles (*Misc. Refl.*, § 136). It is clear that Mandeville blames the clergy for treating worldly comforts as a blessing and for not resisting their craving for them.

Mandeville's thesis "Private Vices, Public Benefits" itself appears to depend on rigorist principles. His definition of the vice of luxury, for instance, is, as he admits, extremely rigorous. So rigorous is it that in some cases we might well with a good conscience refuse to apply it, but this Mandeville will not allow us. In Remark L to the *Fable* he asserts: "If everything is to be Luxury (as in strictness it ought) that is not immediately necessary to make Man subsist as he is a living Creature, there is nothing else to be found in the World, no not even among the naked Savages." He adds: "This definition every body will say is too rigorous; I am of the same Opinion, but if we are to abate one Inch of this severity, I am afraid we shan't know where to stop" (Kaye I, 107). The difficulty he is in is as much a moral one as one of logic or of definition. He is unwilling to give comfort to those who, living in ease, hypocritically profess an other-worldly detachment. The *Letter to Dion* reverts to the problem: "If you tell me, that Men may make use of all these Things with Moderation, and consequently that the Desire after them is no Vice, then I answer, that either no Degree of Luxury ought to be call'd a Vice, or that it is impossible to give a Definition of Luxury, which Every body will allow to be a just one" (p. 42). Yet, Mandeville had gone out of his way in Remark L to the *Fable* to make the admission that luxury no longer seemed to him so heinous in its enervating effects on a nation as it once had seemed (Kaye I, 117-8). His denunciation of luxury as a vice has a somewhat metaphysical or ideal air, for sometimes what he condemns as luxury is not what we should ordinarily condemn as such. On the other hand, even when he is speaking of what all would agree is luxury he does not necessarily show outright disapproval. In his tolerance of luxury for its practical utility he comes close to Bayle's argument in the *Continuation des pensées diverses* (§ 124): "Voulez-vous qu'une Nation soit assez forte pour résister à ses voisins [and this is not a prime consideration in Bayle's view]; laissez les maximes du christianisme pour thème aux Prédicateurs... Conservez à l'avarice et à l'ambition toute leur vivacité..., animez-les d'ailleurs par des récompenses: promettez une pension à ceux qui inventeront de nouvelles manufactures ou de nouveaux moyens d'amplifier le commerce . . . que rien ne puisse arrêter la passion de s'enrichir. Vous accumulerez dans votre pays les richesses de plusieurs autres . . . un luxe modéré a de grands usages dans la République." Like Bayle he maintains nevertheless that "les utilités du vice n'empêchent pas qu'il ne soit mauvais" (*Dict.*, Ajax, fils de Telamon B).

In fact there seems to be some uncertainty in Mandeville's conception of vice and evil. In his *Search into the Nature of Society* he argues that "all [Societies] must have had their Origin from [man's] Wants, his Imperfections and the variety of his Appetites." "How necessary our Appetites and Passions are for the welfare of all Trades and Handicrafts has been sufficiently prov'd throughout the Book, and that they are our bad Qualities, or at least produce them, no Body denies" (Kaye I, 346, 344). And in the second part of the *Fable*, Cleomenes explains: "When I have a Mind to dive into the Origin of any Maxim or political Invention, for the use of Society in general . . . I go directly to the Fountain Head, human Nature it self, and look for the Frailty or Defect in Man, that is remedy'd or supply'd by that Invention" (Kaye II, 128). The defect in man, it appears, is, by social means, "supply'd," showing that it is a lack as much as or more than a fault. Mandeville's arguments seem to pull in two different directions. On the one hand, he seeks to exculpate the legislator from the charge of promoting vice, on the ground that he works with material that is inherently vicious. On the other hand, he gives a definition of vice of such rigour that it includes, without any obvious qualification, basic human appetites, desires and needs, and moderate use of the world's goods. Mandeville seems now to extenuate vice, now to condemn as vice what, to our ordinary way of thinking, is not vice. But his whole picture is ultimately of a corrupt humanity. The most he will allow us (unless we belong to that rather exiguous category of men inspired by divine grace) is the moral neutrality of the instinctive impulse which has good effects but which is not meritorious because it involves no self-denial.

A logical consequence of this view of man is the concept of necessary evils, which has an important role in Mandeville's thought. The idea is implicit in his conception of private vices as sources of public benefits. Just as "dirty Streets are a necessary Evil inseparable from the Felicity of London" (Kaye I, 12), so private vices are evils necessary to prosperity. Here of course the evils are necessary only if prosperity is necessary, and Mandeville has claimed explicitly, if not very persuasively, that he holds primitive frugality to be in principle more desirable than a prosperity based on evil (Kaye I, 12-3). Altogether more plausible is his argument that moral choice will sometimes necessarily be a choice not between good and evil but between two evils. In this case it is proper to speak of a necessary evil.

The transition to the second thesis is effected in Remark H to the *Fable*, when Mandeville first argues for the licensing of brothels. He writes: "it is manifest, that there is a Necessity of sacrificing one part of Womenkind to preserve the other, and prevent a Filthiness of a more heinous Nature. From whence I think I may justly conclude (what was the seeming Paradox I went about to prove) that Chastity may be supported by Incontinence, and the best of Virtues want the Assistance of the worst of Vices" (Kaye I, 100). The thesis is developed in much greater depth, but with a much greater appearance of duplicity, in the anonymously published *Modest Defence of Publick Stews* (1724). This work is so bitterly uncharitable towards the Societies for the Reformation of Manners and the estimable Bishop Gibson who preached to them; [6] it is so ribald and takes so much delight in offending the pious, that Mandeville's attempted reconciliation of Christian principles with his advocacy of licensed brothels is bound to appear disingenuous. And yet it can hardly be denied that the case is seriously argued and argued on genuine moral grounds. It is not impossible that Mandeville is trying to resolve a moral conflict within himself which the ribaldry only partially cloaks. He puts to himself the objection that "although the Welfare and Happiness of the Community is, or ought to be the only End of all Law and Government, yet, since our spiritual Welfare is the *summum bonum* which all Christians should aim at, no Christian Government ought to authorize the Commission of the least known sin, though for the greatest temporal Advantage." He answers with specious logic that if the precepts of the Christian religion are calculated to promote the happiness of mankind in this world as well as the next, then the public breach of any gospel precept cannot be for the temporal good of society and therefore that what is for the temporal good of society cannot be so in breach of a gospel precept. "We may with Confidence affirm, that no sinful Laws

---

[6] "That most edifying Anti-Heidegger Discourse" to which Mandeville alludes in the "Dedication" of his *Modest Defence* is "A Sermon Preached to the Societies for Reformation of Manners at St *Mary-le-Bow* on *Monday* January the 6th, 1723 By the Right Reverend Father in GOD EDMUND Lord Bishop of LONDON." J. J. Heidegger was a Flemish-English adventurer living in London and concerned with the masquerades which Bishop Gibson denounces in his sermon. There is, as Mandeville says, an "exact Account tack'd" to the sermon of the eighty-six thousand offenders punished and the four hundred thousand religious books distributed in the year 1723 through the efforts of the Societies in London and Westminster.

can be beneficial and *vice versa* that no beneficial Laws can be sinful" (p. 69). The logic is, of course, faulty, but there is no solid reason to suppose that Mandeville had his tongue in his cheek. It is unlikely, however, that the argument would have been put forward had it not been for the emphasis which the latitudinarian Christianity of the time placed on the practical and temporal advantages of virtue. Mandeville stresses that he is not defending evil intentions in the legislator. "*Fornication* is, no doubt, a direct Breach of a *Gospel* Precept, and is therefore a Sin; but this Sin, barely as such, concerns the *Government* no more than the eating of Black-puddings, equally prohibited in the same Text. (Acts c.xv, v. 29). [The "black puddings" are apparently Mandeville's whimsical gloss, for the text refers simply to "blood."] Since the Sin of the Intention is entirely out of the *Legislature's* Power, the utmost they can do, with regard to this Sin is, to prevent its being aggravated by actual Commission" (p. 70).

In the *Letter to Dion*, published eight years later, in reply to the superficial and tendentious attack on the *Fable of the Bees* in Berkeley's *Alciphron*, Mandeville defends his good intentions with even more care and with greater feeling. Challenged to show that the benefits conferred by private vices are real benefits, in the sense that they contribute to eternal happiness, he replies that he made no such claim, and that in ordinary usage the word "benefit" does not refer to supernatural blessings but to temporal welfare. No doubt he is right. He nevertheless adds that he would not have described as a benefit the worldly advantage accruing to the actual person who commits a crime. But eternal happiness, Mandeville argues, and here his theology is dubious, appertains only to the next life, whereas his argument is concerned not with personal happiness in the next life but with public welfare in this. And the public welfare in this world may well be owing to the misdeeds of individuals who will be punished in the next. The final stage in the argument is particularly remarkable, for Mandeville asserts boldly, and in full awareness of the shocking character of the assertion, that "the Publick is wholly incapable of having any Religion at all." In the ordinary sense of the words used the statement is plainly false. Mandeville defends it with a behaviouristic argument which no doubt he himself needs to be convinced by, since it appears to protect him from the accusation of advocating immorality. All that can properly be said of public religion, he claims, is that "Mix'd Multitudes of Good and Bad Men, high and low Quality, may join together in outward Signs of Devotion, and perform together what is call'd Public Worship; but Religion itself can have no Place but in the Heart of Individuals" (pp. 38-40). What Mandeville seems to be driving at is that the legislator can determine only outward behaviour and not the convictions of the heart, but this clearly exaggerates the gap between motive and behaviour and underestimates the influence of authority on the citizen's conception of what is good and what is evil. At all events, Mandeville's aim seems to be to show that what is required for the welfare (even the moral welfare) of society may be entirely different from and even opposed to what is required for the moral welfare of the individual. The legislator is not to blame if he institutionalises immorality for the public benefit, since his legislation does not determine the inner convictions of the individual.

Like Bayle and the French Jansenists (and for that matter Hobbes who stands behind them) Mandeville sees the authorities as making disreputable impulses serve the social order. The French writers do not see the whole of public morality in these terms, and if they do isolate a hypothetical social order based wholly on self-regard, it is so that they may hold it up as a mirror to a nominally Christian society. In any case, they see the order which is constructed out of vice as a providential palliation of evil. No doubt much of this is true of Mandeville's conceptions also. But what we do not find these French moralists doing is defending as Christian, and on the ground of the heterogeneity of public and private morality, legislative manipulation of conduct contrary to Christian principles. Mandeville's defence of his legislator in these terms is spurious. We need not suppose Mandeville to be deliberately dishonest (although one is bound to feel uneasy about the *Modest Defence*) but he does seem to be guilty here of a failure of moral judgement.

Bayle observed worldly society from a certain distance; Mandeville was deeply involved in it. Both set out to give an uncompromisingly hardheaded analysis of its moral basis. Bayle sought to warn his fellow-Christians against supposing that the apparent merits of worldly society were due to the practice of Christian virtue. Mandeville claimed to have the same purpose. Both have been accused of intending to subvert Christian principles by insisting too complacently on the merits and efficiency of the unchristian social order of which they wrote. The charge is more plausibly directed against Mandeville, if only because of his very marked approval of worldly prosperity and his irritation with those who toyed with the idea of reverting to a more primitive economic order. In this way he makes a very different impression from Bayle, who advocates luxury as a recipe for a society seeking power in worldly terms but does not express approval of such a society. Mandeville differs also from the French Jansenists, who were inclined to look upon the utilitarian ethic as a more or less estimable *pis-aller* in default of Christian charity, inasmuch as (despite his protests) he gives a strong impression of preferring a society based on self-seeking and self-indulgence to a society based on frugality and selflessness. Since he represents the corruption of society as intrinsic to its nature, his complaint against the lack of self-denial in the worldly must appear incongruous. But there does seem to be a genuine paradoxical rigorism underlying the worldly concerns which pervade much of Mandeville's writing. He condemns man for not performing what of his nature – his corrupt nature – he cannot perform, namely unselfish acts. As with Bayle we are shown little of the life of grace. Only the early Reformers, sadly – or conveniently? – remote from us in time, are held up by Mandeville for our admiration. On the other hand, the hypocrisy of the contemporary clergy, which sometimes provokes in him a genuine indignation, also serves to divert his attention from the defects of his own moral outlook. He may be free from hypocrisy, he is not free of self-deception. In persuading himself that evil is the necessary basis of a flourishing society, in defending the *status quo* against proposed social and moral reforms on the grounds that these are hypocritical, chimerical or both, he hides from himself the extent to which he connives by his arguments at the evils which he claims to be inevitable.

Mandeville tends to blur important distinctions. Christian doctrine, he insists, is to be believed but not, as in Bayle, refined to the point at which acute differences arise among Christians. More damagingly, he plays down when it suits him the gap between Christian morality and the morality of the cunning politician. No doubt it would be more restful to the conscience if, as Mandeville appears to be saying in *A Letter to Dion*, the principles of public morality could be divorced from those of personal morality. But it does not seem possible to accept his claim that the manipulations of private vice for public benefit can be in accord with gospel precepts. That Mandeville should feel the need to argue this thesis reveals the strength of his attachment to the social order that is created out of evil.

It also reveals, however, a moral uneasiness which in its personal aspect is clearly expressed in the preface to the second part of the *Fable*. Mandeville writes of his spokesman:

Cleomenes seemed charitable, and was a Man of strict Morals, yet he would often complain that he was not possess'd of one Christian Virtue, and found fault with his own Actions, that had all the Appearances of

Goodness; because he was conscious, he said, that they were perform'd from a wrong Principle ... He was sure, that the Satisfaction which arose from worldly Enjoyments, was something ... foreign to Religion; and he felt plainly, that as it proceeded from within, so it center'd in himself: The very Relish of Life, he said, was accompanied with an Elevation of Mind, that seem'd to be inseparable from his Being. Whatever Principle was the Cause of this, he was convinced within himself, that the Sacrifice of the Heart, which the Gospel requires, consisted in the uttter Extirpation of that Princi-ple; confessing at the same time, that this Satisfaction he found in himself, this Elevation of Mind, caused his chief Pleasure; and that in all the Com-forts of Life, it made the greatest Part of the Enjoyment (Kaye II, 18-9).

It seems that Cleomenes/Mandeville is in an impossible position. His whole being is necessarily and intrinsically determined by a principle foreign to religion, a principle which cannot be extirpated, though it must be extirpated if he is to be saved. He is one of those who despite their efforts and their good desires appear deprived of saving grace.

Mandeville's conviction that corruption is essential to the nature of man and of society is a source of sorrow to him in moments of pious recollection. But in his moments of pragmatism, which predominate, that corruption seems to him to be the very source of social prosperity and progress. If it is asked what Mandeville "really" believes: that human appetites and desires are evil because self-seeking, or good because they are the source of social welfare and prosperity, one can only reply that he believes both these things, even where they are in contradiction. Deep human sympathies and a strong feeling for the worldly achievements of contemporary society war in Mandeville with a conviction of the profound corruption of human nature. But when he shows emphatically in a series of wide-ranging essays that the corruption of the human heart is no bar to, and indeed may – or even must – be the basis of, the construction of stable and effective social and moral orders, his pessimistic principles can only seem metaphysical and unreal. Yet his uneasy conscience appears real enough, and one may doubt whether his perception of hypocrisy and moral complacency in others would have been so acute without it.

POLITICS AND SOCIETY:

MANDEVILLE AND THE EUTOPIA SEATED IN THE BRAIN

W. A. Speck

"Private Vices, Publick Benefits," the central paradox of the *Fable of the Bees*, is paradoxical because it appears to contradict conventional Christian morality. It seems absurd to ask who was arguing the reverse. But is it? Perhaps because it has been taken for granted that Mandeville's proposition was calculated to outrage traditional moralists, some of his contemporaries whose views might have provoked him have previously escaped notice. These were the members of the Societies for the Reformation of Manners, whose motto could have been "Private Vices, Publick Calamities."

This movement had its origin in the rise of the religious societies which sprang up in Charles II's reign. The first was founded in 1678 to oppose the growth of popery. In James II's reign a community at St. Clement Danes in London established a monthly lecture to combat Catholicism. After the Revolution this community was the nucleus of a movement aimed not just against Catholics but also at irreligion. By the turn of the century there were about forty distinct societies in the capital alone, and other bodies modelled on them began to appear in other towns. Their more zealous members began to prosecute citizens engaged in such immoral practices as swearing, whoring, drunkenness and trading on Sundays. On one occasion they organised a complete purge of the Tower Hamlets district in the City. "They got warrants for search and brought all suspected persons to clear themselves in a legal way." Swearers, drunkards, Sabbath breakers, whores were arrested by the score, Sunday markets, music houses and brothels were closed down. Exhilarated by these successes the zealous citizens formed themselves into more organized groups than the religious societies, bodies which developed into the Societies for the Reformation of Manners. With Royal encouragement and Establishment approval these Societies throve until by 1700 there were about twenty of them in London alone. As well as being concerned with the reformation of manners they were also involved in the charity school movement, and founded some forty schools in the capital for the education of over 1,000 poor children.[1]

The Societies incurred much resentment. Daniel Defoe objected to them on the grounds that they persecuted the poor and left the rich immune to enjoy their vices without fear of the law.

> Thy Magistrates who should reform the Town,
> Punish the poor Mens Faults, but hide their own.[2]

The high church preacher Henry Sacheverell thundered anathemas at them from the pulpit, denouncing the Societies as "mungril institutions" and their members as "sanctify'd hypocrites." [3]

Mandeville, therefore, was not unusual in disliking the Societies, which he clearly did, judging by a passage in the work which he published immediately before the *Grumbling Hive*. The following lines occur in *Typhon; or the Wars between the Gods and Giants*, which appeared in 1704; [4]

> About the middl' of *July*, one day,
> Which, as it happen'd was a *Sunday*,
> The Better day the better deed,
> For 'twas an Age, in which we read
> Of hardly one good Man in twenty,
> An Age, that spoil'd by Peace and Plenty,
> Had no Reformers, under Banners
> Of holy Thirst-encountering Manners;
> Those Champions of Sobriety,
> That watch to keep the world adry;
> Whose Drummers teach one day in seven,
> That the tap-toos the march of Heaven.
> I say 'twas in that wicked time,
> When quenching thirst was thought no Crime.

Mandeville had a tolerant attitude to other vices condemned by the Societies besides drinking and Sabbath-breaking. His *Modest Defence of*

---

[1] Josiah Woodward, *An Account of the Rise and Progress of the Religious Societies in the City of London, etc. and of their Endeavours for Reformation of Manners* (London, 1701).

[2] "Reformation of Manners," *Poems on Affairs of State*, ed. F. H. Ellis (New Haven, 1970), VI, p. 411.

[3] Henry Sacheverell, *The Character of a Low Church Man* (London, 1702), pp. 16-17; *The Communication of Sin* (London, 1709), p. 15.

[4] *Typhon* (London, 1704), pp. 5-6.

Public Stews which was dedicated "to the Gentlemen of the Societies," connived at sins which some of their members considered to be more heinous than murder. In *A Search into the Nature of Society* he wrote: "Gross Vices, as Irreligion Whoring, Gaming, Drinking and Quarreling I won't mention; even the meanest Education guards us against them; I would always recommend . . . the Practise of Virtue, but I am for no Voluntary Ignorance, in a Gentleman, of any thing that is done in Court or City. It is impossible a Man should be perfect, and therefore there are Faults I would connive at, if I could not prevent them, and if between the Years of Nineteen and Three and Twenty, Youthful Heat should sometimes get the better of his Chastity . . . should he . . . drink more than was consistent with strict Sobriety . . . or if . . . he had been drawn into a Quarrel . . . they might be pardon'd or at least overlook'd at the Age I named. . . ." [5] The whole passage ran directly contrary to the precepts and practices of the Societies, who believed in Christian perfectibility, insisted on the citizen's duty of informing on his neighbour's vices, and prided themselves above all on appealing to the youth of the country. [6]

Mandeville's main objections to the Societies, however, differed from the stock complaints of his contemporaries. Unlike Defoe he had no passionate concern for social justice, and while he might have agreed with Sacheverell that the Societies consisted of hypocrites, his chief complaint against them rested on economic rather than on moral grounds. It was one thing for the Societies to wage a moral crusade against the manners of the Age; but it was quite another for them to claim that sin was also detrimental to the material well-being of English society. When they made such claims Mandeville was prepared to refute them.

The leading apologist for the Societies, Josiah Woodward, argued that the reformers were fighting for the economic as well as the moral Salvation of England. He agreed that post-Revolution England was materially prosperous. When dedicating his *Account of the Rise and Progress of the Religious Societies* to "the magistrates, ministers, and all the inhabitants of the kingdom of England" he told them: "I know I need not tell you, that you are inhabitants of a nation, which for its commodious situation, climate, trade, riches and plenty of all necessary accommodations is inferior to few. . . ." This prosperity, however, was in jeopardy.

---

[5] *The Fable of the Bees,* ed. Phillip Harth (London, 1970) [hereafter *Fable*], pp. 341-2.

[6] Woodward, *op. cit.,* p. 91. Their desire to reform the manners of the young was manifested in their sponsorship of charity schools, institutions which Mandeville was later to attack in his *Essay on Charity and Charity-Schools.*

But I must in conscience mind you, that all these great enjoyments are in manifest danger of being lost, by those horrid enormities which have for some years past abounded in this our nation; for indeed they are gross, scandalous, and crying, even to the reproach of our Government, and to the great dishonour of the Christian religion: and therefore I beseech you, even by your hope of mercy in both worlds, that you would effectually set your selves to pull up these pestiferous roots which will produce nothing but gall and bitterness to you and yours in this life, and that to come.

Woodward went on to specify how vice affected the economy.

There is a natural tendency in vice to ruin any person, family, city, or nation, that harbours it. It engenders Sloth, Variance, Profuseness, Pride, Falsehood, Violence, and a neglect and betraying of the Publick Good: It dulls the understanding, takes away the sense of honour, despirits mankind, cuts the nerves of diligence, and destroys the true principles of commerce and just dealing. And by these means it directly tends to undermine and overthrow the prosperity of any nation, City, or publick body.[7]

Another enthusiast for the cause suggested other ways in which private vices could produce public calamities. Edward Stillingfleet preached a sermon on the *Reformation of Manners the True Way of Honouring God* in which he asserted as a self-evident truth

that the sins of a nation do naturally tend to the weakness and dishonour of it. . . . Who can deny that luxury and debauchery, and all sorts of intemperance, not only sink the reputation of a people, but effeminates and softens them, and makes them careless and idle, regardless of any thing but what makes for their own ease and voluptuousness? And in all humane probability, such a nation must sink, when a people of more wisdom and courage and resolution makes it their business to overcome them. So that these sorts of sins are natural causes of weakning the power and interest of a nation.[8]

Both Woodward and Stillingfleet agreed that enormities not only weakened society in the nature of things but that they would eventually call down a judgement from God. "Ruin will persue vice the more swiftly and surely" warned Woodward "because it is push'd on by the just vengeance of Almighty God."[9]

There were therefore three distinct ways in which vice was detrimental to material well-being in the eyes of the reformers of manners, two

[7] Woodward, *op. cit.*, Preface.
[8] Edward Stillingfleet, *Reformation of Manners the True Way of Honouring God* (London, n.d.), p. 15.
[9] Woodward, *op. cit.*, Preface.

natural and one supernatural. Vice naturally made a people indolent, which led to the stagnation of trade and industry. This in turn produced national weakness which left the country a prey to a more powerful enemy. Finally enormous vices would precipitate the intervention of God who would surely punish England as he had done Sodom and Gomorrah.

Mandeville set out to answer Stillingfleet's challenge that nobody could deny that luxury and debauchery weakened a country both internally and externally. On the contrary, in his view such vices as luxury and pride, so far from jeopardizing the country's economy, actually stimulated it. And this in turn strengthened the sinews of war and enabled a nation to maintain itself as a great power.

These propositions, so paradoxical to contemporaries, were conclusions which Mandeville reached not so much by speculating on moral philosophy as by observing social and economic realities in pre-industrial society. He appreciated the simple but vital truth that the generation of wealth depended upon the conspicuous consumption of a small, wealthy, leisured élite. Industrialisation and mass production were later to enhance the living standards of the bulk of the population. This in turn generated spending power amongst the masses, which stimulated production and brought about the consumer society. But until this happened the masses were too impoverished for them to generate significant consumer demand. Consequently growth in most economic areas, especially in the vital luxury trades, could only be stimulated by the purchasing power of the élite.

In early eighteenth century England something like 26 per cent of the national income was in the hands of about 6.5 percent of the population.[10] This minority comprised the aristocracy and gentry, the lawyers and civil servants, and the merchants and traders by sea. It was their spending habits, and not patterns of consumption adopted by the population below them, which generated economic activity in this period. It was the élite which lived "in Luxury and Ease." Most of the rest were

> damn'd to Sythes and Spades,
> And all those hard laborious Trades;
> Where willing Wretches daily sweat,
> And wear out Strength and Limbs to eat. (*Fable*, p. 64)

It was the pride and greed of the élite at the top which provided employment for those at the bottom; luxury

---

[10] Calculated from Gregory King's scheme of the income and expense of the several families of England, published in Peter Laslett, *The World We Have Lost* (London, 1965), pp. 32-3.

> Employ'd a Million of the Poor,
> And odious Pride a Million more.
> Envy it self, and Vanity,
> Were Ministers of Industry;
> Their darling Folly, Fickleness
> In Diet, Furniture, and Dress,
> That strange ridic'lous Vice, was made
> The very Wheel, that turn'd the Trade. (p. 68)

The houses of the rich, with their furniture, tapestries, silverware, porcelain, gardens, coaches, not to mention clothing and catering, created consumer demand which stimulated economic growth

> To such a Height, the very Poor
> Lived better than the Rich before. (p. 69)

Even Mandeville agreed that gracious living scarcely stiffened the sinews of the rich for war. But, he argued, what have "People of any Substance to do with the War, but to pay Taxes. The Hardships and Fatigues of War that are Personally suffer'd, fall upon them that bear the Brunt of every thing, the meanest indigent Part of the Nation, the working slaving People." [11]

As for divine intervention, he agreed that God had punished and destroyed great nations for their sins, "but not without means; by infatuating their Governors . . . of all the famous States and Empires the World has had to boast of hitherto, none ever came to Ruin whose Destruction was not principally owing to the bad Politicks, Neglects, or Mismanagements of the Rulers." [12] The Grumbling Hive came to ruin because its governors were infatuated by Jove with honesty. England would come to ruin if the Societies for the Reformation of Manners had their way. If they succeeded in transforming the ethos of the élite from the concept of conspicuous consumption to the "virtue" of thrift, then the consumer demand which stimulated the economy would be removed at a stroke, and economic collapse would inevitably follow.

Once Mandeville's initial insistence upon the importance to economic growth of the élite's spending habits is appreciated, then the rest of his ideas fall neatly into place. Indeed they now seem almost self-evident. Yet they did not appear so to many Englishmen at the time. Perhaps this was because they failed to appreciate the truth of the initial assumption. Although it now seems obvious that in an underdeveloped economy con-

---

[11] *Fable,* pp. 144-5.
[12] *Ibid.,* p. 142.

sumer demand will be generated more by an élite than by the bulk of the population, this was not immediately apparent to contemporaries. This was partly due to the fact that in the seventeenth century the most impressive economic advance had been made by the most egalitarian society in Europe, the Dutch Republic. As Sir William Temple put it in 1671, "The States of *Holland*, in point both of riches and strength, is the most prodigious growth that has been seen in the world, if we reckon it from their peace with *Spain*." [13] Other Europeans naturally wanted to know how the Dutch had achieved their economic miracle. Many explanations were forthcoming, from their geographic situation to their commercial ethic which put gain before godliness.[14] But in seeking reasons for Dutch prosperity a connexion was commonly found between the economy and the polity of the United Provinces. The Dutch Republic was regarded as the model of an egalitarian society which was conducive to economic growth. This connexion was held to be the main reason why France's economic performance, despite the country's overwhelming natural advantages, had not been as impressive. France appeared as the model of a society with an absolutist form of government and a hierarchical social structure, and the French polity was a positive obstacle to economic advance . Sir William Temple further observed that trade throve under republics, but, although it could prosper "under good Princes and legal monarchies as well as under free States . . . under arbitrary and tyrannical power it must of necessity decay and dissolve, because this empties a country of people, whereas the others fill it; this extinguishes industry, while men are in doubt of enjoying themselves what they get, or leaving it to their children; the others encourage it, by securing men of both: one fills a country with soldiers, and the other with merchants. . . ." [15]

As in the nineteen fifties, when the U.S.A. and the U.S.S.R. seemed to offer other countries the alternatives of Capitalism and Communism as rival patterns for their future development, so in the late seventeenth and early eighteenth centuries France and the United Provinces appeared to provide different models for England to emulate. And as in the Cold War, political predilections unduly influenced English thinking on the respective attractiveness of these two models.

The French model appealed more to the Tories, since it conformed more with their traditional belief in the divine right of kings and support for the royal prerogative, and with their strong connexions with the land-

[13] *The Works of Sir William Temple, Bart.* (Edinburgh, 1854), II, p. 18.
[14] Where Sir William Temple attributed Dutch prosperity to their frugality, Mandeville characteristically countered by attributing it to their extravagance. *Fable,* p. 205.
[15] *The Works of Sir William Temple, Bart.* (Edinburgh, 1854), I, pp. 120-1.

ed elements in society and their dislike of the monied and trading section of the community. The Dutch model was more to the liking of the Whigs, fitting in more appropriately with their preference for the contractual theory of government, and with their links with the business and commercial interests. Not that either party identified completely with the preferred model outside the more extreme propaganda effusions of their opponents. The Tories were not all Francophiles bent on introducing Bourbon despotism into England, despite Whig assertions to the contrary. Nor were the Whigs really attempting to convert England into a Dutch Republic, although many Tories were prepared to say that they were. The parties showed their predilections more by their aversion to the model they disliked than by their advocacy of the one they preferred. Thus the Whigs symbolised their opposition to French culture by carrying effigies of Louis XIV side by side with pairs of wooden shoes in their propaganda processions. Their equation of arbitrary power and poverty could not have been more vividly depicted. Tory detestation of the Dutch model was so marked that the third earl of Shaftesbury once wrote "If you would discover a concealed Tory, Jacobite or Papist speak but of the Dutch and you will find him out by his passionate railing." [16]

Most foreigners, especially Dutchmen, identified with the English Whigs – not surprisingly in view of Tory xenophobia – and Mandeville was no exception. His Whiggism is implicit in the very opening lines of the *Grumbling Hive*. The hive "fam'd for Laws and Arms" is immediately recognisable as post-Revolution England seen, with approval, through Whig eyes. England became famed for arms after 1688. Before that she had been a satellite of France. It was the Revolution which brought her to the forefront of European power politics. The Tories resented this development. They would have preferred England to remain isolated from the continent. The Whigs, on the other hand, applauded it, as clearly did Mandeville. He also eulogised the Revolution Settlement in the lines,

> No Bees had better Government . . .
> They were not Slaves to Tyranny,
> Nor ruled by wild Democracy;
> But Kings, that could not wrong, because
> Their Power was circumscrib'd by Laws.

Although the notion that England was blessed with a better constitution than other countries because she enjoyed a mixed monarchy was axio-

[16] Public Record Office, Shaftesbury Papers 30/24/22/2.

matic with most Englishmen, this was a very Whiggish way of expressing
the sentiment. Tories tended to stress how, in a mixed monarchy, the
ruler could still check the power of the lords and commons, and thereby
preserve constitutional equilibrium. It was the Whigs who usually
emphasised, as Mandeville does here, that the balance between tyranny
and "wild democracy" had been achieved in the Revolution settlement
by circumscribing the powers of the monarch.

The most explicit acknowledgment of Mandeville's commitment to the
Whigs, however, was in a tract he published soon after the Hanoverian
accession which had the ironic title *The Mischiefs that ought Justly to
be Apprehended from a Whig Government*. It took the form of a dialogue between a Tory, "Tantivy" and a Whig, "Loveright." As the very
names imply, this was a strong attack on Tory attitudes and a sturdy
defence of Whig principles. Dealing with the preaching of the high
church Tory clergy, "Loveright" expostulated "to read some sermons
one would think there was no other sin than being a Whig, and nothing
was requir'd towards salvation besides being a Tory and to stand up for
the High Church." [17] He also stood up for the Whig principle of the right
to resist tyrants in the most uncompromising terms. When citing English
precedents in support of the right, most Whigs were content to refer to the
Glorious Revolution of 1688 and the resistance to James II. Few dared
to acknowledge in print that the opposition to Charles I had been justified. Yet at a Time when the Tory cult of Charles king and martyr made
it imprudent to draw precedents from the civil war period, "Loveright"
went so far as to say that "the ship money alone was enough to justify
resistance." [18] On the eve of the General Election of 1715, therefore,
Mandeville revealed himself as a thoroughgoing Whig.

It might be expected that Mandeville's Whiggism would include the
acceptance of Whig views on the United Provinces and France. But, on
the contrary, he could not accept that an egalitarian society generated
more wealth than an aristocratic society. Mandeville, in self-imposed
exile from Holland, was not as infatuated with Dutch models as were
English economists and politicians. And though he disliked the French
form of absolutism, saying of Louis XIV that "he ought to be detested
by all that hate slavery," [19] he could appreciate that France's social struc-

---

[17] *The Mischiefs that ought Justly to be Apprehended from a Whig Government*
(London, 1714), p. 21.

[18] *Ibid.*, p. 23.

[19] *The Virgin Unmask'd: or, Female Dialogues Betwixt an Elderly Maiden Lady,
and her Niece, On several Diverting Discourses on Love, Marriage, Memoirs, and
Morals, &c. of the Times* (London, 1709), p. 127.

ture could create internal economic strength. Where contemporary Englishmen were impressed with the distribution of wealth in the two countries, admiring its evenness in the United Provinces and deploring its unevenness in France, Mandeville was more concerned with its creation. Thus he agreed that "where nations are equal in riches and plenty, the lowest rank of people will not be so poor in a commonwealth, as in a kingdom, and ... they must still be more superlatively mean in am absolute than in a limited monarchy." [20] But he disagreed that the French and the Dutch were equal in riches and plenty. France must not be judged by the poverty of her peasants. The prodigious wealth of her nobility indicated formidable economic potential. "What multitudes of tradesmen and artificers must they not employ in every corner? And the whole being inspir'd with the same gayety and fickleness in their fashions, it is possible but this must, without considering any foreign trade, occasion an incredible circulation of money among themselves." [21]

Mandeville's views on social structure and economic growth, therefore, were at odds with those held by his fellow Whigs. To some extent he was old fashioned. He was not welcoming the emergence of a new capitalist bourgeoisie so much as praising the economic role of the old aristocracy. In other ways he was astonishingly percipient about future trends. The heyday of the Dutch republic was over, its golden era of economic expansion about to be replaced by "the Periwig period." On the other hand France had only recently emerged as the greatest power in Europe and was to remain such for a long time to come. Not the least important source of her strength was the prodigious wealth which her kings were able to tap. Where optimistic Whigs were daily predicting the final collapse of France through sheer economic exhaustion, Mandeville shrewdly realised that she was in fact basically strong.[22]

He was a Whig of his time, however, in his enthusiasm for the profound changes which were affecting English society in this period. For England was rapidly changing from a predominantly landed community to one in which urban life was playing an increasingly important part. The economic dynamic of this change was not industrialisation: that did not occur for another century. It was trade that was transforming England

[20] *Ibid.*, p. 167.
[21] *Ibid.*, p. 168.
[22] Bishop Burnet wrote that in 1705 "all people looked on the affairs of France as reduced to such a state, that the war could not run beyond the period of the next parliament [1708]" Gilbert Burnet, *History of My Own Time* (Oxford, 1823), V, p. 197. Among the few who, like Mandeville, opposed this view was Daniel Defoe, whose *Review of the Affairs of France* began in 1704 to counter those who were arguing that the French economy was cracking under the strain of war.

so rapidly that historians now refer to this period as the time of the Commercial Revolution. At once the greatest stimulus, beneficiary and symbol of this Revolution was the City of London. It is now reckoned that London grew from a city of 200,000 in 1600 to about 575,000 in 1700, at which time it housed a tenth of the total population of England and Wales. The social and economic effects of this growth were dramatic.[23] It was the greatest single cause of the transformation of England from a rural backwater of Europe to the centre of global commerce. Those who lamented these changes, and who sighed nostalgically for a golden age when English society had been completely dominated by an hereditary landed aristocracy with rural values, tended to be Tory. They found their greatest spokesman in Jonathan Swift. Those who welcomed these changes, seeing in them the key to progress, tended to be Whigs. Their greatest spokesman was Danial Defoe; but they found a powerful advocate in Bernard Mandeville.[24]

Although Mandeville could write that he would "prefer a small peaceable Society, in which Men neither envy'd nor esteem'd by Neighbours should be contented to live upon the Natural Product of the spot they inhabit, to a vast multitude abounding in Wealth and Power" it is obvious that he was speaking with his tongue in his cheek.[25] Implicit throughout *The Fable of the Bees* is a rejection of rural life and an enthusiasm for the bustle, wealth and even the squalor of London. Only an enthusiast for town life could argue, as he did, that the very filth in the streets should be tolerated because it was "the result of the Plenty, great Traffick and opulency of that mighty City" [26] Advocacy of the importance of trade could hardly have been taken further. One of his main concerns was to show "How Honesty and Trade agree," and it was the latter and not the former that in his opinion "is the Principal . . . Requisite to aggrandize a Nation." [27] His belief that it had not only aggrandised England but would continue to do so is argued throughout Remark (P), which begins: "If we trace the most flourishing Nations in their Origin, we shall find that in the remote Beginnings of every Society, the richest and most considerable Men among them were a great while destitute of a great many Comforts of Life that are now enjoy'd by the meanest and most humble Wretches: So that many things, which were once look'd

---

[23] E. A. Wrigley, "A Simple Model of London's Importance in Changing English Society and Economy, 1650-1750," *Past and Present*, No. 37 (1967).

[24] Isaac Kramnick, *Bolingbroke and His Circle: The Politics of Nostalgia in the Age of Walpole* (Cambridge, Mass., 1968).

[25] *Fable*, p. 58.

[26] *Ibid.*, p. 57.

[27] *Ibid.*, p. 142.

upon as the invention of Luxury, are now allow'd even to those that are so miserably poor as to become the Objects of publick Charity, nay counted so necessary, that we think no Human Creature ought to want them." [28] The Whig philosophy of Progress was scarcely more confidently expressed by Macaulay.

What most disturbed Mandeville was not that this Progress was under attack from Tory reactionaries, but that many who welcomed it were at the same time deploring the very attitudes and activities which had brought it about. Above all it was threatened by the Societies for the Reformation of Manners, most of whose members probably called themselves Whigs. The latitudinarian outlook which gave rise to their development was more a Whig than a Tory attitude. They even included dissenters in their ranks, a degree of cooperation between Anglicans and dissenters which Tory high churchmen considered reprehensible. The high church clergy disliked the way the Societies dragged offenders before lay magistrates instead of citing them before church courts. The Tory laity might even have felt especially threatened by the Societies, since there was a belief abroad that Tories were more immoral than Whigs, a view emphasised in a tract of 1715 which has been attributed to Defoe: "how do the Morals of our Modern Stanch Tories, agree exactly with those of their Predecessors in King Charles and King James's Reigns, when Loyalty and Vice were in the most flourishing Condition." [29] Whatever the reasons, Tories tended to detest the Societies, and Tory clergy were the most vociferous in their denunciations of them. By contrast, preachers who supported them, notably Gilbert Burnet, Benjamin Hoadly and White Kennett, tended to be Whigs. It was Kennett who preached a sermon on 23 March 1704, *Christian Honesty Recommended,* in which he was "careful to point out that Christian honesty was even more important among the great and influential than it was among those who were prosecuted for small crimes." [30] This was to advocate the conversion of the élite to the principles of the Societies for the Reformation of Manners. It is true that the Societies made little headway against the manners of the élite, most of their prosecutions, as Defoe observed, being brought against the poor. But the movement was aiming at the moral regeneration of the nation's governors. The idea of reform from above was in the air. Queen Mary, King William and Queen Anne all spoke approvingly of the aims of the Societies and issued proclamations for

---

[28] *Ibid.,* p. 188.
[29] *The Immorality of the Priesthood* (London, 1715), p. 59.
[30] G. V. Bennett, *White Kennett* (London, 1957), p. 187.

putting in execution the laws against vice.[31] Mandeville clearly thought
that the universal implementation of such measures would have disastrous
economic effects.

Not that he advocated a complete laissez-faire attitude to vice. On the
contrary, sharing Hobbes' pessimism about human nature, he thought
that the state should step in very firmly to deter men from indulging their
anti-social passions, or civil society would collapse.[32] The difference between him and the members of the Societies lay in the definition of what
constituted an anti-social vice. According to Mandeville the state had
made the distinction when it defined some sins as crimes and punished
them. Crimes like murder and theft, if left unpunished, would dissolve
society.[33] On the other hand, sins like dishonesty, so far from threatening
the foundations of society, actually helped to prop it up. Economic
progress depended on the encouragement rather than the restraint of sin.
The state should encourage, for instance, the demand for luxury goods.
It should discourage vice only when it became criminal.[34] As he put it in
the *Grumbling Hive*:

> *So Vice is beneficial found,*
> *When it's by Justice lopt, and bound.* (p. 76)

Or, as he himself resolved his famous paradox in the *Fable* (p. 371):
"Private Vices by the dextrous Management of a skilful Politician may
be turn'd into Publick Benefits."

The Societies, on the other hand, maintained that sins were no less
dangerous to the community than crimes. Indeed the distinction between
sins and crimes, so clear today, was still vague in the early eighteenth
century. Not much earlier it had been more an administrative than a
legal distinction. Sins were those offences punishable by the church courts,
crimes were those punished in the common law courts. During the course
of the seventeenth century, however, the jurisdiction of the church courts

---

[31] Burnet, *op. cit.*, V, pp. 14-17. Even Swift, who disliked the Societies and was
among the most sceptical about the possibility of general moral improvement, thought
that a royal lead could have an impact; see "A Project for the Advancement of Religion and the Reformation of Manners," *The Prose Works of Jonathan Swift,* ed.
Herbert Davis (Oxford, 1939), II, pp. 51, 57.

[32] Nathan Rosenberg, "Mandeville and Laissez-Faire," *Journal of the History of
Ideas,* 24 (1963), 190.

[33] His "hard" line on crime pervades *An Enquiry into the Causes of the Frequent
Executions at Tyburn.*

[34] Cf. *A Modest Defence of Publick Stews*: "*Fornication* is, no doubt, a direct breach
of a *Gospel*-Precept, and is therefore a sin: but this Sin, barely as such, concerns the
Government no more than the Eating of Black-puddings, equally prohibited in the
same text" (p. 70).

was steadily eroded. This was especially true after the Revolution when the Toleration Act of 1689 made it very difficult to enforce sanctions against sin since so many citizens were effectively outside the grasp of the church courts. Although some form of church attendance was still legally compulsory, even this regulation proved impossible to enforce. Attempts to regulate the morals of Englishmen through the old parish machinery had to be virtually abandoned, especially in urban centres and above all in London. The Societies for the Reformation of Manners were seeking to get the secular power to take over the task of restraining sin which the ecclesiastical authorities were no longer able to perform. In essence they were trying to apply the discipline of rural parishes to the metropolis.

We can therefore identify some of the people Mandeville had in mind when he wrote "Fools only strive to make a Great an honest Hive." They were the members of the Societies for the Reformation of Manners. Their attempts to preserve the simplicity of life in a rural village and at the same time to enjoy the amenities of a large city were incompatible. Men had to choose between honest rusticity and vicious civilisation. They could not have it both ways. Those who tried were inhabiting a dream world of their own imagination.

> *T'enjoy the world's conveniences,*
> *Be famed in War, yet live in Ease*
> *Without great Vices, is a vain*
> Eutopia *seated in the Brain.* (p. 76)

THE POLITICS OF BERNARD MANDEVILLE

H. T. DICKINSON

In recent years there has been a major revival of interest in the work and influence of Bernard Mandeville. Much of this interest has, quite naturally, concentrated on his most famous work, *The Fable of the Bees*, and on the ethical and literary aspects of his writings.[1] Little attempt has been made to analyse his political thought or to establish his attitude towards contemporary politics.[2] The main reasons which have been put forward for this neglect – that little is known about his political activities, that he deliberately avoided getting involved in political controversies, and that

---

[1] Any study of Mandeville's works and influence must begin with F. B. Kaye's edition of *The Fable of the Bees* (2 vols., Oxford, 1924) and the same author's essay "The Influence of Bernard Mandeville," in *Studies in Philology*, XIX (1922), 83-108. The *Augustan Reprint Society* has begun reprinting many of Mandeville's works: so far they have reprinted *A Letter to Dion* (no. 41, Los Angeles, 1955), *An Enquiry into the Causes of the Frequent Executions at Tyburn* (no. 105, Los Angeles, 1964), *Aesop Dress'd or A Collection of Fables Writ in Familiar Verse*, and *A Modest Defence of Publick Stews* (no. 162, Los Angeles 1973). Other recent republications include *A Letter to Dion*, ed. Bonamy Dobrée (Liverpool, 1954), *An Enquiry into the Origin of Honour and the Usefulness of Christianity in War*, ed. M. M. Goldsmith (London, 1971), and two editions of *The Fable of the Bees*, ed. Irwin Primer (New York, 1962) and Philip Harth (London, 1970). Recent important essays, none of which bear directly on his views on contemporary politics, include J. C. Maxwell, "Ethics and Politics in Mandeville," *Philosophy*, 26 (1951), 242-252; Philip Harth, "The Satiric Purpose of *The Fable of the Bees*," *Eighteenth-Century Studies*, 2 (1962), 321-340; Nathan Rosenberg, "Mandeville and Laissez-Faire," *Journal of the History of Ideas*, XXIV (1963), 183-196; Thomas R. Edwards, "Mandeville's Moral Prose," *ELH*, 31 (1964), 195-212; Martin Price, *To the Palace of Wisdom* (New York, 1964), pp. 105-128; F. A. Hayek, "Dr Bernard Mandeville," *Proceedings of the British Academy*, 52 (1966), 125-141; M. J. Scott-Taggart, "Mandeville: Cynic or Fool?," *Philosophical Quarterly*, 16 (1966), 221-232; Elias J. Chiasson, "Bernard Mandeville: A Reappraisal," *Philological Quarterly*, 49 (1970), 489-519; and John Colman, "Bernard Mandeville and the Reality of Virtue," *Philosophy*, 47 (1972), 125-139.

[2] Of the works listed in the previous footnotes, only Rosenberg and, to a lesser extent, Hayek and Maxwell, have discussed Mandeville's political thought. Only Isaac Kramnick, *Bolingbroke and His Circle* (Cambridge, Mass., 1968), pp. 201-204, has made an attempt to link Mandeville directly to the contemporary political scene, but even he only examined Mandeville's works in relation to the political debate during the ascendancy of Sir Robert Walpole.

he never wrote an overtly-political work – will not stand up to close scrutiny. Moreover, simply by examining his major works, it is possible to learn a great deal about his view of Whig-Tory disputes in the reign of Queen Anne, about his attitude towards the Court-Country debate during the years of Walpole's ascendancy, and about his theories concerning the origin and development of political society.

It must be conceded that not much is known about Mandeville's political activities. Nevertheless, what we do know of them would suggest that he was a Whig. Mandeville was a Dutchman who came to England in the 1690s, shortly after the Glorious Revolution. It seems likely therefore that Mandeville supported the Revolution and sympathised with the political principles and aspirations of the Whigs, who had done so much to put Dutch William on the throne and who were staunch supporters of the Dutch alliance. Certainly no Dutchman would have found a welcome in the Tory camp for the Tories were notorious for their hostility towards the Dutch.[3] Little is known of Mandeville's acquaintances, but one of them, Thomas Parker, later Earl of Macclesfield, was a thorough-going Whig. Parker was the most able Whig manager [4] in the celebrated impeachment in 1710 of the high-flying Tory, Dr. Henry Sacheverell, and he was advanced to the posts of Lord Chief Justice and Lord Chancellor by Whig patronage and influence. Unfortunately, there is not enough evidence on Mandeville's relations with Parker to help us determine Mandeville's position on any particular issue.[5]

In trying to ascertain Mandeville's view of contemporary politics another problem presents itself. It has been suggested [6] that there is little evidence in his authenticated works to show that he was much interested in politics and that, on the contrary, he often claimed that he would not be dragged into political discussions. It can certainly be maintained that Mandeville was never a political bigot or an active partisan. This would indeed have been foreign to his ironic, even cynical, view of human nature, his realistic appreciation of human weakness, and his oft-stated opposition to intolerant or extremist views. Moreover, his own words can be quoted to show how reluctant he was to engage in party politics. In his *Free Thoughts on Religion, the Church and National Happiness,*

---

[3] See my essay, "The Tory Party's Attitude to Foreigners," *Bulletin of the Institute of Historical Research,* **XL** (1967), 153-165.

[4] See Geoffrey Holmes, *The Trial of Doctor Sacheverell* (London, 1973), pp. 149-155.

[5] G. S. Rousseau, "Bernard Mandeville and the First Earl of Macclesfield," *Notes and Queries,* **XVIII** (1971), 335.

[6] Paul Sakmann, *Bernard Mandeville und die Bienenfabel-Controversie* (Freiburg, 1897), p. 38.

Mandeville declared: "I despise the very thoughts of a party-man, and desire to touch no man's sore, but in order to heal it." [7] Even more categorical is the statement by Cleomenes, in *An Enquiry into the Origin of Honour and the Usefulness of Christianity in War*, that he will have nothing to do with Whigs or Tories.[8] In the second volume of *The Fable of the Bees*, Cleomenes warns Horatio to avoid party disputes in their conversations: "No disaffection, I beg of you. The difference between past and present times, and persons in and out of places, is perhaps clearer to you than it is to me; but it is many years ago, you know, that it has been agreed between us never to enter into party disputes." [9] At the end of his *Free Thoughts*, Mandeville confessed that he wished that he could cure men of the folly of enlisting in parties:

Could we leave statesmen to fight their own battles, and prove their own virtues and good qualities, abundance of mischief might be prevented. Men have had their heads broke for defending the honesty of a courtier, who at the same time was a bed with another man's wife, or bribing over a bottle of champaign, another minister who was to audit his accompts.[10]

Certainly Mandeville himself, unlike many other writers of his day, refused to sell his pen to any party and, in *A Letter to Dion*, he expressed his contempt for such party-hacks:

Those polemick authors among them, who are party-men, and write either for or against Courts and Ministers, have a greater regard to what will serve their purpose, than they have to truth or sincerity. As they subsist by vulgar errors, and are kept alive by the spirit of strife and contention, so it is not their business to rectify mistakes in opinion, but rather to encrease them when it serves their turn.[11]

Such expressions, however, while they show that Mandeville was opposed to political extremism and critical of party-hacks, do not mean that Mandeville was without political views or void of political commitment. He would not meddle with faction, detested those who would preach rebellion or trumpet sedition, and hoped to heal some of the wounds caused by violent political conflict,[12] but these attitudes were shared by most writers who clearly were heavily engaged in the political debates of the early eighteenth-century. Furthermore, there is clear evi-

[7] *Free Thoughts*, p. 152. All quotations from this work are from the 1723 edition.
[8] *Origin of Honour*, p. 139.
[9] *The Fable of the Bees*, ed. F. B. Kaye, II, 42.
[10] *Free Thoughts*, pp. 362-363.
[11] *A Letter to Dion*, p. 8.
[12] *The Female Tatler*, no. 100 (wrongly printed as no. 97), 22 Feb. 1710.

dence that Mandeville, while he was prepared to condemn partisanship carried to extreme lengths, was one of the few men of the period [13] who appreciated the political benefits conferred by the existence of rival parties:

> Parties directly opposite
> Assist each oth'r, as 'twere for Spight; [14]

Mandeville recognised that an opposing party imposed limitations on the activities of the men in power. Though the former might not be primarily concerned with the liberty of the subject, their hostility ensured that the ministers, who were rarely men of virtue, would not have a free hand to trample on the rights of others:

The envy, strife, and all the feuds and jealousies of courts are so many safeguards to the liberty of the people, they never fail producing severe censors to those at the helm, that watch over all their actions, magnify their failings, and heighten the least oversight into a capital crime; ... When Parliaments are sitting, all the busy part of the year ministers have no great opportunities of doing any considerable damage to the nation, and seldom will attempt it.[15]

The same point was made even more explicitly in the second part of *The Fable of the Bees*:

... should anything be done or attempted, that would be palpably ruinous to the kingdom, and in the opinion of natives and foreigners, grosly and manifestly clashing with our interest, it would raise a general clamour, and throw the minister into dangers, which no man of the least prudence, who intends to stay in his country, would ever run into. As to the money for secret services, and perhaps other sums, which ministers have the disposal of, and where they have great latitudes, I don't question, but they have opportunities of embezling the nation's treasure: but to do this without being discover'd, it must be done sparingly, and with great discretion: the malicious overlookers that envy them their places, and watch all their motions, are a great awe upon them: the animosities between those antagonists, and the quarrels between parties, are a considerable part of the nation's security.[16]

Finally, to maintain that Mandeville showed little interest in contemporary politics, it is necessary to ignore two overtly-political works

[13] Most men defended their own party while hoping to ruin their opponents. Very few were prepared to accept the value or legitimacy of contending parties. See J. A. W. Gunn, "Party before Burke," *Government and Opposition*, III (1968), 223-240.
[14] *The Fable of the Bees*, ed. F. B. Kaye, I, 25.
[15] *Free Thoughts*, pp. 341-342.
[16] *The Fable of the Bees*, ed. F. B. Kaye, II, 334. Cf. *Ibid.*, I, 94-95 and *Free Thoughts*, pp. 355-356.

which have been attributed to him. The first of these, *The Pamphleteers: A Satyr* (London, 1703), may have been written by Mandeville.[17] It is a thorough-going defence of William III and his Whig ministers against the supporters of Popery and arbitrary government:

> Then come the Millions, which are call'd mispent,
> Ill-manag'd by a greedy Government.
> Why did the Nation those vast Sums advance,
> But to protect us against Rome, and France?
> If that be done, as 'tis, and we enjoy
> Our dear Religion, Laws, and Liberty,
> Secur'd from Popish and Tyrannick Sway,
> The Money's well employ'd, not thrown away.[18]

The second work, *The Mischiefs that ought Justly to be Apprehended from a Whig-Government* (London, 1714), is almost certainly Mandeville's.[19] In the tense political atmosphere between the death of Queen Anne and the outbreak of the Jacobite rebellion of 1715 this satirical pamphlet was one of the more moderate defences of the Hanoverian succession. It upholds, without any display of rancour, the main principles of the Whig cause. It supports the Revolution, favours a limited monarchy and rejects the theories of divine right, non-resistance and indefeasible hereditary succession. It is committed to the Protestant succession in the House of Hanover and opposes a Jacobite restoration. It condemns the High-Church extremists and supports the religious toleration granted to Protestant Dissenters. It criticises the Tories for their lukewarm support for the recently-concluded war against Louis XIV and for their decision to desert the allies and sign a separate peace treaty with France. Most significantly of all, in view of its attribution to Mandeville, it makes a special point of arguing that the nation has nothing to fear from a foreign king or from other foreigners who might come into the country.

It would appear from the evidence so far presented that there is not a strong case for maintaining that Mandeville was not greatly interested in,

[17] I have traced three copies of this work to the British Museum, the Newberry Library and the Folger Shakespeare Library. In all three repositories it is catalogued under Mandeville. W. T. Morgan attributes it to Mandeville in *A Bibliography of British History (1700-1715)*, (Bloomington, Indiana 1934), I, 285.

[18] *The Pamphleteers: A Satyr*, p. 9.

[19] The extant copies in the Bodleian Library, the British Museum and the William Clark Memorial Library, are all catalogued under Mandeville. F. B. Kaye, Mandeville's greatest editor, has attributed it to him in "The Writings of Bernard Mandeville: A Bibliographical Survey," *Journal of English and Germanic Philology*, 20 (1921), 448-450 and in *The Fable of the Bees*, I, xxxi, note 5. I hope to argue at greater length elsewhere that Mandeville did in fact write *The Mischiefs*.

or involved in, contemporary political debates. Moreover, even if we ignore Mandeville's friendship with such a staunch Whig as Thomas Parker, acknowledge that he was never a party-hack or a committed partisan, and agree that the two overtly-political works attributed to him should not be used in evidence since it is impossible to identify them positively as the products of Mandeville's pen, it is still possible to say a great deal about Mandeville's politics. From a study solely of his authenticated works it is possible to learn Mandeville's views on the Whig-Tory disputes of the early eighteenth century, his attitude towards the Court-Country debate in the years of Walpole's ascendancy and his ideas on the origin and development of political society.

i

In the early eighteenth century the political nation was clearly divided into two organised parties, Whig and Tory, which opposed each other on a number of important issues.[20] Whereas the Tories were loath to abandon the principles of divine right, non-resistance and indefeasible hereditary succession, the Whigs supported Parliament's right to alter the succession to the crown in order to secure a limited monarchy and to safeguard the Protestant settlement. While the Tories were staunch defenders of the special privileges of the Church of England, the Whigs were ready to extend religious toleration at least to Protestant Dissenters. Already lukewarm in their support for the Revolution settlement the Tories were opposed to the heavy military and financial expenditure needed to secure the Hanoverian succession, whereas the Whigs believed that no expense should be spared to curb the ambitions of Louis XIV, which included a Jacobite restoration in England.

An examination of Mandeville's declared political opinions, in his authenticated works, shows that Mandeville was clearly a Whig on these issues. For example, he openly rejected the Tory notions of divine right, non-resistance and passive obedience, while supporting the Revolution of 1688 and the Whig constitutional ideals of a limited monarchy and a mixed form of government. In chapter eleven of *Free Thoughts on Religion, the Church and National Happiness,* Mandeville expressed his political and constitutional views at some length. While admitting that there could be no perfect form of government and that each form had

[20] Much recent research has clearly established the reality of Whig-Tory divisions in the early eighteenth century. See, in particular, Geoffrey Holmes, *British Politics in the Age of Anne* (London, 1967) and W. A. Speck, *Tory and Whig: the Struggle in the Constituencies 1701-1715* (London, 1969).

its peculiar disadvantages, he expressed his preference for the mixed form of government in Britain. This system combined monarchy, aristocracy and democracy, through the institutions of Crown, Lords and Commons, to such good effect that the benefits of each were secured while the inconveniences normally associated with each of them in their pure form were avoided. Such a constitution could be relied upon to protect the prerogatives of the crown while safeguarding the liberties of the subject. Like all true Whigs, however, Mandeville was more concerned about the threat which an unrestrained monarch might pose to the rights of the people. It was therefore vital to stress that: "The rights and privileges of Parliament, and the liberty of the people are as sacred branches of the constitution as anything the King can claim." [21] While taking care not to encourage the wilful resistance of the people to their lawful sovereign, Mandeville believed that such resistance was less objectionable than the exercise of arbitrary power:

The illegal sway of magistrates is not to be justified from the Gospel, any more than the resistance of the people. Where two parties quarrel, and open animosities are to be seen on both sides, it is ridiculous for either to appeal to the Gospel. The right, which princes have to enjoy their prerogative, is not more divine than that which subjects have to enjoy their privileges; and if tyrants will think themselves more justifiable before God than rebels, they ought first to be satisfied, that oppression is less heinous in his sight than revenge.[22]

The civil war of the seventeenth century, Mandeville maintained, was caused by Charles I rejecting this system of mixed government in favour of an absolute monarchy sustained by the theory of the divine right of kings.[23] Only by abandoning such a dangerous theory, and the associated notions of non-resistance and indefeasible hereditary succession, could the people protect their political liberties in 1688.[24] To secure a mixed government and a limited monarchy, the nation had to abandon James II and welcome William III as the defender of both English and European liberties.[25]

There can be no doubt that Mandeville shared the religious views of the staunch Whigs. Throughout his works he criticised the excessive pretensions of the clergy, accusing them of inciting disputes among the laity

---

[21] *Free Thoughts*, p. 305.
[22] *Origin of Honour*, pp. 170-171.
[23] *Ibid.*, pp. 163-165 and *Free Thoughts*, pp. 298-299.
[24] *Free Thoughts*, pp. 309-315. See also the mock advertisement Mandeville printed in *The Female Tatler*, no. 75, 26 Dec. 1709.
[25] *Free Thoughts*, pp. 321-328.

and interfering in secular affairs. He also constantly advocated a policy of religious toleration among Protestants since he believed that they only disagreed over minor questions of ceremony and organisation. In his *Free Thoughts* and, to a lesser extent, in the *Origin of Honour*, Mandeville savagely attacked the worldly ambitions, the hypocrisy and the intolerance of the Roman Catholic Church in particular, but he did not spare the various Protestant sects. He made a strong plea for men to put an end to the unnecessary and destructive disputes between the clergy of the Church of England and the Protestant Dissenters: "The more one really considers the difference between a Churchman and a Presbyterian, the more easy it seems to heal the score, if those who are intrusted with the cure, would throw by their corrosives, and but cease to keep open the wounds with so much industry and application." [26] Though he was prepared to advocate a policy of toleration for Protestant Dissenters, Mandeville, like nearly all his fellow-Whigs, was unwilling to extend such a policy to Roman Catholics. Since they acknowledged that they owed a higher allegiance to the Pope than to any temporal ruler, they could not be trusted to support the Revolution settlement:

When I speak up for tolleration of different sects, I mean only, such as shall own the Government to be the supream authority upon earth, both in Church and State and have no other master abroad, that may make them plot against our safety. It is on this head only that Papists and Non-Jurors ought to be excluded; but this being the business of the State, the clergy has nothing to do with it.[27]

In his contributions to *The Female Tatler*,[28] written between 1709 and 1710, Mandeville applied himself more directly to the impact on contemporary politics of the religious disputes caused by intolerant clergymen. He showed himself particularly concerned by the political and religious tension created by the notorious sermon of Dr Henry Sacheverell. In St. Paul's, on 5 November 1709, the anniversary of William III's landing at Torbay in 1688, Sacheverell preached a sermon on "The Perils of False Brethren," which attacked not only the Whig ministers then in office, but the Toleration Act and the political principles which underlay the Revolution settlement. Most Whigs, including Mandeville, promptly condemned both the tone and substance of this inflammatory

---

[26] *Ibid.*, p. 57.
[27] *Ibid.*, pp. 241-242.
[28] For the evidence on Mandeville's authorship of these essays, see Paul Bunyan Anderson, "Splendor out of Scandal: The Lucinda-Artesia papers in *The Female Tatler*," *Philological Quarterly*, 15 (1936), 286-300 and Gordon S. Vichert, "Some Recent Mandeville Attributions," *ibid.*, 45 (1966), 459-463.

sermon. Mandeville at once wrote an essay in *The Female Tatler* criti-
cising religious divines who would destroy peace and stability.[29] A month
after Sacheverell's sermon Mandeville inserted this satirical advertisement
after one of his essays in *The Female Tatler*:

There is now in the press and will be speedily publish'd, The Case of Passive
Obedience, truly stated in a sermon preached in the Chief Mosque of Con-
stantinople in the Christian time, call'd St. Sophia; shewing, that the disposition of Mahomet in the year 88 was contrary to the rules of the Alcoran.
By Sache-ali-Verello, a seditious priest, that having no other merits, would
fain have dy'd a martyr for the cause, but was preserved by the lenity of
the successors. Translated by a Non Juror.[30]

Mandeville also shared the Whig conviction that everything possible
must be done to curb the over-mighty power of Louis XIV. In *The
Virgin Unmask'd*, Mandeville's dialogues between Lucinda and Antonia
are full of references to the need for the smaller European powers to
combine in order to curb the ambitions of Louis XIV. Since none of the
other powers, acting alone, was strong enough to defeat France then
their only recourse was to fall on her with their combined force.[31] In their
discussions Antonia is much more prejudiced against Louis XIV and
frequently refers to the sufferings he had inflicted on Europe. Lucinda,
on the other hand, is prepared to acknowledge that Louis XIV had done
much to promote the arts and sciences, but this admission only makes
her condemnation of him appear more convincing:

I wish all that were able, were as willing as I, and taxes should be continu'd
or doubl'd, if it was requisite, one six years longer, to humble his insolent
haughtiness. Can any one love liberty, and not abhor that harden'd monster
of ambition? To whom the greatest losses and calamities of his friends, are
not unwelcome, if they can but advance his glory. That arbitrary fiend, that
knowing himself to be the cause of war and famine, beholds the miseries of
his own people with less concern than you can see a play; the bane of
mankind, that can draw whole schemes of the destruction and devastation
of flourishing cities and plentiful countries, with the same tranquility as I
can play a game of chess, and if it but contributes to his gigantick aim,
esteeming the lives of a hundred thousand of the most faithful of his subjects,
no more than I value the losing of a single pawn, if it forwards my design
upon your game.[32]

---

[29] No. 57, 14 Nov. 1709.
[30] No. 66, 5 Dec. 1709.
[31] *The Virgin Unmask'd: Or, Female Dialogues betwixt an elderly Maiden Lady,
and her Neice* (London, 1709), p. 127.
[32] *Ibid.*, pp. 181-182.

Mandeville had no illusions about the glory of war and frequently ridiculed men who risked their lives in the pursuit of honour and fame,[33] but, during the War of the Spanish Succession, he entertained no doubts about the crucial importance of defeating France. In *The Female Tatler*, Mandeville, using the "Oxford Student" to voice his own ethical views, criticised the vanity of soldiers, but admitted the justice of the war against Louis XIV.[34] On several other occasions Mandeville praised Marlborough and the troops who took the field against the French.[35] He was convinced that the heavy cost of the war must be borne and he believed that it was being borne by all the allies. Unlike the disgruntled Tories, who complained about the heavy land tax of four shillings in the pound and who delighted in Swift's stinging attack on the Dutch in *The Conduct of the Allies*, Mandeville maintained that the Dutch were bearing a greater proportion of the financial burden of the war than the English. He claimed that the Dutch hundred penny tax, paid on a wide range of items, was a heavier tax than the English levy on land.[36]

This defence of the Dutch, who were only popular with the staunchest Whigs in 1709, was not Mandeville's only attempt to combat the xenophobia of the Tories. Later, he deliberately sought to reconcile those, who feared the way George I favoured the foreign servants he brought over with him from Hanover, to this disagreeable but temporary situation:

I will easily grant, that it is not pleasant to a nation, to see so much wealth divided among foreigners, but we have this comfort, that they can only be so for themselves; their posterity will be the same with ours. Most of our fore fathers were once strangers, but the first children, they begot here, were *English*. When courtiers, that are foreigners enrich themselves with our money, their heirs spend it among us, and the sons often with the same application, that the fathers scrap'd it together.[37]

ii

Clearly, in the early eighteenth century, though he was not heavily engaged in the party battle and did not concentrate on political issues, Mandeville nevertheless betrayed a marked Whig bias. Later, in the

---

[33] *The Fable of the Bees*, ed. F. B. Kaye, I, 63; *The Female Tatler*, no. 84, 16 Jan. 1709/'10; and *Origin of Honour*, especially the third dialogue.
[34] No. 84, 16 Jan. 1709/10.
[35] *The Fable of the Bees*, ed. F. B. Kaye, II, 337-339; *Origin of Honour*, p. 139; and *The Virgin Unmask'd*, pp. 133, 148, 151.
[36] *The Virgin Unmask'd*, pp. 138-139.
[37] *Free Thoughts*, p. 351.

years of Walpole's political ascendancy, in the 1720s and 1730s, Mandeville, while never openly declaring his support for either the Great Man
or his critics, still made his distinctive political views quite plain. By this
period the previously sharp distinctions between Whigs and Tories had
become blurred. No longer did such issues as the Protestant succession,
the toleration of Protestant Dissenters or the conduct of war against
France divide the political nation into clearly defined parties. The Tory
party had disintegrated as an effective political force since the last years
of Queen Anne and the remnants could no longer challenge the Whigs
for power. The Whigs too had undergone a significant, though more
gradual, change after 1714. Whereas the Tories were faced with the
insoluble problems created by their internal divisions over the Hanoverian
succession and by their complete exclusion from political office, the
Whigs had to adjust to a virtual monopoly of power. Lacking serious
political rivals to keep a measure of party discipline, and with too many
able and ambitious men competing for power, the leading Whigs fell
prone to personal and factious struggles. The political arena no longer
saw a clash of Whig and Tory parties, but a battle among Whig factions
as to who should be in and who should be out of power. In this contest
the 'ins' looked to the Court for powerful support, while the 'outs' usually
sought a temporary alliance with the Tory or independent backbenchers
in order to force their way into office. These often proved to be short-
lived alliances of convenience rather than of principle. Among the opponents of Walpole, however, there were those, both Whig and Tory,
who opposed the administration on grounds of principle. These spokesmen for a 'Country' or 'Patriot' program made a sustained attack not so
much on Walpole's policies as on his political methods. With some justice
they maintained that Walpole was prepared to use any means, no matter
how corrupt or dishonest, to monopolise power in his own hands and to
perpetuate his ministry. By exploiting the resources of royal patronage in
order to corrupt both electors and M.P.s, Walpole was threatening to
undermine the independence of Parliament. Thus, Walpole was presiding
over a lamentable decline in moral standards while destroying the delicate
balance of the constitution. Walpole's extensive use of bribery and corruption was therefore both a social and a political issue, both an ethical
and a constitutional question. The result was a major debate involving
politicians, pamphleteers and moralists.

It has been suggested that in this debate Mandeville must be considered as a supporter or at least as a defender of the Walpolean system.[38]

---

[38] Isaac Kramnick, *Bolingbroke and His Circle,* pp. 201-204.

There is some evidence to support such an assessment, but it is a rather limited view of Mandeville's distinctive, even unique, contribution to this debate. *The Fable of the Bees* can be characterised as a general defence of money, luxury and corruption and as an attempt to ridicule those who yearned for a return to a simpler, more honest society. Mandeville sought to demonstrate that what appeared to be social evils, such as prodigality and corruption, could have beneficial consequences on society in general. Whereas, if a nation chose to live by a strict code of virtue, men must renounce wealth and power. A powerful and prosperous society could not survive on the virtue of its members; instead, it needed to harness the forces of self-interest and materialism. To condemn corruption and to renounce the new moneyed institutions created by the financial revolution of the 1690s might not only prove undesirable but impossible:

> Then leave Complaints: Fools only strive
> To make a Great an honest Hive.
> T'enjoy the World's Conveniencies,
> Be fam'd in War, yet live in Ease
> Without great Vices, is a vain
> Eutopia seated in the Brain.
> Fraud, Luxury, and Pride must live,
> Whilst we the Benefits receive:
>
> . . .
>
> Bare Virtue can't make Nations live
> In Splendor; they, that would revive
> A Golden Age, must be as free,
> For Acorns, as for Honesty.[39]

Not surprisingly, these sentiments, which were so contrary to those expressed by the Country spokesmen, were strongly condemned by the Opposition's leading journal, *The Craftsman*.[40]

Mandeville's disagreements with the critics of Walpole did not just extend to their sentiments on luxury and corruption. He evidently suspected their political honesty for he questioned whether they themselves were always motivated by lofty principles rather than sordid ambition. In the dialogues between Horatio and Cleomenes, in part two of *The Fable of the Bees*, which appeared in 1729, Mandeville discussed the integrity of such "patriots" as were then bitterly opposing Robert Walpole. He allowed the naive Horatio to defend such politicians:

[39] *The Fable of the Bees,* ed. F. B. Kaye, I, 36-37.
[40] Nos. 291, 312 and 320 for 29 Jan., 24 June and 19 Aug. 1732 respectively.

... there have been Patriots, that without selfish views have taken incredible pains for their country's welfare: nay, there are men now that would do the same, if they were employ'd; and we have had Princes that have neglected their ease and pleasure, and sacrificed their quiet, to promote the prosperity and encrease the wealth and honour of the kingdom, and had nothing so much at heart as the happiness of the subjects.... Are there not in all countries men of birth and ample fortune, that would not accept of places, tho' they were offer'd, that are generous and beneficent, and mind nothing but what is great and noble?

But to this question, the tough-minded, realistic Cleomenes, voicing Mandeville's own attitude, replied:

Yes: But examine their conduct, look into their lives, and scan their actions with as little indulgence as you did those of the cardinals, or the lawyers and physicians, and then see what figure their virtues will make.[41]

In a later dialogue Cleomenes claimed that such men out of power were no better than the ministers they attacked: "For my part, I don't think that, generally speaking, Prime Ministers are much worse than their adversaries, who, for their own interest, defame them, and at the same time, move heaven and earth to be in their places." [42]

It is a mistake, however, to regard such remarks as evidence for Mandeville's uncritical support for Robert Walpole and his political methods. When Horatio claimed that a Prime Minister must be a man of "prodigious genius, as well as general knowledge, and other great abilities," [43] Cleomenes, speaking again for Mandeville himself, was quick to disabuse him. He suggested that there were fifty men in the kingdom with the talent to be a Prime Minister for every one with ability needed to become Lord Chancellor. While he acknowledged that a statesman needed great qualifications, a man with much inferior parts might be Prime Minister: "that an artful man may make a considerable figure in the highest post of the administration, and other great employments, without extraordinary talents, is certain." [44] With all the advantages of this office at his disposal, an active man of tolerable education could perform the necessary duties and get the better of men of much greater capacity. His chief task was simply to penetrate his master's desires and then furnish him with everything he could wish. Provided he remained bold and resolute he could always procure enough support to baffle his op-

---

[41] *The Fable of the Bees,* ed. F. B. Kaye, II, 42, 58-59.
[42] *Ibid.,* II, 336. Cf. *ibid.,* II, 41-42, where, tongue in cheek, Mandeville presents the best and worst assessments of the motives of a Prime Minister.
[43] *Ibid.,* II, 328.
[44] *Ibid.,* II, 340.

ponents and pursue the necessary policies of his administration. It did not even require unusual talent to decide what policies ought to be pursued. Experience and a knowledge of human nature were enough.[45] These were the qualities which enabled the politician, by "dextrous management," to turn private vices into public benefits. The politician does not have to find extraordinary means to repress man's selfishness; he merely has to channel it into directions which will also benefit others.[46] Once the appropriate laws have been devised, to make use of man's selfish passions in order to promote the good of society as a whole, then the political system could be managed by men of ordinary ability.[47] If such regulations were established, neither capacity nor virtue would any longer be required in the nation's politicians:

When once they are brought to as much perfection, as art and human wisdom can carry them, the whole machine may be made to play of itself, with as little skill, as is required to wind up a clock; and the government of a large city, once put into good order, the magistrates only following their noses, will continue to go right for a great while, tho' there was not a wise man in it.[48]

Mandeville therefore does not eulogise Walpole, though, in arguing that a Prime Minister does not need the virtues demanded of him by the Opposition, he does, in a sense, legitimise Walpole's position. There is no effort to magnify Walpole's abilities nor to demand that he should be more than he is.[49]

It appears then that Mandeville held neither Walpole nor his critics in very high esteem. Courtiers and politicians, he maintained, were never renowned for their honesty nor their impartiality. Good men and men of the highest quality rarely offered to serve their country in a public capacity. There had never been a minister without faults nor an opposition prepared to acknowledge what merits he did possess. Therefore, while men should not rely too much on the virtue and probity of ministers, they should also be careful about viewing their actions through the jealous eye of the opposition.[50] Indeed, a minister's policies might be well

---

[45] *Ibid.*, II, 320-321, 328-333, 340.
[46] *Ibid.*, II, 208, 318-319; *Origin of Honour*, pp. 20, 28; *A Letter to Dion*, pp. 36-37, 42, 45.
[47] *The Fable of the Bees*, ed. F. B. Kaye, II, 323.
[48] *Ibid.*, II, 322-323. Cf. *ibid.*, I, 190. For the preceding paragraph, see also Nathan Rosenberg, "Mandeville and Laissez-Faire," *Journal of the History of Ideas*, 24 (1963), 183-196.
[49] See M. M. Goldsmith's introduction to *An Enquiry into the Origin of Honour and the Usefulness of Christianity in War* (London, 1971), p. viii.
[50] *Free Thoughts*, pp. 339-341, 343-344, 355.

conceived and concerted, but still miscarry because of unexpected developments:

A man may be well vers'd in State affairs, have wit, penetration, a perfect knowledge of the world, and every thing requisite to make a compleat politician, and yet not be able to make any tollerable guesses of what will ensue from a thing which is new, and he can get no insight into, either from history or his own experience.[51]

In this remark Mandeville showed some understanding of the difficulties in which a minister like Walpole could find himself, through no fault of his own. On other issues he found himself in agreement with Walpole's most outspoken opponents, particularly with such radical Whigs as John Trenchard and Thomas Gordon. Mandeville's works echoed two of the most persistent themes of the radical Whigs: their attacks on the pretensions of the clergy [52] and their criticisms of the charity school movement.[53]

Clearly Mandeville's political position at this time was neither so biased nor so committed that he can be unequivocally listed in the Court or Country party. As an independent Whig he was able to recognise the faults and merits of Walpole and his critics, most of whom were Whiggish in their politics. In his attitude towards the poor, Mandeville shared the common prejudices of the political nation, whether Whig or Tory, Court or Country. The poor must be inured to work and idleness was the prime vice. In fact, one of Mandeville's principal reasons for attacking the charity schools was because they encouraged the poor to have ideas above their station. The education provided simply created malcontents:

The more a shepherd, a plowman or any other peasant knows of the world, and the things that are foreign to his labour or employment, the less fit he'll be to go through the fatigues and hardships of it with chearfulness and content. . . . every hour those of poor people spend at their book is so much time lost to the society. Going to school in comparison to working is idleness, and the longer boys continue in this easy sort of life, the more unfit they'll be when grown up for downright labour, both as to strength and inclination. Men who are to remain and end their days in a labourious, tiresome and

---

[51] *Ibid.*, p. 346. Cf. *ibid.*, p. 345.

[52] Mandeville's anti-clericalism has already been mentioned. For the anti-clericalism of Trenchard and Gordon see their contributions to *The Independent Whig* between 1720 and 1721.

[53] Mandeville's "An Essay on Charity and Charity-Schools," in *The Fable of the Bees,* ed. F. B. Kaye, I, 253-322, is very similar to John Trenchard's essay "Of Charity and Charity-Schools" in *The London Journal,* Cato's Letter, no. 133, 15 Jan. 1723. Both essays were published in 1723 and both were condemned by the supporters of the charity-school movement.

painful station of life, the sooner they are put upon it at first, the more patiently they'll submit to it for ever after.[54]

While clearly hostile to tyranny, Mandeville opposed any extension of political power to the labouring poor for this would only disturb the delicate balance of the state. The same harsh, anti-egalitarian sentiment was expressed by John Trenchard, who, in other respects, must be regarded as a radical Whig.[55]

iii

Much about Mandeville's political attitudes can be gleaned from a careful examination of his authenticated works, even though none of them deals directly with contemporary politics. He wrote even less about the origin and nature of political society, but it is still possible to show that he had some interesting theories on the subject. Some political theorists in eighteenth-century England still maintained that political society had originated in conquest, though it was generally held that it had been created by some sort of contract, either express or tacit. There was, however, some disagreement as to whether this contract had originally established a paternalistic, monarchical regime or a more democratic system in which every man once had a voice. Mandeville made no mention of an original contract. He was not certain whether man had first been subdued by superior force or had been persuaded to form a civil society, but he evidently believed that monarchy was the first political system in existence. Aristocracy and democracy, he maintained, were two different methods of mending the inconveniences of monarchy, though, like almost all his contemporaries, Mandeville believed that a mixture of all three forms was to be preferred to any of them in their pure form.[56] No form of government, however, was perfect. All constitutional systems might be equally good if all men were honest and did their duty. Since this was too much to expect, then "that is the best constitution which provides against the worst contingencies, that is armed against knavery, treachery, deceit, and all the wicked wiles of humane cunning, and preserves itself firm and remains unshaken, though most men should prove knaves."[57] Mandeville evidently believed that the English constitution, since the Revolution settlement, came closest to satisfying these criteria. It man-

[54] *The Fable of the Bees*, ed. F. B. Kaye, I, 288. Cf. *ibid.*, I, 192-194; II, 351-352 and *A Letter to Dion*, p. 51.
[55] *The London Journal*, Cato's Letter no. 133, 15 Jan. 1723.
[56] *The Fable of the Bees*, ed. F. B. Kaye, I, 347-348.
[57] *Free Thoughts*, p. 297.

aged to preserve the prerogatives of the crown, the privileges of parliament and the liberties of the subject. Sovereignty was vested jointly in
Crown, Lords and Commons and, while these institutions performed
their duty, all subjects must give absolute obedience. Only when these
institutions betrayed their trust could the people exert their right of
resisting arbitrary power.[58]

In presenting such arguments Mandeville was only advancing notions
common to most Whigs. Where he differed most from his contemporaries
was in his theory about the development of political society. It was
generally agreed that a good constitution rested on a set of fundamental
principles and that it was accepted by the people at a particular stage in
their history. This deliberate act might be a recent agreement, such as the
Revolution settlement, but it was more likely to have occurred at the first
creation of political society.[59] This constitution might later be subverted
by ambitious men, but it could be restored to its pristine state if men
returned to the first principles upon which it had been established.
Mandeville disagreed fundamentally with this notion that political society
was created by deliberate actions at a specific point in time. He said
nothing in fact about any original contract, though he appears to have
accepted the notion of an implied or tacit contract between sovereign and
subjects. This contract, however, was not a deliberate act. Rather civil
society had evolved over a long period of time and, indeed, was continually evolving. It was not possible to detect when a particular society had
been created or what were the fundamental principles upon which it
rested, since very often changes had occurred by chance rather than by
conscious design. No man or group of men had ever sat down to devise
a political constitution for their society. On the contrary, constitutions
evolved over a long period and in ways which were rarely planned and
hardly even understood. They might be the result of human action, but
never the product of conscious design. Of the laws and regulations of
society "there are very few, that are the work of one man, or of one
generation; the greatest part of them are the product, the joynt labour
of several ages." [60]

Since most laws were designed to satisfy men's self-interested passions,
it could take many generations to discover what men desired for men
were notoriously blind to their own nature:

[58] *Ibid.,* pp. 297-318.
[59] For disagreements about the date of the original creation of the English constitution which existed in the eighteenth century, see Isaac Kramnick, *Bolingbroke and
His Circle,* pp. 127-136, 177-181.
[60] *The Fable of the Bees,* ed. F. B. Kaye, II, 321-322. Cf. *ibid.,* II, 141-146, 187,
287, 318-319; and *Origin of Honour,* pp. 40-41.

In the pursuit of self-preservation, men discover a restless endeavour to make themselves easy, which insensibly teaches them to avoid mischief on all emergencies: and when human creatures once submit to government, and are used to live under the restraint of laws, it is incredible how many useful cautions, shifts, and stratagems, they will learn to practise by experience and imitation, from conversing together; without being aware of the natural causes, that oblige them to act as they do, viz. The passions within, that unknown to themselves, govern their will and direct their behaviour.[61]

It was the special function of politicians to discover as much as possible about these selfish human desires in order to turn them to the benefit of society as a whole. It is doubtful whether Mandeville expected politicians fully to master this art, but he believed that an effective government required cunning politicians who could detect the multiplicity of man's desires and so gratify them that they accepted the rules and regulations of their society.[62] Such regulations must be so devised that they persuaded men, out of a concern for their own interests, to act in a socially-useful way. Man's pursuit of his own self-interest had to be made consistent with the larger needs of society. To achieve such a satisfactory state of affairs, governments and politicians could not leave men entirely to their own devices; nor must they continually intervene to regulate men's passions. Laws and institutions must create an environment which allowed the individual enough freedom to gratify his own passions and, at the same time, serve the needs of the state. In other words, a general framework had to be created, but then it must evolve under the impulse and actions of men's selfish nature and not be too restrictive. Wise rules needed to be established, but even these evolved and were rarely deliberately invented. Once appropriate laws were in operation, society could virtually run itself for considerable periods of time before further intervention was necessary. New rules would only become necessary when earlier regulations proved defective in some way: "the wisest laws of human intervention are generally owing to the evasions of bad men, whose cunning has eluded the force of former ordinances, that had been made with less caution." [63]

---

[61] *The Fable of the Bees,* ed. F. B. Kaye, II, 139.

[62] *Ibid.,* I, 51, 145, 208; II, 319-321; *Origin of Honour,* pp. 20, 28; and *A Letter to Dion,* pp. 36-37, 42, 45.

[63] *The Fable of the Bees,* ed. F. B. Kaye, II, 319. It will be obvious that in this section I have relied upon Nathan Rosenberg, "Mandeville and Laissez-Faire," *Journal of the History of Ideas,* 24 (1963), 183-196 and F. A. Hayek, "Dr Bernard Mandeville," *Proceedings of the British Academy,* 52 (1966), 125-141. I also accept their views on Mandeville's economic ideas rather than those of Jacob Viner in his introduction to *A Letter to Dion (Augustan Reprint Society,* no. 41, Los Angeles, 1953), pp. 11-15.

MANDEVILLE IN RELATION TO SOME OTHER WRITERS:

MANDEVILLE AND WITHER: INDIVIDUALISM AND THE WORKINGS OF PROVIDENCE

J. A. W. GUNN

The most compelling aspect of Mandeville's thought, to the modern reader at least, is his sensitivity to the complex processes that produce and sustain society. The moral wrench once administered by his paradoxes has long ago been softened by familiarity. It is not then his critique of moral rigorism – the doctrine that true virtue must be both unselfish and dispassionate [1] – or even his supposed departures from economic ortho- doxy that most attracts the historian of social thought. Rather, it is the general mode of analysis, displayed in his discovery of the fabric of society in human frailty. Sumptuary laws, charity schools and the transportation of criminals have ceased to exercise informed opinion. Perhaps the boldest of his hypotheses – the notion of a self-equilibrating market that ensured brothels a supply of ruined women – has also fallen victim to social change. However, the social sciences remain committed to a study of the unintended consequences of human behaviour, finding some of their proudest monuments in the demonstration of counter-intuitive conclu- sions. Here Mandeville was a master – one of the first – and his reflections can accurately be said to embody the habit of mind now called function- alism, here understood as the notion that aspects of social behaviour may best be explained in terms of their contribution to the maintenance of a social system, irrespective of what social actors may think that they are doing.[2]

A great deal of good scholarship has already been directed to the task of placing Mandeville in his context. This was entailed by the nature of

---

[1] The definition is Kaye's. See Mandeville, *The Fable of the Bees,* ed., F. B. Kaye (Oxford, 1924), I, xlviii. Hereafter cited as *Fable.*

[2] For a number of definitions of functionalism, see Don Martindale, *The Nature and Types of Sociological Theory* (London, 1964), pp. 442-47. Those aspects of Mandeville's thought that anticipate modern functional analysis are discussed by Louis Schneider, "Mandeville as Forerunner of Modern Sociology," *Journal of the History of the Behavioral Sciences,* 6 (1970), 219-30.

his satire, which, in his major work, consisted in an initial attempt to be outrageous, followed by efforts to disarm the opposition, without abandoning the case. Kaye rightly saw that an assessment of Mandeville's originality involved tracing comparable phrases and meanings in other, and earlier, writers. The only excuse for adding one more thread between Mandeville and the seventeenth century is my dissatisfaction with what existing literature tells us about Mandeville's treatment of unintended consequences and its meaning for an understanding of Augustan ideas about individualism and providence.

The baseline for the inquiry is the work of George Wither (1588-1667) – poet, part-Puritan and irrepressible moralist.[3] As a subject for comparison with Mandeville, Wither's credentials include striking parallels in medium, metaphor and message. Wither wrote the bulk of his enormous output in rhymed couplets, inferior in vigour to Mandeville's verse, but including lines whose beauty ensures their survival: "Shall I wasting in dispair/Die because a woman's fair?" From his youthful vivacity to the plodding sententiousness of old age, Wither's verse teems with the categories central to Mandeville's moral theory – virtue and vice, public and private – and these abstractions found particular application in activity by denizens of a grumbling hive.[4] For Mandeville was not the first English moralist to write a fable of the bees; these social insects had equally served Wither's intentions.[5] This is perfectly explicable, since both writers probably had the same source of inspiration, the Roman fabulist Phaedrus. Of course, they came to him in different ways. In the year of Wither's death, La Fontaine was only beginning to publish his fables, a number of which – including that of the wasps and the bees – were based on the fables of Phaedrus. It will be remembered that Mandeville published the first substantial English translation of La Fontaine in 1704,[6]

---

[3] For details of Wither's life, see Frank Sidgwick, ed. *The Poetry of George Wither* (London, 1902), I, introduction.

[4] Wither generally referred to industrious citizens as "bees." His "parable" of the bees is contained in his most important political work, "The Dark Lantern, ... Whereunto is annexed, a Poem, Concerning a Perpetuall Parliament" (1653) in *Miscellaneous Works of George Wither: Third Collection,* Spencer Society, Manchester, vol. 13 (reprinted New York, 1967). Further references to Wither's writings are all to this edition.

[5] Mandeville figures prominently in one scholarly account of the place of bees in folklore; there is no mention of Wither. See J. P. Glock, *Symbolik der Bienen* (Heidelberg, 1897). For examples of various English works, including those of Wither, that drew social conclusions from the life of bees, see W. H. Greenleaf, *Order, Empiricism and Politics* (London, 1964), p. 24.

[6] See Mandeville, *Æsop Dress'd or a Collection of Fables writ in Familiar Verse* (1704) introduced by John S. Shea, The Augustan Reprint Society, publication 120 (Los Angeles, 1966). The fable borrowed from La Fontaine is called here "The Wasps and the Bees." For the relevant fable by Phaedrus, see *The Fables* introduction and notes by G. H. Hall (London, 1895), p. 31.

and the next year saw the first version of his own fable, then called *The Grumbling Hive*. No similarities in imagery would detain us, however, were they not accompanied by those of substance.

Social Models

Before tracing parallels in Wither's all-too-ample works, it is useful to consider what modes of reasoning were available to Augustan thinkers who wished to account for the regularity apparent in human affairs. Allowing that few people were interested in analysis of this sort, those who were seem to have been limited to two different strategies or some combination of them. Society, and more especially government, might be seen as the conscious product of decisions by determinate human beings. This had been the characteristic design of a number of seventeenth-century republicans and was quite compatible with leaving some scope for divine involvement, although this factor was not a central one for Harrington and others like him. The approach found a respectable voice among Mandeville's contemporaries in John Trenchard, enemy of corruption and standing armies, when he looked to the day when "our Government would act mechanically and a Rogue will as naturally be hanged as a Clock strike twelve when the hour is come." [7]

This has much in common with the mechanistic elements in Mandeville's work – he sometimes likened government, even social relations, to a machine – except that Mandeville leaned away from reliance upon architectonic designs of rulers in favour of as great an emphasis on gradual development as his mechanistic vocabulary would allow. Thus his description of how social intercourse makes men sociable is one of the most brilliant passages in the early history of social theory.[8] It would be unwise, however, to assume from this that Mandeville did not mean his comments about "dextrous management" by politicians. Sociability developed in society still required external sanctions and if Mandeville chose to see government as a clock or a knitting-frame, which, once constructed, might work well even for incompetents, he was saying no more than Trenchard.[9] It was a matter of believing that if a polity had the right constitution and good laws, even bad men could be compelled to enforce

---

[7] John Trenchard, *An History of Standing Armies in England ... with an incomparable Preface upon Government,* 1st edn. 1698 (London, 1739), p. II. For a similar position, see Mandeville, *Free Thoughts on Religion, The Church, and National Happiness* (London, 1720), p. 342.

[8] *Fable,* II, 188-89.

[9] *Ibid.,* pp. 322-23.

those laws. Allowing that he did not favour regulating foreign trade, there is still no reason to deem his general position as anything other than interventionist, for laws remain immanent in society, able to check human action.[10] It is unnecessary to visualize their being changed; they need only be enforced. In explaining the development of society, Mandeville was concerned with the proper information for the legislator, or lawgiver – that vital figure in the history of political philosophy who founds a political order. But he also readily addressed himself to contemporary lawmakers and moulders of their people, and, while primarily concerned with providing the legal framework within which self-interest could operate, he still believed in the efficacy of laws.

Recent work on English mercantilism has made it clear that many people who believed in the policy of intervention in the economy also believed in the necessity and social benefits of self-interest. They differed from the later liberals chiefly in the mechanisms through which they sought to further the national interest.[11] So Mandeville shared his theory of human motivation even with thinkers more disposed to government intervention than he was. But this is not the most troublesome question; to argue over the relative weight of *laissez-faire* and interventionist sentiments in Mandeville still leaves his understanding of the relation between private and public good undetermined. This matter will more readily be disposed of after a look at seventeenth-century individualism.

Whatever his view of the ends of policy, Mandeville did wish to portray the hidden springs of society, and a mechanical model was an imperfect instrument for that purpose. Fortunately there existed an appropriate vocabulary in which to detail the spontaneous operation of unintended consequences. It was the same that was to serve Adam Smith late in the century – the language of divine providence. The alternative to conscious human purpose was then divine involvement, an answer that antedated the hubris of constitution-makers and persisted long after they had come on the scene. To avoid the presumption and also the wearying detail of classical republicans one need only posit the existence of a divine plan, manifesting itself through human actions, and disposing where they but proposed. This might simply involve the recognition of a mysterious final cause shaping human life and was quite compatible

---

[10] This factor appears to be overlooked in an otherwise perceptive reassessment of Mandeville's economic assumptions. See Nathan Rosenberg, "Mandeville and Laissez-Faire," *Journal of the History of Ideas,* 24 (1963), 183-96.

[11] See William D. Grampp, *Economic Liberalism: Vol. I The Beginnings* (New York, 1965), p. 50 and Donald C. Coleman, ed. *Revisions in Mercantilism* (London, 1969), pp. 12-13.

with attributing most actions to the interaction of codes of human law with an unchanging human nature.

Mandeville wrote frequently of providence, although his great editor, Kaye, consistently minimized the importance of these passages. At times Mandeville placed providence at the beginning of the chain of causation, crediting God with giving men their abilities, but only in the form of potential to be realized in society. The metaphor of the single grape whose vinosity would only appear in the general process of fermentation made clear that providence as the starting-point of an explanation might be too far removed from social activity to explain anything in particular.[12] Kaye dismissed this reference to providence in terms of the need to answer William Law's charge of irreligion.[13] This argument fails, however, when we realize that before he had any critics, or, it would seem, readers, Mandeville had already given a much more prominent role to providence. In the first book of his *Fable* he had visualized providence, not only as the unanswerable "why?" behind experience, but also as immanent in the knowledge gained from an inquiry into the nature of worldly things:

> ... nothing can render the unsearchable depth of the Divine Wisdom more conspicuous, than that *Man*, whom Providence had designed for Society, should not only by his own Frailties and Imperfections be led into the Road to Temporal Happiness, but likewise receive, from a seeming Necessity of Natural Causes, a Tincture of that Knowledge, in which he was afterwards to be made perfect by the True Religion, to his Eternal Welfare.[14]

Kaye explains this passage away by insisting that, whatever its apparent meaning, it must not be taken as evidence that Mandeville was an advocate of the popular "optimism" of Leibnitz, Shaftesbury or Milton. Rather, Mandeville's argument eschewed teleology and his interest was limited to "a matter of worldly fact." The evidence for this interpretation is that Mandeville refused to call many things anything but evil, despite their social utility. It is quite true that he shrank from calling this the best of all possible worlds, although it is indisputable that he also wished to convey the impression that changes sought by some moralists would neither be possible nor, if possible, desirable. To cite another example, Kaye has assumed that Mandeville's reliance upon providence to account

---

[12] *Fable,* II, 185-89.

[13] *Ibid.,* p. 185n. We may accept Kaye's statement here that Mandeville argued against the divine origin of virtue and still take seriously the description of man as ultimately designed for society.

[14] *Fable,* I, 57. The passage does not, of course, mean that sociability or virtue were innate or of divine origin, for this Mandeville denied. It meant rather that men had been created with an innate "Thirst of Dominion," and that quality served better than any natural sociability to produce complex societies. See *Fable,* II, 205, 253.

for the survival of primitive man was satirical in intent.[15] What actually occurs in the passage cited is that Mandeville gradually moves behind an opaque reference to divine interference by miracles to provide a more naturalistic explanation. That explanation proceeds down the hierarchy of causes to deal with social factors, but it is couched nevertheless in terms of providence working through mundane instruments. Kaye has apparently equated providence with references to miracles – an unwarranted assumption as we shall see. Indeed, even Shaftesbury, who was anxious not to reduce God's involvement with society to that of a remote first cause, still declined to cite miracles as evidence of His providence.

It seems that Kaye's disinclination to link Mandeville in any way with teleology proceeded from the unambiguous fact that Mandeville explicitly disagreed with Shaftesbury's moral philosophy, and did so because the latter denied the existence of evil and portrayed mankind as altruistic, instead of irremediably selfish. But this does not mean that references to providence necessarily entailed a denial of the possibility of evil. Wither simultaneously believed in both, as we shall see. Providence would remain an invaluable concept for purposes of expressing social causation, even for writers who were quite unconcerned about the problem of evil. Kaye also saw Mandeville and Shaftesbury as diametrically opposed in their understanding of the relations between individual good and that of the community.[16] This too is worth exploring.

Contrary to Kaye's insistence on the irrelevance of providence to an understanding of the *Fable*, some scholars have already suggested that the root of Mandeville's paradoxes might lie in the doctrine of predestination associated with Protestantism.[17] There have even been suggestions that Weber's hypothesis about the connection between Calvinism and economic conduct was significant for the background to Mandeville,[18]

---

[15] For Kaye's argument, see *Fable*, II, 21n. The passage in question, including Mandeville's definition of providence as an "incomprehensible Chain of Causes," is in II, 237 *et. seq.* Other passages that suggest Mandeville's acceptance of an ultimate cause are to be found in *A Letter to Dion* (1732) introduction by Jacob Viner, The Augustan Reprint Society, publication 41 (Los Angeles, 1953), p. 34 and *Free Thoughts . . .*, p. 3. Mandeville's impatience with talk of providence took the form of denying that it was sensible to pray for divine intervention in those activities, such as war or commerce, where both sides tried to invoke it. See *Fable*, vol. I, p. 398 and *An Enquiry into the Origin of Honour, and the Usefulness of Christianity in War* (1732) introduced by M. M. Goldsmith (London, 1971), p. 190.

[16] *Fable*, I, lxxiii.

[17] See Wilhelm Deckelmann, *Untersuchungen zur Bienenfabel Mandevilles . . .* (Hamburg, 1933), pp. 95, 100, 114 and Louis Schneider, ed., *The Scottish Moralists on Human Nature and Society* (Chicago and London, 1967), p. xlix.

[18] Deckelmann, pp. 100-01.

thus raising the question of the nature of seventeenth-century individualism. This line of inquiry seems valuable, especially if one substitutes
providence for predestination. Mandeville undoubtedly absorbed Bayle's
comments on predestination, but nothing conclusive follows from that.
For one thing, recent studies have reminded us that predestination is a
Christian belief, not exclusively a Protestant one.[19] More importantly,
providence is the more general notion and predestination has normally
been justified in terms of the subjection of all creation to God's inscrutable
purpose.[20] It is not at all clear, therefore, that consideration of the
problem of evil required the dogma of predestination; God's unfathomable providence would suffice. A case can still be made for the Protestant
background of Mandeville's thought, since Protestant writers emphasized
providence in contrast to Catholic asceticism. Turning to seventeenth-
century Protestantism can thus serve both to reveal early examples of
unintended consequences, couched in the language of providence, and a
form of individualism that will cast light on the social philosophy attributed to Mandeville.

Unintended Consequences Before Mandeville

George Wither had little to say about predestination, claiming that he
held a position consistent with the orthodox Anglican doctrine of election,
predestination and free grace. At the same time, he chose to defend a
doctrine of "universal redemption," feeling that any other position presup-
posed that God damned people before they had done either good or evil.
He was aware of the prevalent opinion that such a stand might be called
Arminianism and deemed a novelty. However, he persevered, strengthened by his resolve that on no account must God be taxed with authorship
of evil. God had given the means of salvation to everyone "who first
excludes himself not by his personal sins and impenitency." [21] With that,
he left the subject, having been less candid than Mandeville would be
about the insoluble problem, but no more successful in unravelling it.

   Wither's charitable departure from the implications of predestination
in no way interfered with his recognizing a generous mandate for providence. It might well be that no man, in Wither's opinion, was predestined

---

[19] See C. and K. George, *The Protestant Mind of the English Reformation, 1570-
1640* (Princeton, 1961), pp. 112-13 and John F. H. New, *Anglican and Puritan: The
Basis of their Opposition, 1558-1640* (Stanford, 1964), pp. 17-18.
[20] See Aquinas, *Summa Theologica* I, xxiii, I, 3 and for Calvin's position, as understood by Bayle, and recorded by Mandeville, *Free Thoughts . . .*, p. 116.
[21] Wither, "Parallelogrammaton" (1662), *Spencer Society*, vol. 33, p. 61.

to evil, but man was prone to sin. Always well supplied with enemies, Wither was quite ingenious in finding benefit in their wrongdoing. A recurrent theme was the measure in which one's foes unintentionally did great service, giving occasions for the display of virtue and, in many ways, conferring honour and profit.[22] Such unsought boons figured as prominently as a just man's own virtue in smoothing the way through life. These manifestations of providence did not, of course, weaken Wither's frequently sanctimonious and intrusive concern for virtuous conduct and this was sensible enough. He made it perfectly clear that evil conduct might properly harm the agent; generally it did no permanent damage to anyone else. An anecdote about an ulcer cured by a wound adequately conveys the optimistic message. Wither's exclusion of wrong-doers from the benefit of their acts is not surprising; Mandeville himself was less insistent on this fact, but it was no part of his intention to argue that they would usually profit.[23] When Wither came to write of government, he tacitly qualified his optimism, since he was acutely aware of just how damaging bad government could be. Thus he proffered much gratuitous advice to a succession of English governments.

His characteristic position on sin led Wither to be just as forgiving in specific instances as he was censorious about the general level of morality. Sin must not be condoned, but neither were sinners readily judged by private men, since God might well be using a falling from virtue to his own purposes, founding some "publick mercy" by a "private sin." [24] He could not, consistently, claim that God caused such sin in order to display his mercy and here Wither seems to have been consistent. God simply used opportunities created by human frailty.

The second factor inhibiting moral judgment was the difficulty of inspecting the "motives" of those who did ill, a problem compounded when dealing with those in authority.

> But GOD'S intentions, and the hearts of Kings,
> Are such inscrutable and hidden things,
> That, none can search their bottomes;
>
> .   .   .   .   .   .

---

[22] See "Britain's Remembrancer" (1620), *Spencer Society,* vol. 28, p. 288; "Halel-viah or, Britain's Second Remembrancer" (1641), *Spencer Society,* vol. 26, p. 31 and "Speculum Speculativum" (1660), *Spencer Society,* vol. 22, p. 37. Each item in this last volume has separate pagination. *Cf.* Mandeville's claim that providence, in some way, led criminals to act as instruments of "great Deliverances." *Letter to Dion,* pp. 32-33.

[23] See *Letter to Dion,* p. 39.

[24] "Speculum Speculativum," p. 17.

> Their wayes of working their own pleasures out,
> Are, many times, by wheeling round about,
> By cross and counter-actings, and by those
> Which seemed their own *Designments* to oppose.[25]

According to Wither, one could never assume deeds to be "ill-intentioned" because they had ill effects; even the acts of virtuous men might
require divine guidance in order to be truly beneficial to society. Thus
Wither allowed, with Mandeville, that an amiable passion, such as pity,
might sometimes hurt the "common good." [26]

Despite some moral qualms, Wither was surprisingly receptive to the
proposition that the passions, in general, were in some sense, good – an
idea identified by Kaye as commonly encountered in the writings of such
seventeenth-century French moralists as La Rochefoucauld, Senault,
Nicole, Esprit and Bayle.[27] Kaye cited no source antedating Wither's
earliest relevant publications, but obviously the doctrine was prevalent,
in its strongest form, in Jacobean England.

> But some men have in this opinion stood,
> *That every Passion's naturall and good.*
> Indeed Philosophers the same doe call,
> *A motion of the soule that's naturall.*
> And in some sort, we may not be afraid
> To hold for truth, as much as they have said.[28]

Wither's caveat related, not to the social usefulness of vices, but to their
degree of moral virtue. He denied the crown of virtue to passions produced by man's corrupted nature and so he resisted the claim that "Vice,
assist to perfect virtue can. . . ." [29] However, his examples of immoderate
passions – the usual ones, but untamed by God's teaching – indicated
only that those who had such passions would be unhappy. Again, it
would seem, the wrongdoer was most likely to injure himself. The proposition here presented by Wither certainly fits into Kaye's category reserved for theories of the passions that contained, albeit implicitly, the
claim that vices might be benefits. Wither's own reaction to this idea was
less than whole-hearted agreement. Nevertheless, it would certainly meet
the test for inclusion in another of Kaye's categories – those theories as-

---

[25] "A Triple Paradox" (1661), *Spencer Society*, vol. 13, p. 37 (separate pagination).
[26] Wither, "Abuses Stript, and Whipt: or Satyricall Essayes" (1622), *Spencer
Society*, vol. 9, p. 74 and Mandeville, *Fable*, I, 56, 260.
[27] *Fable*, I, cv, [2].
[28] "Abuses . . . ," p. 152.
[29] *Ibid.*, p. 73.

sociating the passions with benefit, but with the reservation that they also smacked of the flesh and the devil.[30] Wither was certainly capable of approaching the sentiments of Mandeville's most outspoken predecessors, as evidenced by the statement, published as early as 1628, that every vice had "some virtue-like disguises made." Again, the earliest comparable expression that Kaye cites from any English source is an anonymous work of 1701.[31]

The most important consideration to be raised with respect to Wither's use of providence is whether it led him to passive admiration of an order from which evil was banished. The briefest acquaintance with his writings makes clear that his conception of providence was not such as to deny all taint of evil. Recognizing sins of various sorts as beneficial to some of those sinned against, he called the acts sinful nonetheless. All actions, he claimed, might promote God's work, even sinful ones. For Bayle and Mandeville this would, of course, create philosophical problems, but good will triumphed over logic, and Wither seems never to have departed from his claim that God did not cause, or require, evil. It did not follow from Wither's discussion of providence that *all* vices promoted discernible benefit; that was a possible, but not a necessary outcome.

> GOD, who of evil things can make good uses,
> And, by what is *unwholesome*, Health produces,
> Vouchafeth to make passage now and then,
> To *signal blessings*, by the sins of men; . . .[32]

This suggested that God might choose to create blessings from unlikely materials, and then again, He might not. With this in mind, Wither explicitly enjoined his readers to "beware also that ye make not God an Umpire in triviall and indifferent things, which are at your own free choice. . . ." [33]

Significant of the social context in which providence worked was Wither's notion that the use of lots in elections gave room for the reali-

---

[30] *Fable,* I, [2].

[31] "Britain's Remembrancer," p. 230. The eighteenth-century work cited by Kaye was likened by its authors to Continental books of proverbs, but the material was apparently original. See [Thomas Brown *et. al.*], *Laconics: or New Maxims of State and Conversation* (London, 1701), sig. A2.

[32] "Speculum Speculativum," p. 17.

[33] "Letters to Advice" (1644), *Spencer Society,* vol. 12, pp. 10-11. Such cautions were sometimes even applicable to large matters, as when an anonymous writer warned against associating divine intent with any sort of government. See *Providence and Precept: or, the Case of Doing Evil that Good may come of it* (London, 1691), pp. 8-12. The habit, however, persisted. See R. Skerret, *The Restoration the Work of Providence* (London, 1717). The providential character of the Glorious Revolution was a commonplace.

zation of God's will.[34] This served notice that Wither's optimism was not such as to discourage his active concern for improving society. When Wither wrote of election by lot, he was writing before the publication of Harrington's *Oceana*, but Wither was equally under the spell of Venice. There was thus a sufficient worldly reason to visualize this worldly instrument. Indeed, in his most explicitly political work, "The Perpetuall Parliament," Wither said that he wished to demonstrate "How we may concord, out of discords bring, . . ." There followed shortly afterwards a description of the way in which humans constantly made wrong conjectures as to which actions would benefit themselves and the public:

> That others, which we judged might destroy
> Our interest; produc'd what we enjoy.
> That wicked *projects*, otherwise brought forth
> As good effects, as those of *reall worth* . . .[35]

All of this was in the context of a proposal to introduce such reforms as staggered elections, rotation in office and the use of the lot. Here Wither made no reference to providence. Such reforms were intended to break parties that might form in a long-sitting House of Commons and to give England's governors frequent tastes of the role of subject – a means of knitting the interests of government and people, long sought by reformers. Elsewhere in the larger work, of which "The Perpetuall Parliament" is a part, Wither described how God made an harmonious whole out of "discords." [36] In this passage he contemplated reform in a more remote, less concrete fashion, from which viewpoint the process displayed the "chain of conceal'd contingencies" called providence. Providence no doubt guided all things, but when sufficiently supplied with worldly mechanisms, Wither was content to hand the job to them. One is reminded of Mandeville's stubborn defence of naturalistic explanation in terms of proximate causes: ". . . Providence makes use of Means that are visible. . . ." [37]

Wither's frequent resort to the idea of a *concordia discors* well illustrates the way in which providence might figure in quite realistic accounts of social processes. The image of society as a wall or building, preserved by a balance or compound of conflicting forces and interests, was familiar to classical antiquity and was not uncommon in seventeenth-century dis-

---

[34] "Letters of Advice," p. 10.
[35] "The Perpetuall Parliament," p. 43.
[36] "The Dark Lantern . . . ," pp. 10-12, 33.
[37] *Fable*, II, 320. See too *Ibid.*, p. 54.

cussions of providence.[38] Wither was fond of noting how God led sinners to correct and check each other. He also applied the moral to the condition of England during the Protectorate, rephrasing the commonly-heard demand that all interests be accommodated to strengthen the regime.

> We know, that *diffring Simples* put together,
> So Qualifie and so correct each other,
> (Though some are poysonous) that they purge away
> Malignant Humours, which would else destroy
> The life of man . . .
>
> .   .   .   .   .
>
> Ev'n so by them who are *Dissenters* now,
> Our *Publick Buildings* may the firmer grow,
> When they into *One Structure* shall be fixt,
> Well qualified, and rationally mixt.[39]

In this way "discords" would grow into "sympathies." It is not difficult, judging from these lines, to see why Wither's reputation as a poet came to be eclipsed. The effort is valuable, however, in showing that thinkers who habitually wrote of providence were not thereby forced to contemplate harmony based either on human altruism or on the necessary nature of a universe presided over by a perfect sovereign mind. One could start, as Wither did, from the particulars and record how they were joined together through interaction. As Mandeville was to note, "Jarrings" might "in the main agree." [40] The observation is quite as indicative of Wither's vision of society as of Mandeville's own.

Wither's faith in a providence that served as a model for secular balances of interest fitted well into the individualism that pervaded his writings. The combination of these assumptions led him to the convenient conclusion that if Saul could establish a kingdom when merely in search of his father's asses, a persecuted English poet might well contribute to remedying "Publick Grievances" when he intended, at the outset, only to relieve his "personal Oppressions." [41] Here unintended consequences linked the spheres of providence and worldly individualism. Having seen that Wither had a conception of providence useful for generating con-

---

[38] See, for instance, Richard Whitlock, *Observations on the Present Manners of the English* (London, 1654), p. 373 and Owen Felltham, *Resolves: Divine, Moral, Political* (London, 1661), p. 75.

[39] "Fragmenta Prophetica" (published posthumously, 1669), *Spencer Society*, vol. 24, p. 117.

[40] *Fable*, I, 24.

[41] "Epistolium Vagum-Prosa-Metricum" (1659), *Spencer Society*, vol. 12, p. 17.

clusions comparable to some of Mandeville's, a discussion of the nature of Wither's individualism should complete the basis for comparison. For Wither's significance does not end with the parallels he affords to Mandeville; he also reflected a form of individualism against which to measure that of the latter.

Private and Public

Wither's linking of private interest and public benefit, under the benign auspices of providence, was less necessary than his efforts to explain sin and misfortune. To state that personal sin might contribute to public good was paradoxical and illustrated God's mysterious intent; by contrast, it was a simple matter for Wither to demonstrate that legitimate private designs would naturally conform to the common good. Divine intent joined forces with a practical, mundane individualism to secure this result – a result so obvious that its providential aspects did not have to be emphasized.

This is not to say that Wither promoted or even condoned vulgar self-seeking. His was a morality that required deeds done from a good motive – love of justice, concern for country and a regard for the duties appropriate to one's status as a gentleman and a Christian. Thus it was not out of character for him to regret that "Self-Interest" was the object of most human actions. Sometimes his concern for elevated sentiments assumed that tone of energetic gloom, so often associated with Puritanism: "In ev'ry Pleasure, somewhat lurks to fear thee,/ In ev'ry Profit, somewhat to ensnare thee." [42] But such rigorism did not preclude opening doors for self-regard of a sort deemed legitimate and healthy. Indeed, the very stringency of this unrelenting ethic seems to have challenged him to qualify it, without renouncing his moralistic tone.

Thus Wither displays the full repertoire of Protestant casuistry. Severely tested by his financial difficulties – he spent twenty years trying vainly to gain possession of lands granted to him in return for services during the Civil War – he became increasingly tolerant of public benefit built upon individual satisfaction. Logically, the first step in the case for a modest degree of self-promotion was to establish that "particulars" were included in "universals." This might dictate nothing more than seeking one's own profit in the betterment of the public, or, it might lead to stating the converse of the initial proposition – that universals consisted in a collection of particulars.

[42] "Britain's Remembrancer," p. 177.

For since an Universal-weal consists
Of many Individual Interests,
A *perfect Body* cannot be injoi'd,
Where, *One* by *One*, the Members are distroi'd; [43]

Wither referred to the "common good" as a "compound being" and his closest approach to a definition of "publick good" was "that each individual, without wrongs,/ May that posses, which to the same belongs." [44] Such an understanding was not rare in the seventeenth century and it was made all the more plausible by Wither's unambiguous statement that the important political problems were domestic ones, not the international issues that exercised many people.[45] This assumption was crucial for any definition of public good, centred on the rights of private property. When defence and foreign policy entered the picture, as they did with Mandeville, it was much more difficult to sustain an individualistic rendering of the public interest.

Scripture was a useful supplement to logic here – an ally within the fortress of moral rigorism.

He that hath no *self-love*, is as blameable as he which hath too much, because he wants that rule whereby he ought to regulate a Love to his neighbour.

The familiar moral dictum that charity began at home supplied a comparable set of arguments for squaring private advantage and public. At another level, Wither might simply argue how economic relations connected "private-sufferings" to "publike-grievances," thus communicating mischief to the whole community.[46]

This effort at social causation illustrates a major difference between Wither and Mandeville in their respective descriptions of society. Some of Wither's major social insights were provoked by a desire to defend legitimate moral claims, which were connected with the public good in ways not always perceived by the claimants. Mandeville, by contrast, was to apply his insights to what he chose to call "vice." Wither might equally well have seen vice in the private interests defended throughout his writings; some of the interests for which he enlisted his support were im-

[43] "A Sudden Flash" (1657), *Spencer Society*, vol. 13, p. 65.
[44] "Speculum Speculativum," p. 66.
[45] "Prosopapoeia Britannica" (1648), *Spencer Society*, vol. 18, p. 82. For this, and other assumptions central to seventeenth-century individualism, see my *Politics and the Public Interest in the Seventeenth Century* (London and Toronto, 1969), pp. 30-35.
[46] "Fides-Anglicana..." (1660), *Spencer Society*, vol. 22, pp. 28, 40; "Justitiarius Justificutus" (1646), *Spencer Society*, vol. 16, p. 14; "Paralellogrammaton," p. 24.

pure ones. However, Wither chose rather to qualify his rigorism in the name of an acceptable measure of self-interest. Wither's very individualism thus denied him the opportunity of anticipating Mandeville's most ingenious paradoxes.

Wither's belief that true public benefit rested upon the foundation of private satisfaction was most pronounced in documents directed to the government. Thus, urging the restored Charles II to honour debts incurred by the Long Parliament, he could direct himself to the wisdom of satisfying articulated claims, even those that seemed morally flawed.

The only way to settle an universal Peace and Concord, is to satisfie all *Interests,* as much as may be; especially in things necessary to a competent subsistence, even to the answering of their expectations, who are most carnal, so far as they are just; in regard these are likely to be most troublesom.[47]

Wither certainly sought a just government of Godly men, if it was to be had, but his plan of parliamentary reform was directed to the very modest goal of neutralizing the impact of evil personnel through a judicious arrangement of institutions. In addition, he observed how necessary it was to gild the way to virtue with sufficient inducements to ensure its being followed. The vanity of members of Parliament must be cared for, that they might "Pursue the *Publike service,* with delight." [48] Here already, in a non-economic context, was the strategy described by Mandeville – that of arranging institutions so as to make the best use of an ineradicable self-interest.

There is yet another respect in which the two writers may be linked through the categories of public and private. In general, Wither's comments on the substance of political decisions indicate that justice in affairs of state turned on a correct assessment of consequences. This was suggested in his insistence that private men be well-motivated, even though the unpredictable consequences of their ill-intentioned acts might well involve public profit; by contrast, he called "good" some apparently wicked governmental decisions, presumably because they involved an accurate reading of circumstances and because, in retrospect, they had produced good effects.[49] We have already encountered his hesitancy about passing moral judgments on those entrusted with government. Thus he was censorious in treating private vice, but in addressing the government, he deserted ethical homilies for social causation. No doubt, he felt that rulers might be wicked, but the more ample scope of activity in-

[47] "Fides-Anglicana . . . ," p. 40.
[48] "The Perpetuall Parliament," p. 68. *Cf. Fable,* I, 220-21.
[49] "The Perpetuall Parliament, p. 43.

volved in public business made a utilitarian calculus appropriate. The same respect for complexity sustained his argument that the arbitrary acts of the Rump were justified by social necessity.

In adopting a standard for measuring public policy different from that obtaining in private morality, Wither remained committed to the perspective of the private citizen. Indeed, accepting the involvement of the subject in time of public danger, he specifically enjoined each person to manage his own affairs effectively if he wished his opinions on public business to be taken seriously.[50] By contrast, Mandeville not only suggested different standards for the two realms, but also denied that experience in private affairs, those of "*Meum* and *Tuum*," gave citizens a useful basis for understanding great matters of state.[51] Here Mandeville may have been correct and Wither naïve. For present purposes, the contrast simply indicates the distance that Mandeville saw as separating private concerns and those of the public.

Turning from differences to similarities, it is difficult not to conclude that Wither was already embroiled in the moral dilemma that Mandeville was to make explicit. Nor should it be forgotten that we still do not know in what measure the dilemma existed for Mandeville himself, since his satirical intent would be compatible with his seeing merit in both of the moral criteria so deftly juggled throughout his writings. Mandeville explicitly drew the line separating the spheres allotted to motives and consequences at approximately the same place where Wither had drawn it tacitly. The point is most succinctly put in a minor work where Mandeville said that a private member of society could not be excused for doing a certain evil in the hope of promoting ultimate social good; legislatures were not so constrained.[52] No doubt the tension has always existed in all systems of thought, prior to the formulation of utilitarianism, that have dealt with the real business of government in ethical terms. Without either embracing the serpent or casting out the dove, people judged public policy by its effects on private moral claims – i.e. consequences, but they remained aware that the world also paid its compliments to good motives. Certainly it would be natural to propose both standards in a society, such

---

[50] "Vox Pacifia" (1645), *Spencer Society*, vol. 13, p. 34.

[51] Mandeville, *Free Thoughts . . .* , p. 347.

[52] For Jacob Viner's argument that, far from being ambivalent about rigorism, Mandeville's doctrine was purely utilitarian, see Viner's introduction to *A Letter to Dion*, pp. 4-11. Here one can only plead that Wither, who might be expected to be a rigorist, was certainly ambivalent, while there remains the apparent ambivalence expressed by Mandeville in *A Modest Defence of Publick Stews: or, an Essay upon Whoring, as it is now practis'd in these Kingdoms* (London, 1725), pp. 49-50.

as pre-industrial England, already sensitive to the case for economic and political individualism.

Familiarity with seventeenth-century meshing of private and public makes it easy to dispel the myth of Mandeville's individualism, as promoted, for instance, by Kaye. Mandeville seems to have expressed little concern for a public interest consisting chiefly in the protection of private rights to property.[53] Admittedly, that case had already been made by many writers and had apparently triumphed with the Revolution; thus no writer interested in paradoxical novelty would deign to labour it. However, Mandeville's silence regarding that central concern of seventeenth-century individualism is complemented by his clear affirmation that each individual was subordinated to the interest of the whole – an interest associated with "worldly Greatness," national honour and strength, of a sort typical of early mercantilism.

. . . Goodness, Integrity, and a peaceful Disposition in Rulers and Governors of Nations, are not the proper Qualifications to Aggrandize them . . . any more than the uninterrupted Serles of Success that every Private Person would be blest with, if he could, and which I have shown would be Injurious and Destructive to a large society, that should place a Felicity in worldly Greatness . . . and value themselves upon their Honour and their Strength.[54]

It is not then true that Mandeville identified "the personal interests of the members of society" with that of the state, if by "interests" we mean the welfare or satisfaction of the members.[55] Nothing is more emphasized in his writings than his understanding of the public good as a set of conditions qualitatively different from the content of private interests. That private persons might share in public things was unquestioned – the point was precisely that they belonged to everyone. This was tellingly illustrated by his examples of things public – army, fleet, funds, public buildings.[56]

It is true that Mandeville saw public good, even social survival, as built

---

[53] Mandeville makes one reference to the importance of protecting private property, but seems here to perceive it as something different both from the "publick Peace" and the "Interest of the Nation." See *Free Thoughts . . .* , p. 14.

[54] *Fable,* I, 365. Mandeville was careful always to note only that general private happiness was incompatible with greatness. A people might certainly turn its back on greatness, but Kaye is correct in saying that Mandeville thought such a choice was a practical impossibility. See *Fable,* I, xlix-1.

[55] As claimed by John S. Shea in his introduction to *Æsop Dress'd,* p. xi and by Kaye, *Fable,* I, cii. Kaye wrote of the fit between the "selfish good" of the individual and the good of the state. Strong contrary evidence abounds. See *Fable,* I, 347 and especially 354-55 where Mandeville stated that his chief intent had been to explain that paradox whereby the "Welfare and real Happiness" of private families was inconsistent with public good.

[56] See *Free Thoughts . . .* , pp. 118-119. Of these, only the "funds" showed a close connection between private and public interests.

upon personal self-seeking. Intentional, uncoerced sacrifice for the public was neither to be expected nor was it necessary. However, this involved nothing more than indicating how, in particular transactions, self-seeking might be beneficial to the public. This was quite consistent with his serene acknowledgement that the agent who produced the benefit might suffer, not only in the next life, but on the scaffold. Nor were innocent parties spared, since their temporal happiness too might have to be sacrificed on the altar of public good. Not just vice, but also personal disaster, created the foundation of national greatness. Despite his emphasis upon market processes, Mandeville saw much of life as a zero-sum game, in the sense that "the temporal Happiness of Some is inseparable from the Misery of others." Furthermore, he used this observation to reinforce his insistence that the public good was inconsistent with the good of all individuals.[57] The dissociation of public good and private satisfaction was most dramatically displayed in one reference to exchanges between individuals which, while not harmful to the public, were inconsequential: "... the changing of Property from one Man to another, is seldom of any consequence to the Publick...." [58] An historian of economic doctrine has called this conception "medieval" and finds it extremely rare even in English mercantilism.[59]

Mandeville then, was an individualist only in the sense that he saw self-interested activity as often necessary and useful for social life. The mechanisms even then were heavily sanctioned by government, so that many activities, however delightful, were denied to self-indulgent humans. The earlier and more substantial sort of individualism, represented by Wither, saw the public good largely as a compound of private satisfactions – a claim saved from unintelligibility by the central place given to private property and its universal protection. This form of individualism was foreign to Mandeville's general argument.

Mandeville: Providence and Individualism

Mandeville's continuity with earlier English thought is most amply shown by the fact that the notion of providence had long proven useful in ex-

[57] See *Fable*, I, 319; *A Letter to Dion*, p. 39 and *An Enquiry into the Causes of the Frequent Executions at Tyburn* (1725) introduced by Malvin R. Zirker, Jr., The Augustan Reprint Society publication 105 (Los Angeles, 1964), p. 13. In this last, Mandeville discussed "theftbote," or the ransoming of stolen goods, and insisted that innocent tradesmen should have their account books destroyed by thieves, rather than encouraging the crime by paying a ransom.
[58] *An Enquiry into the Causes of the Frequent Executions ...* p. 14.
[59] Grampp, *op. cit.,* p. 96.

plaining social processes. This was how Wither had used it – as a general label calling attention to the unintended consequences of human actions. Usually this involved demonstrating how good might come of evil, whether it was the profit accruing to good men from the actions of their enemies, or the unexpected by-products of war and famine.[60] The hand of providence was least likely to intrude when Wither wished to see specific political reforms or scope for particular private interests, not least of all his own. Thus it played a minor part in his rationale for self-interest, although Wither must have believed that God was responsible for human inclinations, a point allowed in Mandeville's comments on providence. Causes that required political action rather than contemplation of cosmic harmony gained little from an identification with providence.

If the reformer seeks to activate men to improve their own lot, the defender of the *status quo* has an entirely different perspective. In politics Mandeville appears to have been a Whig, but few divine-right Tories can have had more respect for authority.[61] Mandeville's tolerance for licensed vice was quite consistent with a law-and-order orientation. He sought few innovations and none that threatened the stability of society. Like most conservatives, Mandeville enjoined his fellow citizens to cherish anomalies and to find hidden value in apparent abuses. It was this very concern that made conservative social theory analytically superior to radical alternatives, at least until the coming of nineteenth-century socialism. Given this concern, some understanding of providence was useful for inculcating precisely the sort of quietism in the face of personal calamity that was taught by Mandeville.[62] For there is no other useful message in his finding that societies flourished on the ruins of private ambitions. By contrast, Wither generally responded to the presence of undeserved misfortune either by claiming that its consequences would ultimately be benign or by suggesting a remedy.

Misconceptions about Mandeville's supposed individualism are related to a determination of the role that he gave to providence. In dismissing Mandeville's references to providence, Kaye linked his interpretation to his exaggeration of Mandeville's individualism. Both considerations entered into the contrast with Shaftesbury. The latter was said, correctly, to argue that one must "consider the Whole and the individual will then

---

[60] "Britains Remembrancer," pp. 41-42.

[61] Mandeville's Whiggish sympathies are suggested in *The Mischiefs that Ought Justly be Apprehended from a Whig-Government* (London, 1714), p. 40. This is one of the suppositious works. For Mandeville's fear of sedition and his case for "unlimited Obedience," see *Free Thoughts . . .* , pp. 293, 297, 300.

[62] See *Fable*, I, 360-64.

be cared for." Mandeville, by contrast, was held to argue: "Study the individual and the Whole will look after itself." [63] But we have seen that he did not so argue. Rather, insisting firmly upon the priority of the public good, he set out to justify the ways of power to men. In this way, Mandeville addressed himself to that level of concern – a complete system or macrocosm – where, according to Shaftesbury, for instance, the results of providence were most apparent.[64] The Whole, as contemplated by Mandeville, was not Shaftesbury's divine machinery; it was, however, a complex and mysterious chain of relations, a suitable field for an accent on unintended consequences.

Of course, Mandeville wrote of providence chiefly in terms of the mysterious realm of origins, although it figured too as the unfathomable answer as to the place of good and evil in the world [65] – an answer about which man could gain only some hints. Like modern functionalists, Mandeville could afford to de-emphasize the exact course of social development, since he saw the past, including here an ultimate cause, as reflected in the arrangements of existing society. But for all his acuity both in conjectures about the evolution of institutions and in tracing the course of unintended consequences, he was still unable to explain the presence of man himself, that animal with the potential for culture. Man, for Mandeville, had a nature and a potential before he was made civilized by social intercourse, and this human nature was uniform and unchanging – identical, in essence, for the rude savage and the civilized being. Mandeville's incapacity to give a wholly naturalistic account of human origins is understandable and indicates the distance still separating him from modern materialists.[66] Providence could thus usefully be seen as supplying the original human potential, without further need to intervene. It was not necessarily the human governor who was passive in Mandeville's system, but the original and divine legislator.

No clear case can, of course, be made about Mandeville's personal feelings regarding a deity. It suffices to show that what he wanted to say

[63] *Ibid.,* p. lxxiii.
[64] See Stanley Grean, *Shaftesbury's Philosophy of Religion and Ethics* (Athens, Ohio, 1967), p. 55.
[65] See *A Letter to Dion,* p. 34.
[66] Mandeville's many statements on the immutability of human nature are conveniently summarized in J. S. Slotkin, ed., *Readings in Early Anthropology* (Chicago, 1965), p. 260. James Hayden Tufts was surely one of the first scholars to note that Mandeville regarded the individual as a "product" of social forces, not as the unit by which to explain those forces. See *The Individual and his Relation to Society,* Part II (1904; reprinted New York, 1970), p. 14. The judgment is intriguing, but it would certainly be untrue to portray Mandeville, whatever his measure of originality, as arguing, with Marx, that man was but an "ensemble" of social relations.

was consistent with the notion of providence and there is reason to suspect that, whatever he believed, he expected his readers to accept his comments about an ultimate cause.[67] Indeed, even moderns, armed with the notion of natural selection, find it a simpler task to mark the chains of relations sustaining society than to account for their presence. One thus recalls the judgment of a modern anthropologist, Lévi-Strauss, that man obeys laws he did not invent.

---

[67] Support for this conclusion is found in F. Grégoire, *Bernard de Mandeville et la "Fable des Abeilles"* (Nancy, 1947), pp. 111-14.

MANDEVILLE AND DEFOE

JOHN ROBERT MOORE

Nearly thirty years ago an able specialist in eighteenth-century literature wrote: "It appears that, among other things, Mandeville was indulging in the sport of baiting the Defoes of his time and exposing the weakness of their armor of virtue." [1] This statement implies that Defoe was a primary target for Mandeville's controversial writing, and that he was in constant disagreement with Mandeville's ideas. On the contrary, it can be shown that Defoe was more nearly in agreement with Mandeville than any other major writer of the age – with marked similarities to Mandeville in his personal background and interests and literary style. When he differed with Mandeville regarding the paradox of private vice and public virtue it was because Defoe discussed this subject as he did so many others – under mutually exclusive frames of reference, as if they were the two sides of the same coin.

Mandeville was a native of South Holland; Defoe was proudly conscious of his own Flemish ancestry and a lifelong advocate of the unpopular measure of naturalizing foreigners in England. One bit of dialogue from a tract listed by Kaye as probably by Mandeville could have been written by the man who identified himself as "The Author of the True-Born Englishman":

the Bulk of the Nation is made up of Strangers, we have but few very ancient Families among us, and the Forefathers of most of us were Foreigners, once within five hundred Years. The succeeding Generations we see don't remain so, and let a Man come from what Country he pleases, he can but be a Foreigner for himself and his Posterity, if they stay here, he must be *English* in spight of his Teeth; I have always been, and am still of Opinion, that the

---

[1] M. E. Prior, review of *The Eighteenth Century Background* by Basil Willey (*PQ*, 21 [1942], p. 149).

bringing in of Foreigners can never be counted detrimental to the Nation, . . .[2]

The author used some of Defoe's favorite arguments, deploring the handicap of study at the Dissenters' academies [3] and the low salaries of dissenting ministers,[4] and urging more sober conduct among the clergy [5] and the desirability of restraining clergymen from political activity: "Let them preach the Gospel, and leave State affairs to those they belong to." [6] Defoe declared repeatedly that he would gladly subscribe to the Thirty-Nine Articles of the Church of England – except for a few which dealt with inessentials; the author of this dialogue presented the same general idea:

If any set of Men had told the Apostles, that they agreed with them in all material points of Christianity, but that they thought they might confess their Faith as well sit[t]ing towards the West as standing toward the East, and could have no respect for any particular Dress or Ceremony which our Saviour had not recommended to them, do you think they would have call'd them Fanaticks, Schismaticks, and thunder'd out Anathemas against them with as much Fury as our High-Flyers do against the Presbyterians? [7]

A tract which is certainly by Mandeville states the same general idea in words which Defoe would have approved: "almost every thing in nature pleads for toleration, except the national clergy in every country." [8]

In another tract by Mandeville, Cleomenes declares that "it was never pretended, that a Man could be Virtuous and a Coward at the same Time; since Fortitude is the very first of the Four Cardinal Virtues." [9] As early as 1694 Defoe had written: "Courage is, if not the Source, at least the sign of all the other vertues," [10] and he frequently restated the same idea for the next twenty-five years.[11] Many autobiographical allusions in his writings deal with his courage when his life had been threatened; his most earnest apologies are for his rare lapses of nerve.[12]

[2] *The Mischiefs that ought Justly to be Apprehended from a Whig Government* (London, 1714), pp. 12-13.

[3] *Ibid.,* p. 35.

[4] *Ibid.,* p. 36.

[5] *Ibid.,* p. 18.

[6] *Ibid.,* p. 18.

[7] *Ibid.,* p. 20.

[8] *Free Thoughts on Religion, the Church, and National Happiness* (2nd ed., London, 1729), p. 239.

[9] *An Enquiry into the Origin of Honour, and the Usefulness of Christianity in War* (London, 1732), p. 45.

[10] *The Englishman's Choice, and True Interest* (London, 1694), p. 21.

[11] *Review,* VII, 590 (March 6, 1711); *An Apology for the Army* (London, 1715), p. 10; *Augusta Triumphans* (London, 1728), p. 51; *Second Thoughts are best* (London, 1729), pp. 6-7.

[12] *Letters,* ed. G. H. Healey (Oxford, 1955), pp. 1, 474.

Kaye remarked on the "realistic homeliness" of Mandeville's style and on his word-coinage "uncomatable"; [13] Defoe's style was equally homely, and "uncomatable" was one of his words. Like Defoe Mandeville apologized for a digression,[14] and he cited two of Defoe's favorite passages from "my Lord Rochester" and "the incomparable Butler." [15] Leslie Stephen accepted the old tradition that Mandeville "was probably little respected outside of distilling circles"; [16] Defoe had much to say of the importance of the distilling trade and he wrote a tract for the distillers, although (like Mandeville) he deplored the evil of dram-drinking. Defoe was a pioneer in recognizing the injustice of African slavery; [17] Mandeville remarked on the severity of the masters of "the innocent, as well as unfortunate Blacks." [18]

Garman has stressed Mandeville's "preoccupation with economics" and his influence on Adam Smith.[19] Defoe's major concern was with economics and he was apparently the first writer to speak of "the Wealth of Nations." [20] Like Defoe, Mandeville declared that unwrought English wool should not be carried abroad,[21] and one of his characteristic passages might easily be inserted in Defoe's discourses on the inland trade:

what a number of People, how many different Trades, and what a variety of Skill and Tools must be employed to have the most ordinary *Yorkshire Cloth?* [22]

Defoe projected an academy for women; Mandeville wrote that "there is no Labour of the Brain, which Women are not as capable of performing, at least, as well as Men, with the same Assistance, . . ." [23] Both writers were pioneers in advocating higher education in London, and both did so in terms which implied contempt for the snobbery of many graduates of the two English universities. Defoe spoke of the young men sent there

[13] *The Fable of the Bees,* ed. F. B. Kaye (Oxford, 1924), II, 38, note 1; I, 95, note 2.
[14] *Ibid.,* I, 290.
[15] *Ibid.,* I, 219; *A Treatise of the Hypochondriack and Hysterical Passions* (London, 1711), p. 94.
[16] Article on Mandeville in *DNB.*
[17] E.g., *Reformation of Manners* (London, 1702), p. 17; *Atlas Maritimus & Commercialis* (London, 1728), p. 237.
[18] *An Enquiry into the Causes of the Frequent Executions at Tyburn* (London, 1725), p. 48.
[19] Douglas Garman, preface to *The Fable of the Bees or Private Vices, Public Benefits* (London, 1934), p. 19.
[20] *Review,* II, 78 (April 19, 1705) and elsewhere.
[21] *The Fable of the Bees* (ed. Kaye), I, 312.
[22] *Ibid.,* I, 169.
[23] *Ibid.,* II, 172.

"merely to say they have been at Oxford or Cambridge, as if the air of those places inspired knowledge without application." [24] Mandeville raised the same objection:

I know there are strange hidden qualities in the Air, the Soil, and the Water, and have often heard, that some Places yielded Cheese, others Butter, that could not be made as good any where else, tho' they had the same Kine, and to all appearances better Pasture; I believe the same of Brewing, tho' they have the same Malt; but it is the greatest Mystery to me in the World, that it should be the same with the learning of Arts and Sciences, tho' they have the same opportunity.

His spokesman Philopirio went on to ask why

a Young Gentleman of Four or Five and Twenty that has lived Seven or Eight Years at *Oxford*, as soon as he comes hither, should be allow'd to know more of Sick-People than a Man of above Fifty, that has convers'd with them in and about this Populous City, and been in good Business for 25 or 30 Years together.[25]

It was a common saying in the trade that a book's sale was most rapidly promoted if the author stood in the pillory or the book was condemned by legal action. Defoe stood three times in the pillory; *The Fable of the Bees* became a subject of international interest after the edition of 1723 was presented as a nuisance by the Grand Jury of Middlesex.

It is not clear that Defoe was interested in Mandeville's broader speculations regarding society and human nature, but throughout most of his active career he had much to say about the famous paradox concerning private vice and public benefits. As early as 1689 the author of *Taxes no Charge* had argued that the extravagant and debauched paid most of the taxes.[26] Nine years later Charles Davenant rejected "the old Notion, that Luxury and some Excess, may be profitable," [27] although in the next year he acknowledged the mixture of evil and good in foreign trade.[28]

It is not certain that Defoe ever met Mandeville, although he lived for years in Hackney (where Mandeville died) and some of their works were published by the same men – Roberts and Brotherton. Perhaps he did not allude specifically to Mandeville until after the Grand Jury condemned *The Fable of the Bees* in 1723, but from 1704 until 1729 he

[24] *Augusta Triumphans (The Novels and Miscellaneous Works*, Tegg-Talboys ed., London, 1841, XVIII), p. 4.
[25] *A Treatise of the Hypochondriack and Hysterical Passions*, p. 220.
[26] *Taxes no Charge, in a Letter from a Gentleman to a Person of Quality (A Collection of State Tracts*, London, 1706, Vol. II), p. 122.
[27] *Discourses on the Publick Revenues: and on the Trade of England* (London, 1698), Part II, p. 74.
[28] *An Essay upon the Probable Methods of Making a People Gainers in the Balance of Trade* (London, 1699), pp. 154-55.

showed deep interest in the paradox which underlay so much of Mande-ville's writing. Defoe was most often the journalist, dealing with subjects which afforded copy for *ad hoc* treatment rather than with broad moral principles or historical truth. He was undergoing his own second bank-ruptcy and actively engaged in Parliament in support of a bill for the relief of bankrupts when he wrote:

by degrees we have brought Vice and Extravagance to be absolutely neces-sary to Trade; and People become Advocates for the Devil, meerly to save themselves from starving; the Nation seems under an unhappy Necessity to uphold their Follies, in order to preserve their Trade; . . .

The *Medium* to all these Excesses is to be found out, and that is, to bring our Fashions and Customs to such a Government, as may at the same time that they Correct Extravagancies, not overthrow Decency: Reform Ill Man-ners, and not Destroy Trade; . . .[29]

Two weeks later he attempted a more precise distinction:

In the open, Large, and Plentiful Living . . . is that Luxury Maintain'd, which I say however it may be a Vice in Morals, may at the same time be a Vertue in Trade, and of this, I confess I cannot be forward to say, I would have it Suppress'd, a great share of our Trade, and for ought I know, two Millions of our People Live by it, and depend wholly upon it.

The Excursions, the Nusances, the Vicious part of this Trade may be restrain'd, and so far as it touches our Morals, they ought to be Restrain'd; but to bring down all those common Excrecencies of Mode, Habit, Fashion, and Custom in Apparel, which are in the General Practice of Trade, become a very considerable part of the Employment of our People, would be to Unhinge the whole Nation, load every Parish and Town with Starving People, Ruin'd Tradesmen, and the Rich would hardly be able to support the Poor.[30]

Five months later he remarked that "an unknown Hand" had sent his publisher a satire including the line "As *Satan's* Logicians prove Vertue, is Vice." [31] Six years afterward he wrote:

I am not now about *Reforming* your Manners and Morals, but *Regulating* your Trade, and if I may speak in the Language of Trade, I must bring in your Vices, and acknowledge some which are really Vices, to be vastly Advantageous to the Common Wealth: . . .

Since then our Vices are by Necessity, thus made Vertues in our Trade, we must allow those Things we call Superfluities, to be Necessaries in Trade; and it is manifest, that he who would go about to Reform effectually, the common Vices and Luxury of the Nation, at the same time begins the Ruin

[29] *Review*, III, 42-43 (Jan. 24, 1706).
[30] *Ibid.*, III, 66 (Feb. 7, 1706).
[31] *Ibid.*, III, 343 (July 18, 1706).

of our Trade; and by that Time he has brought us to be a Nation of Saints, will be sure to make us a Nation of Beggars–[32]

In the year before *The Fable of the Bees* was published, he anticipated its subtitle in his defense of the Treaty of Commerce with France: "*When casual Fire seizes on the Town,/ Some Houses are blown up, and some pull'd down;/ None blame the Evil, for 'tis understood,/ A private Mischief for a publick Good.*" [33]

As a moralist Defoe rejected Dr. Mead's argument that strong drink would have helped to prevent the plague in 1665; [34] *as a journalist* he could say that "as no Man can merit the just Character of an impartial Writer, without producing what can be said on both Sides of a Question, it is fit I should enumerate all the Benefits accruing to the Publick from this *private publick* Vice." [35] Nowhere did he attempt such a psychological analysis of the motives of human conduct as Mandeville did; but frequently he outlined the arguments on both sides of a question,[36] stressing his consciousness of two different frames of reference. For example: "To say, let Luxury and Extravagance *abate*, it will reform the Town, is to say nothing, for the *Question* does not lye that way: It is not whether Luxury will abate, but will our Trade abate or not; if the *Trade abates*, as it certainly will, my argument is good." [37]

Perhaps Mandeville never referred to Defoe, but there are several allusions to Mandeville in Defoe's writings. Aitken pointed out that in the title of *Everybody's Business is Nobody's Business; Or, Private Abuses, Publick Grievances*, "Defoe had in mind Mandeville's 'Fable of the Bees, or Private Vices Publick Benefits,' which had recently been reissued." [38] As an anonymous correspondent of *Mist's Weekly Journal* Defoe took issue with *A Modest Defence of Publick Stews*:

The Treatise Intitled *The Fable of the Bees*, perhaps, has as much good and bad reasoning in it as ever were seen in the Writings of the same Author.

[32] *Ibid.*, VIII, 739 (May 27, 1712).
[33] *Ibid.*, [IX], 196 (May 21, 1713).
[34] *Due Preparations for the Plague* (Aitken ed., London, 1895), p. 43.
[35] *A Collection of Miscellany Letters, Selected out of Mist's Weekly Journal* (London, 1727), IV, 172.
[36] E.g., *The Complete English Tradesman* (London, 1726), p. 68; *The Compleat English Tradesman* (London, 1727), II, Part II, 102, 110-11, 169-76; *Augusta Triumphans* (Tegg-Talboys ed., Vol. XVIII), p. 31; *Atlas Maritimus & Commercialis* (London, 1728), pp. 173-74; *A Plan of the English Commerce* (London, 1728), pp. 196-97; *Some Objections Humbly offered to the Consideration of the Hon. House of Gommons, Relating to the present intended Relief of Prisoners* (London, 1729), pp. 21-22.
[37] *Ibid.*, p. 18.
[38] *Romances and Narratives by Daniel Defoe* (London, 1895), X, xii.

This Gentleman I take to be the first amongst us who has argued for a publick Toleration of Vices. He seems a great Admirer of the Policies of the *Dutch*; but as there is no Government without some Errors, he has (for the Ostentation of shewing his Parts) chosen to recommend the Licence which is given to publick Lewdness amongst them, imitating herein a Lawyer, who is Council for a Felon at the Bar; he knows his Client is a thorough-pac'd Rogue, and will certainly be found guilty; however, he has the Vanity of making the most of a bad Cause.[39]

Later, writing as a journalist in *Some Considerations upon Street-Walkers*, he presented both sides of what had become an intensely controversial issue for which no easy solution had been found:

In *Rome, Naples,* and other great Cities abroad, Common Whores are kept in a sort of decent Order; certain Places are allow'd them from which they must not depart, and certain Rules of Behaviour prescrib'd to them which they must keep up to; so that in effect they give no Scandal, tho' they commit some Sin. That the same was practis'd here formerly, we have Reasons to believe from some old Laws, which we find regulating the Apparel and Behaviour of Whores, and the Keepers of Stews; and from these Arguments, several warm Gentlemen would infer the Fitness and Necessity at once of tolerating Fornication and restraining the Irregularities of Harlots. These Gentlemen are for applying Lenitives, which perhaps may succeed; while our Street-Reformers, who are inclin'd to make human Weakness no Allowances, think of no Cure for Lewdness, but Amputation: . . . and they have cut and slash'd with so little Distinction, that the peccant Humours have escap'd them, mingled with the Mass, and render'd the Malady incurable.[40]

Defoe was fond of intelligent conversation, and he was at his best in private discussions of public issues. Sometimes he attended such conferences in disguise; more often he appeared in his own person, in the presence of king or queen, of nobleman or commoner. Once he wrote to assure some of his bitter opponents, who had spoken too freely before a stranger, that he would not betray their confidence.[41] If Mandeville and Defoe ever conversed in the shops of Roberts and Brotherton, it is a pity that we have no record of it. Their conversation might well have proved as interesting to us as the dialogues of Horatio and Cleomenes.

[39] *A Collection of Miscellany Letters* (London, 1727), IV, 237-38.
[40] *Some Considerations upon Street-Walkers* (London, n. d. [1726]), pp. 4-5.
[41] *Letters*, p. 106.

MANDEVILLE AND SHAFTESBURY:
SOME FACTS AND PROBLEMS

IRWIN PRIMER

Beginning with his doggerel verse in *The Grumbling Hive* (1705) and concluding vigorously with *A Letter to Dion* (1732), Bernard Mandeville elaborated his famous "selfish system" in publications which span a period of twenty-seven years. In 1714, a year after the death of the third earl of Shaftesbury and three years after the publication of the first edition of Shaftesbury's *Characteristicks*, Mandeville amplified his *Grumbling Hive* with many pages of prose "remarks" which elaborated upon specific passages in the reprinted poem. This enlarged work was renamed *The Fable of the Bees*. It is almost impossible to believe that Mandeville by 1714 had not yet encountered, either directly or indirectly, the central tenets of Lord Shaftesbury's ethical system, the so-called "social system." [1] Nevertheless the simple fact remains that Mandeville's first overt reference in print to Lord Shaftesbury's works appeared in 1720 in the first edition of *Free Thoughts on Religion, the Church, and National Happiness*.[2] Here Mandeville cites Shaftesbury's *Characteristicks* with obvious approval in three separate passages. Not until 1723, when he added "A Search into the Nature of Society" and other essays to his expanding *Fable of the Bees*, did Mandeville publicly oppose Shaftesbury's social system.[3] During the rest of the eighteenth century the Mandeville-Shaftes-

[1] The three volumes of the *Characteristicks of Men, Manners, Opinions, Times* (1711, revised 1714) comprise Shaftesbury's personal collection of his writings, one of which appeared unauthorized in 1699. For the publishing history of this omnibus work, see William E. Alderman, "English Editions of Shaftesbury's *Characteristics*," *Publications of the Bibliographical Society of America*, LXI, 4 (1967), 315-34.

[2] The first edition of the *Free Thoughts* was reissued in 1721 and 1723, and a so-called second edition appeared in 1729. A French translation by Justus Van Effen appeared in 1722 and was reissued in 1723, 1729 and 1738. *F.T.* was also translated into Dutch (1723) and German (1726). See F. B. Kaye, ed., *The Fable of the Bees: or, Private Vices, Publick Benefits* (Oxford University Press, 1924), I, xxxi. All future references to this invaluable edition will be abbreviated to "Kaye."

[3] Kaye (I, lxxii-lxxv) notes (a) that "Mandeville's first references to the *Characteristicks* occur in his *Free Thoughts* (1720), pp. 239-41 and 360, and are favourable,"

bury debate remained alive and influential, not only in Britain but on the Continent and in the American colonies as well.

The impression conveyed in traditional surveys and summaries of eighteenth-century English literature and of the development of Enlightenment thought is that Mandeville's importance lies precisely in his vivid antagonism toward Shaftesbury. Shaftesbury generally emerges as an optimistic idealist, a Stoic moralist, a harbinger of "the return to nature," and also the butt of the ridicule of a libertine and pragmatic Mandeville. Astute scholars have recognized, however, that while the fundamental appeal of these authors is accentuated by the ever-pertinent debate between Mandevillean egoism and Shaftesburian altruism or benevolism, striking similarities and concurrences in some of the positions taken by these two authors are unrecognized or ignored.[4] It is the purpose of this paper to focus upon Mandeville's dependence upon Lord Shaftesbury, particularly in the *Free Thoughts*, in which he borrowed much more from the *Characteristicks* than he openly acknowledged. It is well to warn the reader that this information will not produce any major reinterpretation of Mandeville's positions on ethics, politics, economics or religion. But it may have a considerable bearing on the reinterpretation of the Mandeville-Shaftesbury relationship.

In his *Free Thoughts* Mandeville appears to be a party writer enlisted in the Whig cause. He argues that those who urge unlimited submission or passive obedience to the throne do so "without taking the least Notice

and (b) that Mandeville "began his systematic attack on the *Characteristicks*" in the 1723 additions to his *Fable of the Bees*. In order to demonstrate certain resemblances between both writers, Kaye observes that "Shaftesbury . . . joined with Mandeville in decrying philosophical systems, and agreed that private advantage harmonized with the public good. These agreements," Kaye adds, ". . . are really superficial." Part of the purpose of this essay is to modify Kaye's conclusion. Though I happen to stress the variety and extent of Mandeville's indebtedness to Shaftesbury, I do not mean to suggest that we ought to cease emphasizing their differences. As Martin Price observes, "Both were considered dangerous freethinkers in their day. . . . But their difference strikes us more sharply today" (*To the Palace of Wisdom* [N. Y., 1964], 105). Price's illuminating remarks on Shaftesbury and Mandeville demonstrate that in the hands of a sensitive critic a much-studied controversy can be made to supply new insights. The particular virtue of Price's chapters on these two authors is that he avoids a point-by-point comparison in order to grasp creatively the vital features and tone of each writer as a self-contained entity.

[4] Among the accounts that have stressed the convergence of Mandeville's and Shaftesbury's ideas, one of the most pointed comments is this by Donald Greene: "It is usually said that Mandeville's book [*The Fable of the Bees*] was an attack on Shaftesbury: insofar as it mocks Shaftesbury's admiration of the primitive life of nature, it is. But this is only an incidental part of Shaftesbury's teaching. In fact, Mandeville and Shaftesbury are basically in agreement: what both are saying, in effect, is 'Trust human nature, and all will be well.' . . . both are satisfied that men do very well when left to the guidance of their own instincts" (*The Age of Exuberance* [N.Y., 1970], 118-19).

of the Constitution, and the Agreement between the King and the People." [5] He defends the contract theory, and briefly refutes the vestiges of monarchist zeal and patriarchalism. As for "unlimited obedience," it is indeed due to "the highest, the supreme Power" in the nation, a power which "is possess'd by the three Estates, the King, Lords and Commons" when they jointly agree.[6] The King's office is to guard and superintend the laws; he is to require obedience to the laws and "to promote, and every way encourage the Execution of them. . . ." [7] He is the nation's chief executive, but he is powerless to alter, abrogate or remove the laws. In times of emergency, and only temporarily, the suspension of the Habeas Corpus Act will increase the King's power, but by no means does he then become absolute. "The Rights and Privileges of Parliament, and the Liberty of the People are as Sacred Branches of the Constitution as any thing the King can claim." [8] Mandeville continues to the end of this chapter, "Of Government," with further commonplaces upon England's limited monarchy.

A comparison of the theologico-political views in Mandeville's *Free Thoughts* and Shaftesbury's *Characteristicks* reveals a broad agreement in many areas. The kind of approval Mandeville accorded to Shaftesbury in this book seems like conventional Whig panegyric. In their denunciations of superstition, religious fanaticism and Tory clergymen who hungered for civil and political power, their agreement was virtually complete. Both supported limited religious toleration, both affirmed their adherence to the Church of England, both relied upon the writings of such esteemed Latitudinarians as Bishop Jeremy Taylor and Archbishop Tillotson, and both testify strongly to the influence of Pierre Bayle in England. Their criticisms of the Church of Rome were far from mild, but on this score Mandeville, perhaps because of his Dutch legacy and Calvinistic background, was much more persistent and vitriolic.[9] Mande-

---

[5] *Free Thoughts* (1720), 298. Unless otherwise noted, all subsequent references to this work are to the 1720 edition, abbreviated *F.T.*

[6] *F.T.* 300.

[7] *F.T.* 301-02.

[8] *F.T.* 305.

[9] Shaftesbury's writings exhibit some of the traditional English Protestant vituperations against Rome, but he can still find a kind word in behalf of his contemporary, Pope Clement XI, as an encourager of learning and the arts. See J. M. Robertson, ed., *Characteristics* (London, 1900), II, 305n. (I use this edition of this work throughout.) Mandeville's remarks on the Roman Catholic Church may sound intolerant, but some, at any rate, may wish to excuse him on the grounds that he attempted to expose the intolerance of that church. Most of his anti-Catholic passages derive from Bayle's *Dictionary*. In the 1720's the motivation for such polemics could well have been primarily political. Hanoverian apologists strove to keep anti-Roman sentiments alive, ostensibly to counter the plotting of the Jacobites.

ville, who devoted many pages and at the end of his career an entire book
to dissecting the history and operation of the principle of "honour," was
preceded by Shaftesbury in the exercise of denouncing false honor which
ignores or tramples upon virtue.[10] On the whole, it can be said that in
his *Free Thoughts* Mandeville quoted with approval and respect from
the *Characteristicks*, and that in basic questions of church and state,
religious authority and individual freedom, Mandeville maintained consistent agreement with Shaftesbury's position. His subsequent quarrel with
Shaftesbury developed within the context of their basic convictions on
the nature of human nature, and Mandeville disagreed radically with
Shaftesbury on such related issues as the origin of evil, the sociableness of
man and the origin of human society.

Much closer to the surface of the *Free Thoughts* than the materials
from Shaftesbury, and in much greater profusion, are the many extracts
from Pierre Bayle's massive *Dictionnaire Historique et Critique*. Because
Mandeville's method in employing the words and thoughts of Bayle has
a direct bearing upon his uses of Shaftesbury, his statement about his
use of Bayle deserves close attention:

THOSE who are vers'd in Books, will soon discover, that I have made
great Use of Monsieur Baile, without mentioning him. I confess, he is the
learned Man I speak of in Page 93. The citations likewise which I have
borrow'd from that Author, without naming him, are many. Had this been
done out of Vanity to compliment my self, or disregard to the Honour of
that Great Man, I would have been wise enough not to have spoke of it now.
The Reasons I had for doing as I have done, are more than one: In the
first Place, Monsieur Baile's Dictionary is not common, but among Men who
have great Libraries, and quoting it would have signify'd little to the greatest
part of my Readers. .... Besides, I imagin'd that it would be unpleasant, if
not disgustful, to see the same Name so often repeated in the Notes, especially to those who are unacquainted with the Vastness of that Work.[11]

Though he acknowledged his extensive borrowings from Bayle, Mandeville neglected to indicate a similar use of Shaftesbury's writings.[12] Per-

---

[10] For Mandeville on "Honour," see the index to *The Fable of the Bees* (Kaye) and
his *Enquiry into the Origin of Honour, and the Usefulness of Christianity in War*
(1732; second ed., London, 1971, ed. by Maurice Goldsmith). For Shaftesbury, see
Charact., I, 307.

[11] *F.T.*, xv-xvi.

[12] In his study, *Untersuchungen zur Bienenfabel Mandevilles und zu ihrer Ent-
stehungsgeschichte im Hinblick auf die Bienenfabelthese* (Hamburg, 1933), 121n.,
Wilhelm Deckelmann briefly listed most of the passages in the *Free Thoughts* that
Mandeville had silently taken from Shaftesbury. These passages become more signifi-
cant, as I shall show, when examined in the light of A. O. Aldridge's work on
Shaftesbury two decades later.

haps he felt that such an admission was unnecessary because what he borrowed from the *Characteristicks* consists mainly of extensive quotations from other writers; nevertheless, such borrowing must be regarded as theft. Whether this unacknowledged debt to Shaftesbury should be regarded as one of the factors that made Mandeville turn upon and attack this noble author in print three years later, is a query perhaps better left to the professional psychologists, but it will remain an interesting sidelight on the Mandeville-Shaftesbury relationship. Another relatively neglected common ground in these authors is their admiration for Bayle. Before pursuing this thread further it will be helpful to present specifically the location and the tenor of each of the passages that Mandeville plundered from Shaftesbury, as well as those which he properly acknowledged in his footnotes.

ii

Mandeville's borrowings from Shaftesbury in the *Free Thoughts* may be roughly divided into three groups: first, the quotations for which he properly identified his source; secondly, passages which Shaftesbury himself had quoted from others but which reappear unacknowledged in the *Free Thoughts*; and thirdly, subject matter and phrases which Mandeville could well have derived from similar passages in the *Characteristicks*.

(A) Direct Quotations clearly drawn from Shaftesbury

The first of these presents Shaftesbury's acidly satirical comment that "a moderate and half way persecution" is politically ridiculous and also inhumane. In the second quotation Shaftesbury deplores the "mere threats made [by clergymen] without power of execution. . . ." The third quotation affirms that persons zealous in the conversion of others probably have private ends of their own in the matter.[13] Here Mandeville was exploiting a passage in Shaftesbury which reveals that this noble author by no means imagined all mankind as following the dictates of a rational ethic, or their "natural affections," as he put it. Shaftesbury was well aware that in practice self-interest was an irrepressible force in human motivation, no matter how well one refuted the philosophy of self-interest in Hobbes, Lord Rochester or La Rochefoucauld. Mandeville's choice of

---

[13] For these quotations, in order, see *F.T.*, 239 and *Charact.*, II, 222; *F.T.*, 240-41 and *Charact.*, II, 224; and *F.T.*, 360 and *Charact.*, II, 222.

this passage in Shaftesbury was of course perfectly in keeping with his general outlook in the first edition of *The Fable of the Bees* (1714).

(B) Mandeville's Unacknowledged Borrowings from Shaftesbury

The first author whom Mandeville silently appropriates from Shaftesbury is Bishop Jeremy Taylor, and the passages involved are all from Taylor's *Treatise on the Liberty of Prophesying* ("printed in his *Collection of Political and Moral Discourses*," as both Shaftesbury and Mandeville remark). In these passages Taylor urges "the Exercise of mutual Charity and Tolleration" among expositors of the "great Mysteries" and of controversial passages in the Scriptures. He argues that "Scripture, Tradition, Councils and Fathers are the Evidence in Question, but Reason is the Judge. . . ." And if a man cannot judge or decide whether the evidence is acceptable to reason, "he is not bound under the tye of necessity to know anything of it." The reader may well wonder how any passage so rationalistic and faith-eroding as this could have been written by the good bishop. The fact is, as A. O. Aldridge has demonstrated, that Shaftesbury himself was more than a bit underhanded here, for in this and in other quotations he manipulated his texts selectively so that they would come closest to saying what Shaftesbury, and not Taylor, meant to say.[14]

Another author and esteemed Anglican leader whom Mandeville found in the *Characteristicks* is Archbishop Tillotson. In a footnote Shaftesbury quotes a lengthy passage from Tillotson's *Rule of Faith*. Mandeville not only cites the same title and page number, but follows Shaftesbury's quotation so faithfully that all of the hiatuses that occur there are repeated in the *Free Thoughts* without modification. The passage was bound to appeal to all those who feared or simply despised the Jacobite cause with its threat of another Catholic ruler for Britain, for it delivers a rationalistic analysis of how the mystery of Transubstantiation could have been introduced into the Roman Catholic faith. Tillotson, as quoted here, sarcastically comments upon the anti-rational aspects of this mystery: "And for the contradictions contained in this doctrine, it was but telling the people then (as they do in effect now) that contradictions ought to be no

---

[14] For each of the quotations from Taylor which Mandeville found in Shaftesbury, see: *F.T.*, 68 and Charact., II, 356; *F.T.*, 77 top and *Charact.*, II, 357; *F.T.*, 77 and *Charact.*, II, 358n.-59n.; and *F.T.*, 78-9 and *Charact.*, II, 359n. Regarding Shaftesbury's misrepresentations, see A. O. Aldridge, *Shaftesbury and the Deist Manifesto*, in *Transactions of the American Philosophical Society*, New Series, vol. 41, pt. 2 (Philadelphia, 1951), 364-65.

scruple in the way of faith; that the more impossible anything is 'tis the fitter to be believed. . . ." As we observed in the preceding exhibit, Shaftesbury again manages his source so that it will say what *he* wants it to say.[15]

The third of these stolen passages is a letter entitled "Julian to the Bostrens" (Julian's Epistles, No. 52). Again Mandeville delivers precisely what he found in the *Characteristicks*, and again Shaftesbury has tinkered with his source for his own ends. After Shaftesbury's selective editing, the Emperor Julian's message to the Bostrens turns out to be a plea for toleration and peacefulness; he regrets that "those . . . whom they call clerics" have driven "the mere people" to riots and seditions. One sentence at the end succinctly summarizes one of Shaftesbury's and Mandeville's persistent themes: " 'Tis by discourse and reason, not by blows, insults, or violence that men are to be informed of truth and convinced of error." [16]

Further evidence of Mandeville's unacknowledged debts to Shaftesbury appear in references to Herodotus, Diodorus Siculus, Harrington, and Gregory the Great. Shaftesbury notes (Robertson ed., II, 185) that "the property and power of the Egyptian priesthood in ancient days arrived to such a height as in a manner to have swallowed up the state and monarchy." He identifies his sources as Herodotus and Diodorus, and in the same paragraph (II, 186) he cites Harrington's famous dictum as follows: "So true it is, 'That dominion must naturally follow property.' " These details are repeated by Mandeville in similar order. He too sends us to Herodotus and Diodorus Siculus. He too tells us "that the *Ægyptian* Priesthood . . . arrived to such a height, as in a manner to have swallow'd up the State." A few lines later we read, "Dominion ever follows Property. . . ." [17] Mandeville repeats this important tag later on, with some modification: "So true it is [Shaftesbury's introductory phrase], that Dominion always follows Property, and that, where the one is wanting it will ever be impracticable for any long Continuance to enforce the other." Harrington's dictum has a direct relevance to Shaftesbury's and Mandeville's thoughts on church and state, for they both desired to separate the clergy from dominion; both feared that disturbances might erupt if any religious faction were to attempt to gain

[15] *F.T.*, 81-3 and *Charact.*, II, 362n.-63n.; and A. O. Aldridge, *loc. cit.*

[16] *F.T.*, 162-64 and *Charact.*, II, 211n.-12n. Note also the repetition of Shaftesbury's words "virtuous and gallant" (describing Julian; II, 210n.) in *F.T.*, 162. According to Aldridge (p. 365), Shaftesbury deleted a passage concerning the expulsion of Bishop Titus, and for this some critics accused him of trying to make Julian appear more tolerant than he was. But Aldridge thinks that Shaftesbury's pruning "is hardly enough to substantiate a charge of duplicity or falsification."

[17] *F.T.*, 143-44.

more power or dominion than King, Lords and Commons agreed it should have.[18]

(C) Possible Borrowings from Shaftesbury

The sources for Mandeville's references to Gregory the Great appear, for the most part, in Bayle's article on this Pope, but one passage – in which Mandeville repeats the old charge that Gregory ordered the destruction of many statues and books of pagan antiquity – seems to have been taken from Shaftesbury's similar passage on Gregory. Shaftesbury cites "Vita D. Gregorii ex Joan. Laziardo Coelestino" as his immediate source; Mandeville cites "Vita D. Georg. ex Joanne Laziardo Coelestin."; but Bayle's article on Gregory seems not to mention this author at all.[19] Did Shaftesbury and Mandeville independently read this Latin life of Gregory? Probably not, given the previous evidence of Mandeville's plagiarism. This instance therefore is classed among the materials Mandeville probably appropriated from Shaftesbury without acknowledgement. In another instance of this kind, both writers affirm that the clergy ought not to call themselves "Ambassadors [of God]" but rather ought to describe themselves as "Messengers." [20]

In the last exhibit two passages are juxtaposed, both reflecting the same general idea without strongly suggesting direct verbal influence:

It was heretofore the wisdom of some wise nations to let people be fools as much as they pleased, and never to punish seriously what deserved only to be laughed at, and was, after all, best cured by that innocent remedy.

(*Characteristicks*, I, 12)

---

[18] *F.T.*, 314. This maxim is one of the fundamental assumptions in James Harrington's *The Commonwealth of Oceana* (1656): "... such ... as is the proportion or ballance of dominion or property in Land, such is the nature of the *Empire*;" cited from S. B. Liljegren's edition (Heidelberg, 1924), 14-15. J. G. A. Pocock in his noteworthy article "Machiavelli, Harrington, and English Political Ideologies of the Eighteenth Century," in *William and Mary Quarterly*, Third Series. V. 22 (Oct., 1965) lists Andrew Fletcher of Saltoun, Walter Moyle, John Toland, Viscount Molesworth, John Trenchard and Thomas Gordon, and even the Tory Viscount Bolingbroke (during his *Craftsman* period) as neo-Harringtonians. Perhaps, by virtue of the references supplied above, and another in *Charact.*, I, 14, Shaftesbury and Mandeville ought also to be included in this list.

[19] *F.T.*, 151 and *Charact.*, II, 303n.-04n.

[20] *F.T.*, 265 and *Charact.*, II, 364-66. Mandeville in this case could have gone directly to the source that Shaftesbury probably used, Matthew Tindal's *The Rights of the Christian Church Asserted* (1706). For the idea that the clergy are the "ambassadors of Christ," see 2 Corinthians 5:20. Again I am indebted to A. O. Aldridge, *Shaftesbury and the Deist Manifesto*, 348-50.

... when Men run into Errors, because they are Fools, it is wrong for wise
Men to be angry with and punish them, as if they were Knaves.

(Free Thoughts, 186)

iii

Having reviewed the evidence of Mandeville's plagiarism – in some
cases certain, in others merely probable or possible – what may we legiti-
mately deduce from it? I believe that in the *Free Thoughts* Mandeville
intended to honor the memory of Lord Shaftesbury in the same way that
he honored Pierre Bayle: by quoting a little with proper acknowledge-
ments and by stealing verbatim or with minor alterations many more
passages from these two authors. Whether either of the two deceased
authors would have been flattered by such a resuscitation in a book that
was not a memorial but a rather obvious piece of political propaganda
is another matter. Mandeville's only reply to the charge of plagiarism
from Shaftesbury would probably have been that he never borrowed
Shaftesbury's own words in this manner; he merely used passages that
Shaftesbury himself had quoted from other authors and to which others
had just as much right.

If we consider the affinities of Bayle, Shaftesbury and Mandeville,
their confluence in such a work as the *Free Thoughts* will scarcely seem
unexpected. Like Erasmus in some ways, Bayle also became a famous
"philosophe de Rotterdam." In Rotterdam Mandeville spent most of
his earlier life and there he attended the Erasmian School. It was quite
possible for Mandeville to have studied under Bayle before emigrating
to England in the 1690's. Shaftesbury came to know Bayle intimately
during two sojourns in Holland, in 1698-99 and 1703-04. His admiration
for Bayle has frequently been noted and is usually demonstrated by citing
his letter to Jacques Basnage, written soon after Bayle's death in 1706.
In that letter Shaftesbury wrote, "... I am sure, no one in particular
owed more to him than I or knew his merit better." [21] Both Shaftesbury
and Mandeville cited Bayle's famous paradox of the atheist of unblemish-

---

[21] Further on in this remarkable letter, Shaftesbury says, "Whatever opinion of
mine stood not the test of his piercing reason, I learned by degrees either to discard as
frivolous, or not to rely upon with that boldness as before; but that which bore the
trial I prized as purest gold." From *The Life, Unpublished Letters, and Philosophical
Regimen of Anthony, Earl of Shaftesbury,* ed. B. Rand (N.Y., 1900), 373-74. For
further comment on Bayle's relationship to Shaftesbury and Mandeville, see Leo P.
Courtines, *Bayle's Relations with England and the English* (N.Y., 1938) and C.
Louise Thijssen-Schoute, "La diffusion européenne des idées de Bayle," in *Pierre
Bayle: Le Philosophe de Rotterdam,* ed. Paul Dibon (Amsterdam and Paris, 1959),
174-76.

ed morality.[22] Though Mandeville appears to lean far more upon Bayle's writings than upon Shaftesbury's, it is well to remember that the impact of Bayle upon both was profound. There is, ultimately, a deliberate consistency in Mandeville's use of Bayle and Shaftesbury in his *Free Thoughts*, and in this book he in a sense exemplifies their liberal spirit and memorializes their friendship. In such a work as this Mandeville would want to present that aspect of Shaftesbury which would redound to the credit not only of Shaftesbury but of the Whig tradition as a whole. And in such a work, his disagreement with Shaftesbury on the nature of human nature – if he had yet worked it out – would appear to be unneccessary and contradictory.

In view of Mandeville's considerable debt to, and apparent respect for, Shaftesbury in the *Free Thoughts*, the reader is faced with a distinct problem when considering Mandeville's downright antagonism to Shaftesbury in 1723. As for his ridicule of Shaftesbury's social system, Mandeville's position is clear, consistent and not unexpected. Mandeville objected to the social system not only on moral and possibly religious grounds, but also from a utilitarian standpoint.[23] What might be unexpected, however, was Mandeville's *ad hominem* attack. Why did Mandeville in 1723 proceed to attack not only Lord Shaftesbury's social system but even his personal character and reputation? Perhaps the answer is simply that this was the way of satire. In ancient times, as we learn from Archilochus and others, the satirist not only meant to kill his enemies but had the power of execution in his words. If there is a deeper or hidden reason behind Mandeville's attack on Shaftesbury's character and career inserted into "A Search into the Nature of Society," that evidence is not yet available.

For the sake of a firm delineation of the problems arising from Mandeville's attack on Shaftesbury, the bibliographical events and attendant problems will be presented in chronological order, beginning with the *Free Thoughts*:

1720 – The *Free Thoughts* contains Mandeville's first references to Shaftesbury; much silent pilfering, as noted above; publishers, T. Jauncy and J. Roberts.

1721 – *Free Thoughts* reissued by T. Warner (French translation by Van Effen in 1722; reissued 1723).

[22] *F.T.*, 4 and *Charact.*, I, 275.
[23] Kaye, I, 331-33. "That boasted middle way, and calm Virtues recommended in the Characteristicks, are good for nothing but to breed Drones, and might qualify a Man for the stupid Enjoyments of a Monastick Life, or at best a Country Justice of Peace, but they would never fit him for Labour and Assiduity, or stir him up to great Atchievements and perilous Undertakings" (I, 133).

1723 – *Free Thoughts* reissued, this time by J. Brotherton. In this year
Mandeville openly attacks Shaftesbury in an amplified edition of *The
Fable of the Bees*, specifically in "Remark T" and in a new essay
entitled "A Search into the Nature of Society," in which he opposes
the doctrine of the natural goodness and benevolence of man and attempts to refute the social system delineated in the *Characteristicks*.
While Mandeville's critique of the social system follows directly from
his own position on man's nature, it has a more specific polemical aim
as a theoretical support for his notorious attack on the charity schools.
This attack first appeared in another section of the newly amplified
Fable entitled "An Essay on Charity and Charity-Schools." Mandeville was apparently not satisfied with merely ridiculing Shaftesbury's
central doctrines, for he proceeded to personal denigration in a devastating character of that lord. Why, he asks, did not Lord Shaftesbury
actively participate in English politics to fight corruption? Because, he
insinuates, his Lordship chose to rationalize the indulgence of his
appetites by writing the praises of retirement and by flattering himself
with a generous view of the nature of mankind. Once again, what
prompted Mandeville to attack the character of this lord ten years
after his death? Was there a personal or political motive for his using
Shaftesbury so unmercifully? Neither Kaye nor any other commentator
has offered an explanation beyond that of the conventional motivation
of the satirist and Mandeville's disagreement with Shaftesbury's social
system.

1724 – The third edition of *The Fable of the Bees* reprints Mandeville's
attack on Shaftesbury, and this reappears in

1725 – the fourth edition of *The Fable* and in

1728 – the fifth edition of that work.

1729 – In this year we find a repetition of a situation that had already
occurred in 1723. In each of these years, 1723 and 1729, it was possible
for a reader to purchase current reprints of both the *Free Thoughts*
and *The Fable*, and so find different attitudes toward Shaftesbury
expressed by the same author. In 1729, too, Mandeville first published
Part II of his *Fable of the Bees*, a separate volume containing six dialogues primarily between Cleomenes, who is generally a spokesman
for Mandeville, and Horatio, who begins by maintaining Shaftesbury's
position but finally accepts Mandeville's. At the end of the sixth dialogue Mandeville, through the voice of Cleomenes, again attacks
Shaftesbury, thus making the entire set of six dialogues appear to be a
unified refutation of Shaftesbury's social system. This passage, though

quite familiar, deserves closer examination within the present context:

Hor. And what say you of Lord Shaftesbury?

Cleo. First, I agree with you, that he was a Man of Erudition, and a very polite Writer; he has display'd a copious Imagination, and a fine Turn of thinking, in courtly Language and nervous Expressions: But as, on the one hand, it must be confess'd, that his Sentiments on Liberty and Humanity are noble and sublime, and that there is nothing trite or vulgar in the *Characteristicks*; so, on the other, it cannot be denied, that the Ideas he had form'd of the Goodness and Excellency of our Nature, were as romantick and chimerical as they are beautiful and amiable; that he labour'd hard to unite two Contraries that can never be reconcil'd together, Innocence of Manners and worldly Greatness; that to compass this End he favour'd Deism, and, under Pretence of lashing Priestcraft and Superstition, attack'd the Bible it self; and lastly, that by ridiculing many Passages of Holy Writ, he seems to have endeavour'd to sap the Foundation of all reveal'd Religion, with the Design of establishing Heathen Virtue on the Ruins of Christianity.[24]

In this passage, which brings the augmented *Fable of the Bees* to a conclusion, we find (1) that Mandeville, in passing, praises Shaftesbury's libertarian sentiments, (2) that he again emphasizes the errors of Shaftesbury's views on human nature and the public good, and (3) that he introduces an attack upon Shaftesbury's deism, more specifically upon his free criticisms of the Bible on moral grounds. The second of these three points is obviously the heart of Mandeville's case against Shaftesbury, but in this passage it is the third point – presented in the order of climax – that was probably intended to be the most damaging. Mandeville, who by then had acquired a considerable reputation as a cynical freethinker, knew that at least some of his readers would find it ironic that one freethinker should accuse another of being a deist. Some modern scholars, one should add, are taking Mandeville's professed accord with Christian principles with greater seriousness than has been the case until the past few years.[25] This is not the place to undertake a

[24] Kaye, II, 356-57.

[25] See Thomas R. Edwards, Jr., "Mandeville's Moral Prose," *ELH*, 31 (June, 1964), 195-212, and Gordon S. Vichert's unpublished doctoral dissertation, *A Critical Study of the English Works of Bernard Mandeville (1670-1733)*, U. of London, 1964; and E. D. James's article elsewhere in this volume. Significant recent scholarship on Bayle appears to diverge from the formerly popular view that his profession of faith merely a cloak for his skeptical undermining of religious institutions, but the emphasis on Bayle as primarily a skeptic is still strongly in view. For a useful annotated bibliography identifying the opposing points of view on the question of Bayle's sincerity,

detailed inquiry into the affinities between Mandeville's doctrines and
those of Toland, Collins or Tindal, but we may note that Mandeville's
name appeared regularly in lists of deistic writers by the pen-wielding
controversial divines. Bishop Berkeley was not interested in the precise
distinctions between the positions of Shaftesbury and Mandeville when
he roasted both authors in his *Alciphron* (1732).[26]

The passages that Mandeville acquired from Shaftesbury were quite
consonant with deistic attitudes in that age. What needs to be emphasized,
however, is that Mandeville, like his mentor Bayle, argued from a position
of Christian skepticism. He never posed as a deist, though others loosely
regarded him as such. In particular, Mandeville exploited his heritage of
rigorism to ridicule and undermine the sentimental benevolism that
characterized Shaftesburian deism. One can find passages in the *Free
Thoughts* which both the deist and the divine might regard as deistic, but
these do not permit us to apply that label to Mandeville. One such
passage reveals simultaneously Mandeville's close affinity with Shaftesburian deism and the precise limit he chose in that direction: "It is evident then, that there is no Characteristick to distinguish and know a true

---

see Richard H. Popkin's edition of Pierre Bayle, *Historical and Critical Dictionary:
Selections* (Indianapolis, 1965). The revaluations which picture Bayle as a sincere
believer have clearly influenced recent opinion concerning Mandeville's sincerity, so
that it can now be said that we have two well-defined positions interpreting Mandeville's religious faith. On the one hand, there are F. B. Kaye, Jacob Viner and their
followers who argue that Mandeville exploited his Christian rigorism in order to show
how little of true Christianity actually survived in the world and how unrelated it is
to the modern "aggrandized" society that is Mandeville's chief concern. On the other
hand, Gordon J. Vichert, E. D. James and Elias J. Chiasson prefer to accept, more or
less, Mandeville's professions of faith as basically sincere statements. My own view is
that Mandeville simply maintains a paradoxical stance. Through his mouthpiece
Cleomenes (*Fable,* II) and elsewhere in his writings he adheres unswervingly to faith
in Providence. On the other hand, by his minute attention to the operations of the
"passions" – our irrational drives and instincts – and in his case *for* luxury, he most
often gives the impression of a man concerned with the health and prosperity of mankind in this world. His non-medical writings are not manuals of devotion or piety:
they are statesmen's handbooks. Nevertheless, he nowhere admits to stepping over the
line from Christian faith to a bland or a radical deism, and only a reckless fool it is
in Mandeville's age would dare to profess atheism publicly. If the tag is at all permis-
sible, there appears to be sufficient reason for regarding Mandeville as a Christian
libertine. See further Jacob Viner, *The Long View and the Short* (Glencoe, Ill.,
1958), 339, and Elias J. Chiasson, "Bernard Mandeville: A Reappraisal," *Philological
Quarterly,* 49 (1970), 489-519.
[26] In *A Letter to Dion* (1732), his retort to Berkeley, Mandeville defended only
his own position. Another example of the linking of Shaftesbury and Mandeville in a
typical onslaught against the deists occurs in the title of a work attributed to Philip
Skelton, *Deism Revealed. Or, the Attack on Christianity Candidly Reviewed In its
real Merits, as they stand in the celebrated Writings of Lord Herbert, Lord Shaftesbury, Hobbes, Toland, Tindal, Collins, Mandeville, Dodwell, Woolston, Morgan,
Chubb, and others,* 1749, second ed., 1751.

Church from a false one." [27] From the deistic point of view, all churches represent more or less the one ultimate truth. But it is not the idea of universal religious truth that Mandeville continues to develop in this paragraph. He observes, rather, that all churches will be punitive or tolerant to the extent to which they command or lack the power to enforce their wishes. The emphasis is mainly political. Mandeville agreed entirely with Shaftesbury and the deists that religion and the state must be divorced; no church may impose its will by any kind of force or coercion, clerical or secular; and only those sects can be tolerated which, unlike continental Roman Catholicism, pose no political threat to the nation.

Given the information now available, it appears that Mandeville alternately praised and blamed Shaftesbury throughout the decade of the 1720's. We should have a clearer view, very likely, if more details were available on the publishing history of the second edition of the *Free Thoughts* in 1729. Though Mandeville added a remark to his preface suggesting that this second edition had been significantly revised and augmented, collation of the two editions reveals only minor changes in diction and correction of typographical errors.[28] This edition was entirely reset and printed on a smaller page, thus yielding a book that was fifty pages longer than the first edition. We cannot be certain that Mandeville was primarily responsible for or even involved in this deliberate deception. The main purpose of this new edition could well have been the stimulation of new sales. In 1729, with a major amplification of his *Fable of the Bees* freshly published, Mandeville was probably riding the crest of his popularity: what better time to resuscitate his earlier writing? If he had wished to take a positive stand by firmly asserting his rejection of Shaftesbury's system in his second edition of the *Free Thoughts*, he could have done so easily. But we cannot even be sure that it was Mandeville himself who supervised and corrected this second edition. In any event, the quotations and borrowings from Shaftesbury reappeared intact. Notwithstanding his vilification elsewhere of Shaftesbury's personal conduct and his attack on the social system, he apparently continued to share with the earl the vital assumptions and principles that united all Augustan Whigs.

What emerges from our new evidence about Mandeville's use of his sources is not new as a literary strategy; Kaye noted similar tactics by

---

[27] *F.T.*, 234.
[28] For a more extended discussion of this problem, see my "Bibliographical Note on Bernard Mandeville's 'Free Thoughts,' " *Notes & Queries* (May, 1969), 187-88.

Mandeville in parts of *The Fable of the Bees*, and sometimes contemporaries of Mandeville, acute readers like William Law, located stolen passages in Mandeville's prose. But none of his contemporaries detected, or
at least revealed in print, the extent of Mandeville's hidden debt to Shaftesbury. Our awareness of that borrowing complicates and forces us to
reconsider the full relationship as it has crystallized in history. The most
that we can venture, perhaps, is that Mandeville's awareness of how he
had raided the *Characteristicks* to fill out his own book may have been
one of the factors that caused him to turn against that noble lord. And
yet, even though he succeeded in becoming the most celebrated opponent
of Shaftesburian benevolism, he continued to show the influence of
Shaftesbury in his later writings. This influence is clearly apparent, for
instance, in the form of Part II of *The Fable of the Bees* (1729). The six
dialogues comprising Part II lead finally to the conversion of Horatio
from adherence to Shaftesbury's system to his acceptance of the Mandevillean account of man and society. Interestingly, these dialogues scrupul-
ously ape the elegance and gentility of Shaftesbury's much-admired dialogues in *The Moralists* (1709; Treatise V in the *Characteristicks*). Part
I of *The Fable* contains many passages in which the speaker presents
"low" comparisons and images; as a stylistic device they complement his
views on the fallen, degenerate state of human nature. Men are, in
Mandeville's view, far closer to the animal world than some divines and
philosophers are willing to admit. Their ideas of the dignity of man are
mere "romantick" fancies, and Mandeville repeatedly mocks this hunger
for the sublime by importing low and homely comparisons. The change
in form which occurs in Part II – miscellaneous "Remarks" or essays
giving way to well-bred dialogue – is accompanied by a significant elevation of tone. It is as if Mandeville had decided to compete with Shaftesbury not only with respect to substance and idea but also in the exercise
of a particular genre, the classical philosophic dialogue. This presents the
interesting situation in which Mandeville uses the form of *The Moralists*
to convince his readers that the doctrines in that work, comprising the
social system, are fundamentally unsound.

It is true that Mandeville need not necessarily have elected the dialogue form in Part II of *The Fable* because of the influence of Shaftesbury; the models from classical antiquity were doubtless well known to
Mandeville. Nevertheless, considering the extent of his earlier uses of
Shaftesbury, I am tempted to believe that his later uses of the philosophic dialogue were inspired primarily by the example of Shaftesbury.
On the whole, Mandeville's collective debt to Shaftesbury turns out to be

considerably more extensive and various than was generally imagined. Shaftesbury provided Mandeville not only with a view of human nature that easily lent itself to the satirist's ridicule, but with much more. In more ways than we have suspected, Shaftesbury's *Characteristicks* shaped Mandeville's thinking and writing: he had imbibed Shaftesbury too well and too often to repudiate him entirely. Whatever success was earned by Mandeville as a provocative writer in his own age and posthumously, a significant part of that success derives from his ambivalent attachment to the writings of Lord Shaftesbury.

MANDEVILLE AND VOLTAIRE

A. Owen Aldridge

Voltaire is perhaps a less puzzling figure than Mandeville even though more learned, versatile and sophisticated. Voltaire contributed to every major literary genre of the eighteenth century and produced at least one masterpiece in each genre, but Mandeville was a one book man to all but narrow specialists in Augustan literary history. Voltaire's purpose in most of his writing was to further the ideals of what is now called the Enlightenment, that is, the promotion of general intellectual tolerance, the adoption of scientific method in philosophic inquiry, and in religion the substitution of reason for authority and superstition. These ideals are inseparable from virtually any work of Voltaire. The aims of Mandeville's *Fable of the Bees*, however, are less clear. Some critics believe that Mandeville also sought to advance Enlightenment philosophy, but others believe that he cared only to shock his fellow citizens and to amuse himself with his brilliant paradoxes. Everyone recognizes that he established his system of psychology on the premise that men are inherently selfish and his system of economics on the premise that luxury is highly beneficial to society, but opinions are divided concerning his motives for advancing these notions and concerning his sincerity. Voltaire is frequently cynical or ironical in particular works or specific passages, but the general purpose of his thought is apparent. With Mandeville, it is his personal philosophy which is debatable.

Previous scholarship has been devoted to ascertaining how much Voltaire derived from Mandeville and at what periods in his intellectual career the borrowing took place. While Voltaire was residing with Emilie du Châtelet at her château in Cirey in 1735, the latter wrote a preface to a translation of the *Fable of the Bees*, which she presumably had begun in the same year. Although no proof exists that Voltaire was personally involved in this translation, it is quite possible that she began the task at his suggestion. A full treatment of her work is given in Ira O. Wade's book *Voltaire and Madame du Châtelet* (Princeton, 1941). Sometime between September 1735 and the following January, Voltaire published his poem *Le Mondain*, which presents many parallels with Mandeville's *Fable*, but no evidence of actual borrowing. This material has also been dealt with exhaustively by Professor Wade and other scholars, and I have no intention of going over it once more or attempting to arrive at a "final evaluation" of Mandeville's influence.[1] Instead I shall confine myself to Voltaire's general attitude toward the Mandevillean philosophy. It is my thesis that Voltaire's occasional and non-committal borrowings from the *Fable of the Bees* indicate that he was intrigued and amused by Mandeville, but that he did not accept the latter's basic tenets. Voltaire used him for his shock value, in order to amaze timorous minds. This does not mean that Mandeville's contribution was negligible. He revealed to Voltaire the value of a blunt, forceful and idiomatic approach to ideas, which Voltaire could use to balance his own polite and formal style. Voltaire regarded the *Fable*, moreover, as a clever example of how concepts unacceptable to the mores of society could be made palatable, or at least presentable in print. This is certainly the drift of his comment to Helvétius in 1762: "Il y a des choses que tout le monde sçait, et qu'il ne faut jamais dire, à moins qu'on ne les dise en plaisantant; il est permis à La Fontaine, de dire que Cocuage n'est point un mal mais il n'est pas permis à un philosophe de démontrer qu'il est du droit naturel de coucher avec la femme de son prochain. [*De l'esprit*, II, iv] Il en est aussi, ne vous déplaise de quelques petites propositions de vôtre livre; l'autheur de la fable des abeilles vous a induit dans le piège." [2]

A very revealing footnote concerning Mandeville appears in Mme. du Châtelet's preface to her translation of *The Fable of the Bees*. After describing Mandeville as the English Montaigne but with the reservation that he possessed more method and a more wholesome conception of things than Montaigne, she added, "C'étoit le petit fils d'un refugié françois. Il prouve par son example que les esprits françois ont besoin d'estre transplantés en Angleterre pour acquérir de la force." [3] One does not know where Voltaire's mistress acquired the notion that Mandeville was the grandson of a French refugee, but this is of minor importance. The part of her comment indicating that French intellectuals need to

---

[1] *Studies on Voltaire* (Princeton, 1947).

[2] 13 August 1762. Theodore Besterman ed., *Voltaire's Correspondence*. Letter No. 9834.

[3] Wade, *Voltaire and Madame du Châtelet*, p. 232.

go to England to obtain mental vigor strongly suggests that she was thinking of Voltaire's self-imposed exile to London in the 1720's, and it is possible she even had in mind the influence of Mandeville on Voltaire's style.

The Latin Epitaph of Marlborough

Mandeville's style in Latin was as bold as that in English, if we judge by an epitaph on the Duke of Marlborough appearing in "Dialogue VI" of *The Fable of the Bees.* Here Mandeville presents his epitaph in a disjointed manner, distich by distich interspersed with conversation. Voltaire was so impressed with the epitaph that he copied it as a complete poem in one of his notebooks. Since Voltairean scholars have done no research on this subject, I shall make a few comments.[4] The epitaph celebrates Marlborough for his achievements in war and peace and suggests that even the ancients had not produced his equal. One of the characters in Mandeville's dialogue remarks that "It is worth all his *Fable of the Bees* in my Opinion." Its literal meaning is as follows: Those who in former centuries have prayed to the stars have created man and the gods with the virtues of war or peace; mendacious Greece, which gave birth to Mars without a father and to Minerva without a mother, may boast of illustrious ancestors; here lies, placed in this urn, the man whom England gave birth to, one such as the ancients have not had even among their gods.

Mandeville supplied his own verse translation, attributed to "a gentleman of Oxford."

> The grateful Ages past a God declar'd,
> Who wisely council'd, or who bravely war'd:
> Hence Greece her Mars and Pallas deify'd;
> Made him the Hero's, her the Patriot's guide.
> Ancients, within this Urn a Mortal lies;
> Shew me his Peer among your Deities.

(Kaye's ed., II, 338-39)

One of Mandeville's characters remarks that "what is aimed at in the Latin is rather more clearly expressed in the English," but Voltaire copied only the Latin version. It may be that Voltaire was less interested in Mandeville's Latin style than in the tribute to Marlborough as such, but

---

[4] The epitaph is printed without editorial gloss in Theodore Besterman ed., Voltaire's Notebooks, vol. 81 of *The Complete Works of Voltaire* (Geneva, 1968), p. 340.

this is doubtful. He copied it along with a variety of other epitaphs, clearly for their paradoxes and epigrammatic qualities.

Unfortunately the date of the notebook in which Voltaire transcribed the epitaph for Marlborough cannot be precisely fixed. A number of his notebooks were printed in the Moland edition of his works under the general, but inexact title of *sottisier*.[5] The material was assembled in its present form by Voltaire's secretary Wagnière, and, therefore, it is impossible to ascertain when Mandeville's epitaph first caught Voltaire's eye.

The same collection contains a comment disagreeing with Mandeville's theory of the political original of morality. "Les politiques ne sont pas les inventeurs de la relligion. Ceux qui ont mis les tauraux au joug ont trouvé leurs cornes touttes faittes." [6] Obviously this observation cannot be unequivocally interpreted as a reference to Mandeville since Voltaire is speaking of the origin of religion whereas it is morality which Mandeville attributes to the invention of politicians, and even in this doctrine he had been preceded by Bayle. The doctrine of the political origin of virtue had nothing specifically to do with Voltaire's deism since even the most rabid of the deists declared that religion was the invention of priests, not politicians. Whether or not Voltaire had Mandeville specifically in mind, he was denying one of the latter's major notions, and for once taking a position more cynical than Mandeville's. Voltaire is implying that the politicians had no need of inventing religion since it grew naturally out of human stupidity or superstition.

The Concept of Luxury

One of the most vigorous repudiations of primitivism in all human thought is Voltaire's satirical poem *Le Mondain*, 1736, which conversely presents a good-natured vindication of luxury and the amenities of civilized living. As one French scholar aptly remarks, Voltaire's poem is "une apologie de la vie épicurienne, légère, optimiste, élégante et heureuse; une sorte d'hymne à la vie de Paris, parmi les choses délicates signées d'artistes connus, de fins dîners, de joyeux soupers, et de jolies femmes" ["an apology for the epicurean existence, volatile, optimistic, elegant and happy; a sort of hymn to the life of Paris, among the delicate productions signed by known artists, joyful suppers and beautiful women"].[7] More

---

[5] Theodore Besterman ed., *Notebooks*, vol. 81 of *The Complete Works of Voltaire* (Geneva, 1968), p. 22 ff.

[5] *Ibid.*, p. 351.

[7] A. Morize, *Le Mondain et l'apologie du luxe au XVIII° siècle* (Paris, 1909), p. 25.

space has been devoted to this subject than to any other aspect of the relations between Mandeville and Voltaire. Professor Wade has concluded on the basis of the date of Madame du Châtelet's translation of *The Fable of the Bees* that Voltaire knew Mandeville before writing his poem.[8] The question of direct influence is complicated by the fact that a famous French economic treatise by J. F. Melon, *Essai politique sur le commerce*, 1734, covers essentially the same ground as Mandeville. According to F. B. Kaye, "It may be said that he offers no basal arguments that are not in the *Fable*, and omits no essential ones that are in the *Fable*." [9] Professor Wade, after painstaking analysis and comparison, comes to the conclusion that *Le Mondain* does not contain a single verse which can be traced to the *Fable*.[10] Nor does it really have much in common with Mandeville's defense of luxury on economic grounds. Fundamentally Voltaire is ridiculing the major presumptions of primitivism, that the best life is the simplest or that based on the bare essentials. He asserts a purely personal zest for the refinements and pleasures of civilization.

> J'aime le luxe, et même la mollesse,
> Tous les plaisirs, les arts de toute espèce,
> La propreté, le goût, les ornements.

Mandeville, even his most ardent admirers will admit, shows very little concern for "propriety, taste, and ornaments," and, if anything, is opposed to indolence. The primary link between *The Fable* and *Le Mondain* is in the general theme of the two works, but this is, nevertheless, rather close. Mandeville explains in his Preface that his "main Design . . . is to shew the Impossibility of enjoying all the most elegant comforts of Life, that are to be met with in an industrious, wealthy and powerful Nation, and at the same time be bless'd with all the Virtue and Innocence that can be wish'd for in a Golden Age." [11] Voltaire in the first two lines of *Le Mondain* similarly refers to the commonly-praised primitive state of man and suggests his conclusion that modern civilization is vastly to be preferred.

> Regrettera qui veut le bon vieux temps,
> Et l'âge d'or, et le règne d'Astrée.

---

[8] *Voltaire and Madame du Châtelet*, p. 25. Also *Studies on Voltaire*, p. 27.
[9] *Fable of the Bees*, I, cxxxvi, n. 3.
[10] *Studies*, p. 31.
[11] Kaye's ed., I, 6-7.

Because of the clamor raised by pious minds against some irreverent references to Adam and Eve in *Le Mondain,* Voltaire wrote a vindication of his ideas on luxury in another poem to which he gave the title *La Défense du Mondain, ou l'apologie du luxe.* Here he shifted to primarily economic arguments, but since these are common to both Mandeville and Melon it is once more impossible to pinpoint a direct influence. The paradoxical flavor of Mandeville, however, is reflected in the following couplet:

> Le goût du luxe entre dans tous les rangs:
> Le pauvre y vit des vanités des grands.

Voltaire expanded, moreover, from *Le Mondain* the concept of progress, which he had merely hinted at in the earlier poem. The Romans were poor in comparison to the inhabitants of a modern city, he argued, and therefore it is erroneous to describe the Roman way of life as virtuous when it was merely barren. The deliberate linking of luxury to the idea of progress was a typical Voltairean refinement completely independent of Mandeville, although Mandeville certainly recognized the anti-primi-tivist concept that modern civilization is superior to life in the remote past. In his *Siècle de Louis XIV*, Voltaire greatly expanded his notion of luxury as progress. "A voir l'aisance des particuliers, ce nombre prodi-gieux de maisons agréables bâties dans Paris et dans les provinces, cette quantité d'équipages, ces commodités, ces recherches qu'on nomme *luxe*, on croirait que l'opulence est vingt fois plus grande qu'autrefois . . . Il n'en coûte guère plus aujourd'hui pour être agréablement logé, qu'il n'en coûtait pour l'être mal sous Henri IV" [Chap. xxx]. Mme de Staël quoted the opinion of one of her contemporaries that *Le Mondain* had given the notion of perfectibility to humanity and that it epitomizes "tout ce qu'il y a de meilleur dans les longues théories sur cette perfectibilité." Mme de Staël disagreed with this opinion.[12] In the article "Luxe" of his *Dictionnaire philosophique*, 1752 [?], Voltaire made explicit the con-nection between luxury and progress as he saw it. "Si l'on entend par luxe tout ce qui est au-delà du nécessaire, le luxe est une suite naturelle des progrès de l'espèce humaine; et pour raisonner conséquemment, tout ennemi du luxe doit croire avec Rousseau que l'état de bonheur et de vertu pour l'homme est celui, non de sauvage, mais d'orang-outang."

Voltaire completely shared with Mandeville the view that luxury was a virtually unmitigated benefit to society, and he certainly went as far as any passage in *The Fable of the Bees* in the direction of governmental

---

[12] Preface to second edition of *De la littérature.*

control of the economic sector. Voltaire strongly believed in state opulence as well as individual consumption. In all of Voltaire's political writings, and particularly in his *Le Siècle de Louis XIV*, he exalts public buildings, monuments, boulevards and other constructions as not only exterior symbols of the greatness and glory of a nation but also as means of attaining economic strength. Mandeville and many others indicated individual luxury, but Voltaire was almost unique in glorifying conspicuous consumption on the national level. What is more, he realized that massive government expenditures had to be financed by the entire population, and Voltaire was more than willing to bear his own share.

The best statement of Voltaire's theory of social luxury appears in a letter to Jean Baptiste Machault d'Arnouville, the French minister of finance in 1749, on the subject of a proposed income tax of one-twentieth (*le vingtième*) to be levelled against all social classes including the clergy. Voltaire was strongly in favor of this tax, and his letter combines arguments in favor of domestic luxury with those in favor of public works. In his letter, Voltaire speaks of a day spent in Mauchault's house. He recalls with pleasure the vast amounts of money lost there at cards, the elegance of the furnishings, the lavishness of the dinner, and the conversation in which it was agreed that the host was perfectly right in paying his chef a salary of 1500 livres, which was 500 more than he gave to the tutor of his son and nearly 1000 more than he gave to his secretary.[13] When a man of sour humor (comparable to the *maître cafard* of *La Défense du Mondain*) objected that there were many families in the upper stories of the building who had very little to eat, the others silenced him by proving that there must always be poor people in society and that the magnificence of a house like Machault's was enough to support at least 200 workers with what they earned from him. It was next remarked that what made Paris the most flourishing city in the world was not so much the number of magnificent buildings (*hôtels magnifiques*) which display opulence with a certain ostentation, but rather the extraordinary number of private homes, where the inhabitants lived with a degree of comfort unknown to their ancestors and to which other nations had not yet arrived. Since Voltaire's motive was primarily to support the *vingtième*, enabling the state to become the major spender, rather than simply to vindicate private luxury, Voltaire diverted the argument from private to public expenditures; perhaps to persuade wealthy land owners that they need not fear losing their opulence should the tax be put into effect. "Ce ne sont point les impôts qui affaiblissent une nation, c'est, ou la ma-

---

[13] Theodore Besterman ed., *Voltaire's Correspondence,* Letter No. 3394.

nière de les percevoir, ou le mauvais usage qu'on en fait. Mais si le roi se sert de cet argent pour acquitter des dettes, pour établir une marine, pour embellir la capitale, pour achever le Louvre, pour perfectionner ces grands chemins, qui font l'admiration des étrangers, pour soutenir les manufactures et les beaux-arts, en un mot, pour encourager de tous côtés l'industrie, il faut avouer qu'un tel impôt, qui parait un mal à quelques-uns, aura produit un très grand bien à tout le monde. Le peuple le plus heureux est celui qui paye le plus et qui travaille le plus, quand il paye et travaille pour lui-même." Both Mandeville and Voltaire were exponents of the economic benefits of luxury, but their perspectives and practical applications differed widely. Mandeville instead of praising the elegance of a household such as Machault's cites as an example of prodigality the son of a greedy statesman, who feeds "an infinite number of Dogs of all Sorts and Sizes, tho' he never hunts," keeps "more Horses than any Nobleman in the Kingdom, tho' he never rides 'em," and gives "as large an Allowance to an illfavour'd Whore as would keep a Dutchess, tho' he never lies with her" [Remark K]. We can imagine Mandeville extolling lavish expenditures while drinking beer in a tap-room, and Voltaire doing the same while sipping champagne in a château.

Voltaire has much less to say than Mandeville about the other end of the social scale, the laboring poor, but he gave the subject some thought. Mandeville in opposing the educating of poor orphans expressed a social philosophy which to many critics of his time and ours seems callous. "Abundance of hard and dirty Labour is to be done," he remarked, "and coarse Living is to be complied with: Where shall we find a better Nursery for these Necessities than the Children of the Poor?" [14] Earlier in the same essay he expressed the principle that only necessity makes people work. "No Man would be poor and fatigue himself for a Livelihood if he could help it: The absolute necessity all stand in for Victuals and Drink, and in cold Climates for Clothes and Lodging, makes them submit to any thing that can be bore with. If no body did Want no body would work." [15] Voltaire agreed with Mandeville in principle, but felt that the poor should, nevertheless, be protected from exploitation. In his *Siècle de Louis XIV*, he commented on the problem without offering suggestions for its solution. "Le manoeuvre, l'ouvrier, doit être réduit au nécessaire pour travailler: telle est la nature de l'homme. Il faut que ce grand nombre d'hommes soit pauvre, mais il ne faut pas qui'il soit misérable" [Chap. xxx]. Voltaire's *Siècle de Louis XIV* incorporates both of

[14] *An Essay on Charity and Charity-Schools,* in Kaye's ed., I, 311.
[15] *Ibid.,* I, 287.

Mandeville's economic principles, that opulence and luxury bring prosperity to all classes and that civilization requires that a body of workers be kept poor.

The Talking Lion

In Remark P of *The Fable of the Bees*, a gloss on the principle that the modern poor live better than the rich of earlier times, Mandeville starts out by vindicating modern civilization against the doctrines of primitivism, but soon branches off into a discussion of the eating of animal flesh and the natural repulsion which all people feel to the shedding of animal or human blood. On the surface his apparently sincere protest against cruelty to animals seems to reflect a much more compassionate spirit than a famous passage in his *Essay on Charity and Charity-Schools* in which he denies that any virtue exists in feeling distress at the sight of an infant torn limb from limb and devoured by an overgrown sow. Actually, however, both passages reflect the notion that man has a repugnancy to killing proceeding from "a real passion inherent in our nature." In Remark P Mandeville uses these precise words, and in his essay he affirms that "not one of the species has a heart so obdurate or engaged that it would not ache" at the sight of the child being mauled. Mandeville concludes Remark P with the fable of a merchant, cast ashore with his slave off the coast of Africa, who falls into the power of a lion. The latter not only speaks several languages but is thoroughly acquainted with human affairs. Voltaire closely imitated this parable in a humorous poem, and for this reason I shall present it in summary. A comparison of Voltaire's version with Mandeville's reveals that the two authors emphasized quite different elements.

Mandeville's lion assures the quaking merchant that he will not be touched provided he is able to furnish convincing reasons for being spared. The merchant, taking courage, cites the "Excellency of Man's Nature and Abilities" as evidence that he was designed for a better use than to be devoured by savage beasts. The lion indignantly retorts that if God had given him this alleged superiority, he should have no need to beg his life of an inferior. Then in terms resembling Gulliver speaking to the Houyhnhnms, the merchant replies that superiority rests in the mind, not in physical force, and that God has given man an immortal soul. The lion answers that he is not interested in the merchant's soul, only his body; the merchant pleads that he has a family to take care of; the lion retorts that he also has young and must provide food for them. He questions, moreover, the sincerity of man's profession of concern for his kind and affirms that it extends no further than "the Share which every one's Pride has in it for himself." The lion, making no claims to being born with compassion, observes that he is satisfied with eating animals already dead, that he hunts the living only when the dead are not available. It is only "mischievous Man" who turns death into a sport; man's appetite is languid and needs to be titllated, but the lion's is always fierce. A single lion is an imposing creature of some consequence; a single man, of none. The lion concludes that since men have never acknowledged superiority without force, he also will not do so; and since the Gods have given him the strength to overcome, he proposes to use it. At these words the merchant faints away. Reverting to his own character, Mandeville reflects on the justice of the charge that man is cruel toward other animals and presents a moving description of the suffering of a slaughtered bullock. "What Mortal can, without Compassion, hear the painful Bellowings intercepted by his Blood, the bitter Sighs that speak the Sharpness of his Anguish, and the deep sounding Grones with loud Anxiety fetch'd from the bottom of his strong and palpitating Heart; Look on the trembling and violent Convulsions of his Limbs; see while his reeking Gore streams from him, his Eyes become dim and languid, and behold his Strugglings, Gasps, and last Efforts for Life . . . ?" Mandeville concludes that such undeniable proofs of suffering completely refute Descartes' theories of animal insensibility.

This is one of the most sober sections of the entire *Fable of the Bees*. It contains only a restrained note of satire, and Mandeville's purpose seems genuinely to be a protest against hunting and other cruelty to animals, as sincere as the more sentimental approaches in the essays of Addison and Steele. His entire emphasis seems superficially to be on physical strength, yet his conclusion calls on the reader for the exercise of pity – even though he does not use that particular word which is reprobated in other sections of his work.

Voltaire created a complete poem out of Mandeville's parable to which he gave the title "Le Marseillois et le Lion," 1768. It is printed among the author's satires, and its major targets are Christian theology and the cupidity of the merchant classes, neither theme having any relationship to Mandeville's parable.

Voltaire takes up where Mandeville left off by refuting Descartes on the theory of animal insensitivity, but he does so on quite different grounds from his source, arguing that the entire Cartesian system, including the theory of the beast machine, is absurd. The poem is accompanied by lengthy prose footnotes devoted primarily to ridiculing the traditions of Christianity. Both in his text and notes, therefore, Voltaire scoffs at the notion that animals have the power of speech. The early part of Mandeville's narrative, Voltaire follows quite closely. Specifying merely that the merchant is a native of Marseilles, he describes the encounter with the lion, the latter's offer to apply reason to the situation, and the merchant's argument that the law of nature has appointed man to reign over all the animals on earth. Instead of answering this argument with more words, the lion, who had the right to laugh at such an absurdity, proceeds to do so and at the same time with a blow of his paw tears off all the merchant's clothes. This is more humorous and dramatic than Mandeville's unrelieved dialogue. Voltaire next supplies a comic description of man's puny physique, attributing all of his grandeur to his real master, but begs him to control his anger on the grounds that "a king is not loved if he is not debonair." In similar vein he alleges that in the wig and clothes. The merchant is forced to admit that the lion is the days of Noah's ark God gave all the animals an injunction not to harm man, who is created in the image of God. In the notes Voltaire casts doubt on the entire flood tradition and points out that in Genesis man and animals are considered as equals and subject to identical laws, a strongly anti-Biblical accusation, made also in Voltaire's notorious *Sermon des cinquante*. The lion himself questions the authenticity of the Noah legend, demands documentation, and indignantly denies that man is the image of the creator. His teeth and claws he takes as more reliable evidence of the nature of things. Once more closely reverting to Mandeville's original text, Voltaire has the lion contrast disparagingly the delicate human digestive system with his own hardy one. Man's "chétives dents" and "débile estomac" require that he depend on the arts of cookery.

> Le pacte universel est qu'on naisse et qu'on meure.
> Apprends qu'il vaut autant, raissonneur de travers,
> Etre avalé par moi que rongé par les vers.

Voltaire carries over from Mandeville the merchant's protest that he has an immortal soul, but unlike Mandeville has the lion reply that he as a lion also has one; he indicates moreover that he does not wish to eat the merchant's soul, merely his body. Voltaire's merchant follows Mandeville's in appealing to the lion to pity his children; the response also is the same – the lion has his own young to feed.

Mandeville brings his narrative to a speedy close by having his merchant collapse in a faint, a turn of events which does nothing but reflect on human cowardice, if it can be said to do even that. Voltaire, however, exposes the craftiness of the merchant by having him strike a bargain with the lion for his freedom; he promises to send two sheep a day for two months and to leave his servant as a hostage. Voltaire's formal conclusion has no connection whatsoever with Mandeville's in style or theme. In a tone resembling the formal conclusion of many of La Fontaine's fables, Voltaire remarks that lions from time immemorial have concluded bargains at the expense of sheep.

The spirit of Voltaire's poem is light-hearted and humorous in contrast to the sobriety of Mandeville's parable. Voltaire's targets are the familiar ones of Christian superstition and the facts of human fallibility; whereas Mandeville is concerned with the reasons for some human attitudes. Although the two authors are telling exactly the same story and although several ideological parallels exist, Voltaire's themes of cupidity, egotism and theological absurdities have absolutely nothing to do with Mandeville's concern over cruelty to animals. As a matter of fact, Voltaire's complete works reveal scarcely any affectionate references to animals or even any treatments of animals as actual creatures of nature. By and large they appear as in "Le Marseillois et le lion" merely as symbols for human beings.

Human Vices and the Selfish System

So far we have hardly touched on the major doctrines associated with Mandeville, particularly that vices of individuals are necessary for the well being of society and that man is a fundamentally selfish creature. Voltaire gave to the first a guarded assent but rejected the second. He recorded his opinion of Mandeville's paradox that private vices are public benefits in the article "Abeilles" of his *Dictionnaire philosophique*, 1752 (?), after a 21-line doggerel poem summarizing Mandeville's "Grumbling Hive."

Il est très vrai que la société bien gouvernée tire parti de tous les vices; mais il n'est pas vrai que ces vices soient nécessaires au bonheur du monde. On fait de très bons remèdes avec des poisons, mais ce ne sont pas les poisons qui nous font vivre. En réduisant ainsi la fable des Abeilles à sa juste valeur, elle pourrait devenir un ouvrage morale utile.

The other principle of man's alleged selfishness Voltaire takes up at some length in a number of his works, first of all in Chapters VIII and IX of his *Traité de métaphysique* which he began working on around 1734. Professor Wade in his discussion of Madame du Châtelet's trans-

lation of *The Fable of the Bees* points out several verbal parallels with
Voltaire's *Traité* and comes to the conclusion that Voltaire may have
used her translation as the basis of his discussion. I have no wish to deny
this conclusion, since I believe it is demonstrated by the fact that a
passage which is not in Mandeville at all but was added silently by Mme.
du Châtelet to her text was adopted in essence by Voltaire in the *Traité*.[16]
I merely wish to add that other evidence exists to show that Voltaire also
drew directly from the *Fable*. He ascribes importance, for example, to
statistics showing a preponderance of males over females born each year,,
a circumstance he interprets as a contrivance of nature to compensate for
the numbers of men killed in wars. This is precisely the argument of
Mandeville in Dialogue V of his *Fable*, but it is not comprised in Mme.
du Châtelet's translation limited entirely as it is to the *Enquiry into the
Origin of Moral Virtue*. Voltaire also refers to another passage in Mandeville not covered by Mme. du Châtelet's translation even though he uses
it as an illustration of one of her principles. She argues against Mandeville that there is virtue inherent in a desire to save an infant from perish-
ing by fire, an illustration drawn from Mandeville's *Enquiry into the
Origin of Moral Virtue*. Voltaire, however, offers as his illustration of
man's inherent benevolence the uncomfortable sensation which we feel
in seeing "un joli enfant prêt d'être dévoré par quelque animal," probably inspired by Mandeville's notorious description in his *Essay on Charity
and Charity-Schools* of the infant torn limb from limb by an overgrown
sow. It is worth noting, moreover, that Mandeville does not dispute the
existence of "anxieties" or "pity" on such an occasion, and Voltaire does
not specifically declare against Mandeville that this pity or uncomfortable
sensation is virtuous. His point is limited to proving that we have "cette
bienveillance qui vous dispose à l'union avec les hommes." It is perhaps
equally important to note moreover that Madame du Châtelet incorporated in her commentary on Mandeville an illustration which she acquired directly from Voltaire – that concerning the intrepidity of soldiers
at the siege of Phillipsburg, who bowled with cannon balls.[17]

Throughout the final two chapters of his treatise, Voltaire presents an
ingenious mixing of Shaftesbury and Mandeville, the theories of benevolence of one, and theories of selfishness of the other. He begins his discussion with a consideration of the attachment of parents and their
young as an illustration of natural benevolence, an attachment which
both Mandeville and Shaftesbury accept. Mandeville calls it "an instinct

---

[16] *Voltaire and Madame du Châtelet,* p. 32.
[17] René Pomeau, *La Religion de Voltaire* (Paris, 1969), p. 196.

of nature" in his parable of the lion and the merchant in Remark P. After next citing the uncomfortable sensation produced by seeing a child devoured by an animal as evidence of inherent benevolence to our species, Voltaire admits that this benevolence is relatively weak as an impulse to make us live in society. He argues, therefore, that a more powerful motivation is required for the foundation of great empires or flourishing cities. To explain the great passions which are required for this end, he turns to Mandeville's theory of pride and the political nature of virtue. He affirms that the furor to acquire wealth leads to progress in all the arts, and that envy disguised as emulation overcomes laziness or inspires activity.

In taking up the question of virtue and vice, Voltaire adopts Mandeville's relativity, giving a series of illustrations to show that the conception of virtue and vice changes according to climate and social variants. The only point of common agreement among nations consists in considering conformity to the laws virtuous and disregarding them criminal. The laws themselves, according to Voltaire, are of minor importance; what matters is that they be obeyed. Virtue and vice, he emphasizes in an italicized maxim, consist entirely in that which is useful or harmful to society, an uncompromising empiricism which is the essence of Mandevilleanism. Despite the obvious disagreements from one milieu to another concerning what is called virtue and vice, Voltaire still argues that there are certain "natural laws" of universal application.

In his concluding paragraph, Voltaire cleverly joins the Mandevillean and Shaftesburian philosophies as he discusses motives to virtue. He follows Mandeville in observing that God has given us pride which will not allow us to endure the hate or contempt of other men, and he follows Shaftesbury by affirming that every man of reason will conclude that it is visibly to his own interest to be virtuous. Finally, Voltaire cites a register of men of rigid virtue, including Shaftesbury, who have been motivated not only by the fear of being condemned by other men but also by the love of virtue itself.

This is the closest Voltaire ever came to open espousal of the Mandevillean system of virtue. Later in his *Poème sur la loi naturelle,* 1752, he indirectly repudiated it. In his preface, Voltaire described the poem as a refutation of a hedonistic discourse by La Mettrie, entitled *Anti-Sénèque, ou le souvereign bien.* The doctrine of the *Anti-Sénèque* strongly resembles that of *The Fable of the Bees* and Voltaire himself had even been mistaken for the author of the *Anti-Sénèque.* Voltaire remarked that La Mettrie's work should have been called *Du souvereign mal* because of its doctrine that neither virtue nor vice exist and that remorse represents a frailty induced by education which should be repressed. Voltaire retorted as his own opinion, "Ceux qui disent que ce retour d'humanité n'est qu'une branche de notre amour-propre font bien de l'honneur à l'amour-propre." In his correspondence Voltaire revealed that he also considered his *Poème sur la loi naturelle* as a refutation of a poem by a Swiss naturalist and theologian Albrecht von Haller *Die Falschheit menschlicher Tugenden* (The Falsehood of Human Virtue), dedicated to proving that virtue does not exist in the human race. The relevance of this to Mandeville is obvious; the latter repudiated human morality on cynical empirical grounds with the same rigor which Haller and staunch Calvinists revealed in repudiating it on theological grounds. One of Mandeville's French precursors, Jacques Esprit, published in 1678 a book with exactly the same title as Haller's, *De la Fausseté des vertus humaines* [Of the Falsehood of Human Virtues]. In his Preface, Esprit declared: "I wish that those in whom these Moral, Civil and Heroick Virtues shine, seeing the Vanity and Meanness of the Motives of their actions, may correct their Errors, and conceive that the Virtues they glory in are only false and sham Virtues, and that far from fancying themselves Hero's and demy Gods, they may acknowledge that they are covetous, envious, vain, weak, fickle and inconstant as other men are." [18]

Voltaire intended his poem as a defense of human virtue against all those who questioned its existence. Like Shaftesbury, he argues that there exists a moral law independent even of the supreme being (a doctrine he had ridiculed in his *Traité de métaphysique*), but that God nevertheless manifests himself to humanity through the universal law of human conscience.

> Cette loi souveraine, à la Chine, au Japon,
> Inspira Zoroastre, illumina Solon.
> D'un bout du monde à l'autre elle parle, elle crie:
> "Adore un Dieu, sois juste, et chéris ta patrie."

Voltaire's argument hits equally all those who presumed to attack man's moral virtue, including Jacques Esprit, Julien La Mettrie, Albrecht von Haller and Bernard Mandeville.

---

[18] English translation by William Beauvoir, *Discourses on the Deceitfulness of humane virtues* (London, 1706); quoted by A. O. Lovejoy, *Reflections on Human Nature* (Baltimore, 1961), p. 28.

STYLE, SATIRE AND PARADOX:

"WHAT PIERCES OR STRIKES": PROSE STYLE IN THE FABLE OF THE BEES

ROBERT ADOLPH

All favourite Expressions in *French* are such, as either sooth or tickle; and nothing is more admired in *English,* than what pierces or strikes.[1]

In the introduction to his edition of *The Fable of the Bees* Professor Kaye describes Mandeville's political theory as "utilitarian:" "Mandeville decided upon the public results of private actions according to utilitarian standards. That which is useful, that which is productive of national prosperity and happiness, he called a benefit." As for private morality, though, "He judged the private actions themselves according to an anti-utilitarian scheme, whereby conduct was evaluated, not by its consequences, but by the motive which gave it rise. . . . The paradox that private vices are public benefits is merely a statement of the paradoxical mixing of moral criteria which runs through the book" (I, xlviii-xlix).

It seems to me that Professor Kaye is correct here. Furthermore, it is the tension between utilitarianism on one hand and a despair about the human condition on the other that generates the paradoxes of Mandeville's style and, indeed, whatever interest he holds for us today as an artist in his most interesting work stylistically, the first volume of the *Fable.*

Public benefits can only flow from private vices but, as Mandeville says several times, it does not necessarily follow that we must approve of vice for its own sake. "If I have shewn the way to worldly Greatness, I have always without Hesitation preferr'd the Road that leads to Virtue" (I, 231). If Mandeville had been of a certain cast of mind, such an outlook would have led to a deeply tragic view of life. In a Calvin, a Pascal, or a Kierkegaard such an awareness of the necessary sinfulness of man without God led to profound anguish. Not so with the satirist Man-

---

[1] Bernard Mandeville, *The Fable of the Bees: or, Private Vices, Public Benefits,* ed. F. B. Kaye (Oxford, 1924), II, p. 297. All references are to this edition.

deville, who temperamentally was no voyager into the existential abyss, but a debunker of human pride, especially the pride that would hypocritically deny the practical, if not moral, necessity of evil. In the end, as Basil Willey notes, "His main plea . . . was for honesty and realism." [2] His style is a reflection of the tensions and paradoxes in his thought and his attempt to cut through them in forceful debunker's language which "pierces or strikes." Without his style, at once paradoxical and blunt, he would be read today solely by students of the history of political and economic theory for what he superficially seems to be, a forerunner of such modern eighteenth-century advocates of the virtue of selfishness as Ayn Rand and Barry Goldwater.

Mandeville's style is both "correct" and satiric. The "correct" side is a product of attitudes towards communication which became prevalent around the time of the Restoration in which prose became normally a vehicle of utilitarian instruction rather than self-expression or elegant artifice for its own sake. Uniformity, objectivity, precision, and clarity became the universally accepted goals of the new style. Historians of style, especially those influenced by linguistics, do well to remind us of the dangers in such high-order abstractions as "Restoration style" or "Augustan prose." But it seems to me that in Mandeville's time literary prose had become so standardized that apart from a few giants like Swift or Defoe only a specialist in the period can identify prose writers by their style. "Unformity," "objectivity," "precision," and "clarity" meant for the Restoration and early eighteenth century the following: First, we have firmly balanced or antithetical syntax to suggest balanced, considered judgement, and the certainty of mathematical ratios. Second, there is a predominance of abstract nouns (almost invariably capitalized) over colorless verbs, with the implication that each noun is a clear and distinct idea or technical term whose meaning is unaffected by any context and therefore is understood by all right-thinking folk who will of course have the correct definition in their heads. As Mandeville's spokesman Cleomones says in book two of the *Fable*, "The true and only Mint of Words and Phrases is the Court; and the polite Part of every Nation are in Possession of the *Jus & norma loquendi.* . . . Whatever is not used among them, or comes abroad without their Sanction, is either vulgar, pedantick, or obsolete. Orators therefore, Historians, and all wholesale Dealers in Words, are confin'd to those, that have been already well receiv'd . . . but they are not allow'd to make new ones of their own"

---

[2] Basil Willey, *The Eighteenth Century Background* (London, 1940), p. 99.

(II, 292-293). People are understood as bundles of these abstract nouns (e.g., Envy, Reason, Shame, Honour) called Passions, Qualities, or Faculties. Very often each Passion, Quality, or Faculty will be balanced off against another, like parts of a machine or a mathematical ratio. Third, there is a good deal of apparent agreement as to what constitutes "low" versus "polite" diction; in general, "low" diction has reference to whatever is physically concrete. Fourth, we find "polite" metaphors and similes in which the relations between tenor and vehicle are self-consciously "unfolded" or spelled out in one-to-one relationships so that all is balanced and nothing left to uncertainty. For example:

Authors are always allow'd to compare small things to great ones, especially if they ask leave first. *Si licet exemplis,* &c. but to compare great things to mean trivial ones is unsufferable, unless it be in Burlesque; otherwise I would compare the Body Politick (I confess the Simile is very low) to a Bowl of Punch. Avarice should be the Souring and Prodigality the Sweetning of it. The Water I would call the Ignorance, Folly and Credulity of the floating insipid Multitude; while Wisdom, Honour, Fortitude and the rest of the sublime Qualities of Men, which separated by Art from the Dregs of Nature the fire of Glory has exalted and refin'd into a Spiritual Essence, should be an Equivalent to Brandy (I, 105).

The intention of this style is to present objective arguments, with an emphasis on mechanical and causal relationships and close analysis, rather than subjective states of mind. Let us look at the opening paragraph of the *Fable*:

Laws and Government are to the Political Bodies of Civil Societies, what the Vital Spirits and Life it self are to the Natural Bodies of Animated Creatures; and as those that study the Anatomy of Dead Carcases may see, that the chief Organs and nicest Springs more immediately required to continue the Motion of our Machine, are not hard Bones, strong Muscles and Nerves, nor the smooth white Skin that so beautifully covers them, but small trifling Films and little Pipes that are either over-look'd, or else seem inconsiderable to Vulgar Eyes; so they that examine into the Nature of Man, abstract from Art and Education, may observe, that what renders him a Sociable Animal, consists not in his desire of Company, Good-nature, Pity, Affability, and other Graces of a fair Outside; but that his vilest and most hateful Qualities are the most necessary Accomplishments to fit him for the largest, and, according to the World, the happiest and most flourishing Societies (I, 3-4).

The paragraph seems "correct" and "polite" enough. The antithetical ratios and "unfoldings" of metaphor are carefully spelled out: "Laws and Government" are to "Political Bodies" as "Vital Spirits and Life"

are to "Natural Bodies;" then "the chief Organs and nicest Springs . . .
of our Machine" (the man-as-machine comparison is here made explicit)
are to "small trifling Films and little Pipes" as "Good-nature, Pity, Affability, and other Graces of a fair Outside" are to "most hateful Qualities."
There are other ratios, e. g., "Those that study the Anatomy of Dead
Carkasses" are to "Vulgar Eyes" as "they that examine into the Nature
of Man" are to the "Vulgar Eyes" of Mandeville's opponents, who do
not see Man as he really is. "Man" is defined technically, as a "Sociable
Animal," to be understood as a constellation of Qualities or (superficially, because too dependent on simple observation rather than by
analysis of the underlying clear and distinct Abstractions) the "Graces of
a fair Outside." These Qualities are to be seen only in terms of causal
relationships observable only to the trained eye of the scientist accustomed
to dealing with the world as extended body in motion. Just as the motion
of the human Machine is caused by trifling Films and little Pipes, so
our physical exterior is really accounted for by invisible abstractions within, the psychological equivalents of the Primary Qualities of Galileo and
Locke. It is worthwhile noting here the appeal to objective, minute
scientific analysis in a word like "Anatomy" and the Films and Pipes
that are overlooked by non-scientists. The ultimate appeal, however, as
Professor Kaye rightly argues, is to Utility, to "necessary accomplishments to fit [Man] for the largest, and, according to the World, the
happiest and most flourishing Societies."

The paragraph is the stylistic outcome of what Whitehead, defining
and stigmatizing the prevalent seventeenth- and eighteenth-century meta-
physic, called the Fallacy of Misplaced Concreteness. It illustrates many
of the techniques and presuppositions underlying "correct" and "polite"
prose. Yet it has another dimension, for there is the tart Mandevillean
thrust, brought in with characteristic casualness: "and according to the
World." Potentially there is a profound despair about the whole human
condition – "the World" – locked up in that aside, undercutting all the
confident, one-dimensional decorum we have so far encountered; but
Mandeville will not take the plunge into the void. Does Mandeville himself agree with the World and its idea of happiness, its utilitarian ethos?
Is his target the corrupt values of the World, or the World's hypocritical
refusal to recognize its own essential vices? Around such questions swirls
the modern discussion of his thought. The difficulties come from his
refusal to answer them explicitly. Instead he leaves us with his paradoxical satire. It is difficult to summarize Mandeville because, as Professor Colie explains, "A paradox cannot be paraphrased. If it can, it is

flat and dull; if it is flat and dull, it is not a paradox." [3] Especially in the first volume of the *Fable* the style is not only "correct" but also "pierces and strikes."

Mandeville's pessimism with regard to human nature could not become a tragic view of life because he was a thoroughgoing antiheroic utilitarian. Satire was therefore the logical mode of expression for him for, while allowing for pessimism, satire banishes both tragic heroism and despair by creating a detached *persona* or speaker who is outside the contradictions and struggles he sees everywhere. The point of view of this satiric speaker may be what Northrop Frye calls "low normal," as in *Catch-22* or *The Adventures of Huckleberry Finn*, which "takes for granted a world which is full of anomalies, injustices, follies, and crimes, and yet is permanent and indisplaceable. Its principle is that anyone who wishes to keep his balance in such a world must learn first of all to keep his eyes open and his mouth shut." [4] In "high normal" satire the speaker looks down on a world which he regards as a grotesque, absurd nightmare, as in Juvenal, the Elizabethan *flyting*, and *Gulliver's Travels*. In between is the category to which, it seems to me, Mandeville belongs, in which the speakers have a "sense of the value of conventions that had been long established and were now harmless" and a "distrust of the ability of anyone's reason, including their own, to transform society into a better structure. But they [are] also intellectually detached from the conventions they [live] with, and are capable of seeing their anomalies and absurdities as well as their stabilizing conservatism." Their ethic is utilitarian, "a tactical defence of the pragmatic against the dogmatic." [5]

The speaker of the *Fable* – who apparently is not to be distinguished from Mandeville himself – is indeed pragmatic. He is neither the naive *ingenu*, tongue-in-cheek bumpkin, or picaresque rogue characteristic of low-normal satire, in which vice is evaded, nor the bitter idealist of high-normal satire, in which vice is attacked. The chief object of Mandeville's satire in fact is not human vice at all, but the refusal to recognize the useful principle that private vices lead to public benefits. Most satirists are appalled that human existence falls so far short of what it could be. John Bullitt begins his study of Swift with the observation that, "In its most serious function, satire is a mediator between two perceptions – the unillusioned perception of man as he actually is, and the ideal perception,

---

[3] Rosalie Colie, *Paradoxia Epidemica* (Princeton, 1966), p. 35.
[4] Northrop Frye, *Anatomy of Criticism* (Princeton, 1957), p. 226.
[5] *Ibid.*, p. 232, 234.

or vision, of man as he ought to be." [6] But Mandeville's satire works the
other way around: it is the idealism, not man as he actually is, that is his
target, not because the ideals are wrong in themselves, but because they
are used hypocritically, and are ruinous to the economy. In the end, to
be sure, it could be said that Mandeville, like most other satirists, is
attacking vice, the vice of hypocrisy; but for him this vice consists of not
recognizing the usefulness of vice! That is a paradox, and paradox –
the seeming contradiction that hides a truth – is his principal stylistic
device to express his vision of a world in which private morality and
public benefits must be in eternal opposition. Anyone who thinks otherwise is, in Swift's famous definition of happiness, in *"a perpetual Possession of being Well Deceived. . . . The Serene Peaceful State of being a
Fool Among Knaves."*

Paradox is quite unlike irony. The ironist means the opposite of what
he says; the paradoxical writer means precisely what he does say.
Throughout the *Fable* Mandeville defends his use of paradoxes, insisting
that they be taken seriously, despite their traditional light-heartedness.
As satirists go he is not very ironic. To be sure he does have many of the
attitudes of the Socratic *eiron* common in satire: a detachment that sees
the world not as tragic or comic but as contemptible or at best amusing,
populated chiefly by strutting *alazons* or blind mechanical robots regu-
lated by custom in a universe which, unknown to them, is utterly indifferent; a determination to *nil admirari*, with the concomitant refusal to
propose new solutions; and the poise of the foxy outsider who can laugh
from a private corner. But he is not at bottom ironic. There is no *persona*
developed at great length standing for the opposite of the author, no
modest proposer, Chaucerian *naif*, or mocking Hardyan President of the
Immortals. He makes little use of the ironical devices traditionally at the
disposal of the satirist: burlesque, parody, lampoon, exaggeration, understatement, allegory, insult, or the mock-heroic. When he does use them –
as in the comparison of the Body Politick to a bowl of punch or the
contemplation of the tortures awaiting him at the hands of his critics if
charity-schools are abolished – it is always with an apology, in contrast
to his defense of the paradox. He should be regarded as a kind of compulsive debunker of received opinion rather than as a satirist in the great
tradition. Paradox has always been the resort of such debunkers, the
defenders of the indefensible "private vices." Mandeville has the sociologist's instinct to reveal "what really goes on" under the surface rather

---

[6] John Bullitt, *Jonathan Swift and the Anatomy of Satire* (Cambridge, Mass.,
1961), p. 1.

than the outrage emanating from a moral center which characterizes most satire. At times he refused to see himself as a satirist. What he says about his verses could also apply to the succeeding "Remarks" which form the bulk of the *Fable*: "I am in reality puzzled what Name to give them; for they are neither Heroick nor Pastoral, Satyr, Burlesque nor Heroi-comick; to be a Tale they want Probability, and the whole is rather too long for a Fable" (I, 5).

Irony is always indirect. For the most part Mandeville, though too much the Augustan to resort to simple invective, presents himself in the *Fable* as the opposite of indirect, as the blunt, no-nonsense, clear-sighted middle-normal satirist. Where ironists delight in first "caressing the object they wish to demolish," [7] his procedure is usually the opposite. He de-molishes the object first, then turns around in a witty paradox to undo his own negation, leaving the reader with an unresolved tension, for "paradoxes are profoundly ... self-critical ... they comment on their own method" (Colie, *Paradoxia*, p. 7). "What the Establishment have traditionally applauded is really done from vicious motives – but the vice is essential." The essence of such paradoxes is surprise, the sudden burst of unexpected honesty, and the most forceful way to express such surprise is the aphorism. Therefore the stunning paradox may occur as a sardonic aside but more often as an aphorism occurring, in his best paragraphs, at a rhetorical climax created, in turn, by a massive list or catalogue. The paradox, the surprise, the aphorism, and the list are the rhetorical underpinnings of Mandeville's satire. For example:

Those that ever took Delight in Plays and Romances, and have a spice of Gentility, will, in all probability, throw their Eyes upon the *Stage,* and if they have a good Elocution with tolerable Mien, turn *Actors.* Some that love their Bellies above any thing else, if they have a good Palate, and a little Knack at Cookery, will strive to get in with *Gluttons* and *Epicures,* learn to cringe and bear all manner of Usage, and so turn *Parasites,* ever flattering their Master, and making Mischief among the rest of the *Family.* Others, who by their own Companions Lewdness judge of People's Inconti-nence, will naturally fall to Intriguing, and endeavour to live by Pimping for such as either want Leisure or Address to speak for themselves. ...

These are certainly the Bane of Civil Society; but they are Fools, who not considering what has been said, storm at the Remisness of the Laws that suffer them to live, while wise Men content themselves with taking all imaginable Care not to be circumvented by them, without quarrelling at what no human Prudence can Prevent (I, 60-61).

Here the Latinate "Some ... Other ... Those ... Others" characteristic of the prose of utility, creates a feeling of firm clarity, preparing the

[7] David Worcester, *The Art of Satire* (New York, 1960), p. 135.

reader for the combined summary and paradox of the second paragraph. Again:

No States or Kingdoms under Heaven have yielded more or greater Patterns in all sorts of Moral Virtues than the *Greek* and *Roman* Empires, more especially the latter; and yet how loose, absurd and ridiculous were their Sentiments as to Sacred Matters? For without reflecting on the extravagant Number of their Deities, if we only consider the infamous Stories they father'd upon them, it is not to be denied but that their Religion, far from teaching Men the Conquest of their Passions, and the Way to Virtue, seem'd rather contriv'd to justify their Appetites, and encourage their Vices. But if we would know what made 'em excel in Fortitude, Courage and Magnanimity, we must cast our Eyes on the Pomp of their Triumphs, the Magnificence of their Monuments and Arches; their Trophies, Statues, and Inscriptions; the variety of their Military Crowns, their Honours decreed to the Dead, Publick Encomiums on the Living, and other imaginary Rewards they bestow'd on Men of Merit; and we shall find, that what carried so many of them to the utmost Pitch of Self-Denial, was nothing but their Policy in making use of the most effectual Means that human Pride could be flatter'd with (I, 50-51).

Here the paradox – with its blunt, debunking "put-down" – concerns the real motivations underlying the supposed "Fortitude, Courage, and Magnanimity" and the pompous monuments which commemorate these virtues. Mandeville's heavy triplets ("Fortitude, Courage, and Magnanimity," "the Pomp ... the Magnificence ... their Trophies, Statues, and Inscriptions," "their Military Crowns, their Honours ... other imaginary Rewards") are the rhetorical equivalents of the very vanity in question. They set up the fine rhetorical swelling culminating at "utmost Pitch of Self-denial," which Mandeville immediately punctures with the sudden honesty at the end.

In place of a single tight aphorism, but having much the same force, many of the best paragraphs (or large rhetorical units in general) end with a flat assertion of blunt honesty. Sometimes a cluster of paradoxical aphorisms will themselves comprise a list, with the unresolved tension tacked on at the end. At such times Mandeville reads like Wilde or Shaw:

The only thing of weight that can be said against modern Honour is, that it is directly opposite to Religion. The one bids you bear Injuries with Patience, the other tells you if you don't resent them, you are not fit to live. Religion commands you to leave all Revenge to God, Honour bids you trust your Revenge to no body but your self, even where the Law would do it for you: Religion plainly forbids Murther, Honour openly justifies it: Religion bids you not shed Blood upon any Account whatever: Honour bids you fight for the least Trifle: Religion is built on Humility, and Honour upon Pride: How to reconcile them must be left to wiser Heads than mine (I, 221-222).

Of course, Mandeville is not always so elegant. As in much of the best satire, his diction combines the scholarly formal – as if mocking the pretentious *alazons* of this world – and the "low," pungent colloquial of the debunking *eiron*. The "low" side of Mandeville's style shows him bursting through the unresolved tensions and paradoxes of his thought by an appeal to realism, honesty, and utility.

The Multitude will hardly believe the excessive Force of Education, and in the difference of Modesty between Men and Women ascribe that to Nature, which is altogether owing to early Instruction: *Miss* is scarce three Years old, but she is spoke to every Day to hide her Leg, and rebuk'd in good Earnest if she shews it; while *Little Master* at the same age is bid to take up his Coats, and piss like a Man (I, 71-72).

Nothing is more destructive, either in regard to the Health or the Vigilance and Industry of the poor than the infamous Liquor, the name of which, deriv'd from Juniper in *Dutch,* is now by frequent use and the Laconick Spirit of the Nation, from a Word of middling Length shrunk into a Monosyllable, Intoxicating Gin, that charms the unactive, the desperate and crazy of either Sex, and makes the starving Sot behold his Rags and Nakedness with stupid Indolence, or banter both in senseless Laughter, and more insipid Jests: It is a fiery Lake that sets the Brain in Flame, burns up the Entrails, and scorches every part within; and at the same time a *Lethe* of Oblivion, in which the Wretch immers'd drowns his most pinching Cares, and with his Reason all anxious Reflection on Brats that cry for Food, hard Winters Frosts, and horrid empty Home. (I, 89)

How can I believe that a Man's chief Delight is in the Embellishments of the Mind, when I see him ever employ'd about and daily pursue the Pleasures that are contrary to them? *John* never cuts any Pudding, but just enough that you can't say he took none; this little Bit, after much chomping and chewing you see goes down with him like chopp'd Hay; after that he falls upon the Beef with a voracious Appetite, and crams himself up to his Throat. Is it not provoking to hear *John* cry every Day that Pudding is all his Delight, and that he don't value the Beef of a Farthing? (I, 151-152)

"Low" writing, when extended, produces jaunty passages in which academic pretentiousness is undercut:

I could swagger about Fortitude and the Contempt of Riches as much as *Seneca* himself, and would undertake to write twice as much in behalf of Poverty as ever he did, for the tenth Part of his Estate: I could teach the way to his *Summum bonum* as exactly as I know my way home: I could tell People that to extricate themselves from all worldly Engagements, and to purify the Mind, they must divest themselves of their Passions, as Men take out the Furniture when they would clean a Room thoroughly; and I am clearly of the Opinion, that the Malice and most severe Strokes of Fortune can do no more Injury to a Mind thus stript of all Fears, Wishes and

Inclinations, than a blind Horse can do in an empty Barn. In the Theory
of all this I am very perfect, but the Practice is very difficult; and if you
went about picking my Pocket, offer'd to take the Victuals from before me
when I am hungry, or made but the least Motion of spitting in my Face, I
dare not promise how Philosophically I should behave my self. (I, 152)

Here is Bernard Mandeville in the classic middle-normal debunker's pose,
man-to-man, ready to defeat all comers, including the reader, as easily
as he disposes of the hypocritical Seneca with one quick left jab ("for
the tenth part of his Estate").

As we would expect in so down-to-earth a writer Mandeville's examples often expand into anecdotes or sharply dramatized sketches. These
can take on a marvelous life of their own, but the satiric aim is always
held in view. The best of them display human happiness as the "perpetual possession of being well deceived." Usually there is a mutual gulling,
for all men, it seems, are both Fools and Knaves, as with jealous Molly
and her baby sister in the *Enquiry into the Origin of Moral Virtue*; the
merchants Decio and Alexander in Remark B; the con-artists associated
with the gin-trade in the great Hogarthian digression on it in Remark G;
the virtuous women, whores, magistrates, and general public in Remark
H; the ascetic parson, his adoring flock, and his starving family in
Remark O; the inhabitants of the kingdom in which quenching thirst
is regarded as a "Damnable Sin" in Remark T; the seemingly lazy porter
and his master in Remark V; the do-gooders and their hangers-on in the
Essay on Charity-Schools; and the obsequious tailor and his rich female
customer in *A Search Into the Nature of Society*. Such anecdotes and
sketches are often in the form of dramatic dialogues in the manner of
Horace or Juvenal in which hypothetical speakers pop up from nowhere
to accost Mandeville or one another. When Mandeville himself bursts
onto the scene it is never for very long, and almost never as an ironic
persona representing the opposite of himself. He always appears as the
man of blunt horse sense.

At other times he resorts to more static forms, such as the Montaignes-
que piece on the superiority of animals in Remark P or familiar essays
on abstractions like Shame or Envy or "characters" in the style of Addison
and Steele. These characters work much like the best of his lists, for even
in these less dramatic forms there is the same juicy vigor. Perhaps the
greatest of them is the Veblen-like portrait of the Rich Man in Remark O.

On the larger scale satire, especially the disorderly, rambling "Menippean" variety,[8] traditionally pierces or strikes by discarding regular struc-

---

[8] See George Hind, "Mandeville's *Fable of the Bees* as Menippean Satire," *Genre*,
1 (1968), 307-315.

ture in favor of informality. Mandeville follows this tradition by writing what is essentially a series of glorified footnotes or "remarks" appended, as if in an afterthought, to a verse fable, itself a "little Whim" and a "few loose Lines with the Name of Poem" (I, 9, 5). As we have already seen, he professes not to know or even to care to what genre his collection of anecdotes, moral essays, characters, and tracts in economics belongs. The *Fable* is informal in another sense of that word in that in it we meet the author with his shirt-sleeves rolled up, apparently thinking off the top of his head (when he feels like it he digresses to ride such hobby-horses as vegetarianism and his admiration for the Dutch) as example is spun out into anecdote and brief note becomes essay. The range of topics is immense, for the subject of satire is *quicquid agunt homines.*

The energy, variety, and informality to be found in the *Fable* has been associated with satire – and related forms including the epigram, epistle, and essay – ever since its ultimate origins in the dialogues of the first true *eiron*, Socrates. The aim of such a mode is urbane self-revelation. As Morris Croll described it:

Its function is to express the individual variances of experience in contrast with the general and communal ideas which the open design of the oratorical style is so well adapted to contain. Its idiom is that of conversation or adapted from it, in order that it may flow into and fill up all the nooks and crannies of reality and reproduce its exact image to attentive observation.[9]

Mandeville's satiric style is united with the methodical, "correct," more public style in which he also wrote. Satire, it has been said many times, flourishes in periods like Mandeville's when social, moral, and stylistic norms are very strongly felt among the literate. If your intention is to pierce or strike, it is convenient to have a univerally accepted standard to attack or to attack *from*. Mandeville had it both ways. He created satire by writing within the Augustan canons of uniformity, objectivity, precision, and clarity to which he fully subscribed yet introducing against this background of smooth judiciousness a trenchant awareness of both the perplexities and hard realities of an existence too rich and paradoxical to be explained in a few easy formulas.

---

[9] Morris Croll, *Style, Rhetoric, and Rhythm: Essays by Morris W. Croll,* eds. J. Max Patrick, Robert O. Evans, John M. Wallace, and R. J. Shoeck (Princeton, 1966), p. 61.

THE CANT OF SOCIAL COMPROMISE: SOME OBSERVATIONS ON MANDEVILLE'S SATIRE

ROBERT H. HOPKINS

Let any Man observe the Equipages in this Town; he shall find the greater Number of those who make a Figure, to be a Species of Men quite different from any that were ever known before the Revolution; consisting either of Generals and Colonels, or of such whose whole Fortunes lie in Funds and Stocks: So that *Power*, which, according to the old Maxim, was used to follow *Land*, is now gone over to *Money*. . . .

Jonathan Swift, *The Examiner,* No. 13 (Nov. 2, 1710)

It is my belief that we must ultimately read Mandeville as a comic satirist and that we shall never fully understand him through an ossified history-of-ideas approach which in cataloging likenesses loses Mandeville's devastating sardonic tone. The current trend of dealing with Mandeville as first and last a satirist should do much to restore to him his historical identity; for if, as Edward Rosenheim insists, satire attacks "discernible, historically authentic particulars" and if the critic has an obligation to identify these particulars we shall be forced to relate Mandeville's satire to its historical context.[1] If we can show, furthermore, how *The Fable of the Bees* and *An Enquiry into the Origin of Honour* satirize certain ambiguities in Mandeville's world that have not diminished in time and that are still very much a part of our contemporary experience, these works may still be found to be very pertinent indeed. In this essay I shall focus on what one recent critic has aptly termed the "sense of the pressure of the social scene" and try to show through the study of several words and phrases occurring in Mandeville's works how this "pressure

---

[1] *Swift and the Satirist's Art* (Chicago: Univ. of Chicago Press, 1963), p. 25. See Phillip Harth, "The Satiric Purpose of *The Fable of the Bees*," *ECS,* 2 (1968-69), 321-40; and "Introduction," *The Fable of the Bees,* ed. Harth (Harmondsworth, Middlesex, England: Penguin Books Ltd.), pp. 7-46. All references to *The Fable of the Bees* in this essay will be by volume and page number in the text to *The Fable of the Bees,* ed. F. B. Kaye (Oxford: Clarendon Press, 1924).

of the social scene" results in some of Mandeville's most effective satire.[2]

Only in the last several years has a critic suggested a really plausible motive for Mandeville's writing the initial verse pamphlet that led to *The Fable – The Grumbling Hive: or, Knaves Turn'd Honest* (1705). Isaac Kramnick drew attention to a number of verse pamphlets written in the 1690's-1700's attacking the corruption of English society by money and identified *The Grumbling Hive* as Mandeville's answer to this verse convention in defense of what historians now call The Financial Revolution.[3] This Financial Revolution is established by the development of long-term public borrowing, the creation of "a whole range of securities in which mercantile and financial houses could safely invest, and from which they could easily disinvest (unlike land mortgages)," and a transition from a primarily agrarian economy to a mercantile economy centered in London around urban monied interests. If Kramnick's conjecture is valid, Mandeville's initial effort in the writing of *The Fable* would seem to place him on the side of the moneyed interest as opposed to the landed interest although in a very little time the landed interest itself came to be what Raymond Williams has termed England's "first really ruthless capitalist class." [4] Mandeville felt compelled later to expound on his verses through essays and prose remarks in the 1714 first edition of *The Fable*, and then again in the 1723 edition. It was the "Essay on Charity, and Charity-Schools" added to this later edition, however, which finally exploded the time-bomb and made *The Fable* one of the most vexing works in all of eighteenth-century English literature.

It is my belief that all of the radical elements which were present in the 1714 edition were not really noticed by Mandeville's contemporaries until history itself caught up with the work. Urban capitalism with all of its ambiguities was becoming the dominating mode of life, but its implications had yet to penetrate fully into the consciousness of Mandeville's contemporaries. The sin of Mandeville's wit was that he had stated more explicitly than any other writer yet had the unstated assumptions and hypocrisies of a social compromise which his society had tacitly agreed upon in order to live with the Financial Revolution.[5] Mandeville had

[2] Elias J. Chiasson, "Bernard Mandeville: A Reapprasal," *PQ*, 49 (1970), 504.
[3] *Bolingbroke and His Circle: The Politics of Nostalgia* (Cambridge: Harvard Univ. Press, 1968), p. 201, p. 303, fn. 40. The phrase is that of P. G. M. Dickson, *The Financial Revolution in England: A Study in the Development of Public Finance* (London: Macmillan, 1967).
[4] "Ideas of Nature," *TLS*, Dec. 4, 1970, p. 1421.
[5] Long ago F. W. Bateson interpreted Swift's "Description of the Morning" as an implicit satire on "the *laissez-faire* individualism of urban capitalism" implying the Christian point "that we are members of one another." See *English Poetry: An Introduction* (London, 1950), p. 177. I hope to show that the phrase "possessive individual-

had the unmitigated nerve to depict these hypocrisies under the guise of traditional satire by relying on a norm of Christian rigorism which at times appears itself a target of satire. Whereas Swift clearly seemed to be writing his satire from a base of Christian value, Mandeville seemed to be using the guise of Christian value to expose the impossibility of a compromise between his affluent society and that value, only then to cast his lot with that society in all of its negative as well as positive aspects. Mandeville's contemporaries responded to his satire not by examining Leviathan's goals and priorities but by making Mandeville himself the scapegoat. (It is the classic reaction in all societies to the world's great satirists.) The amazing over-response (overkill?) to the 1723 *Fable* by John Dennis, Richard Fiddes, William Law, George Bluet, Francis Hutcheson, and later in 1732 by George Berkeley, had the curious result of broadcasting Mandeville's satire to a much wider reading audience until it was not necessary to have read *The Fable* in order to know its central themes. This unintentional broadcasting of *The Fable* by its enemies so as to make it a central presence in the literary consciousness of the middle decades of the eighteenth century has not been stressed enough. We may also use these attacks on *The Fable* as a valuable index to those aspects of Mandeville's satire which seemed to vex most his contemporaries.

The "State of Nature" and The "Nature of Society"

One of the most vexing phrases in *The Fable* was the "State of Nature." It is first encountered in the "Introduction" to "An Enquiry into the Origin of Moral Virtue." After complaining that "most Writers are al-

ism" is both more appropriate and historically accurate than Bateson's phrase. The urban nature of this capitalism has been ably discussed by John Loftis, *Comedy and Society from Congreve to Fielding* (Stanford: Stanford Univ. Press, 1959), pp. 1-19. Swift's poem appeared in *The Tatler,* a periodical slanted towards the middle and upper classes most involved in the development of urban capitalism. As is well known, *The Spectator* attempted to effect a social compromise by improving the morals of the aristocracy and the gentry while refining the manners of a growing middle class. In its level of style, its didacticism of purpose, and its eschewal of potentially risqué or coarse subject matter and language, *The Spectator* tends in retrospect to be genteel. That is to say, it self-consciously simplifies the complexity of eigtheenth-century experience by means of a class-consciousness so that its imagination is limited by that consciousness. Addison and Steele tended to romanticize the monied interest and to emphasize only the affirmative aspects of the Financial Revolution. Mandeville satirizes this genteel consciousness by a deliberately coarse style and by stressing the negative aspects of the Financial Revolution. F. B. Kaye was struck by the literary resemblances between *The Spectator*, No. 69 and a passage in Mandeville's *The Fable of the Bees* but then noted that Addison, unlike Mandeville, had "made little attempt to deduce economic principles" (I, 357, n. 1). I believe that Mandeville's satire is directed towards the negative aspects of this social compromise including both its political and economic implications insofar as it is based upon an optimistic view of human nature.

ways teaching Men what they should be, and hardly ever trouble their heads with telling them what they really are" (I, 39), Mandeville proceeds to state that men are governed primarily by their passions and that this truth is intrinsic to "a flourishing Society." Mandeville intends to discover how Man might "yet by his own Imperfections be taught to distinguish between Virtue and Vice": *"And here I must desire the Reader once for all to take notice, that when I say Men, I mean neither* Jews *nor* Christians; *but meer Man, in the State of Nature and Ignorance of the true Deity"* (I, 40).

"An Enquiry" proper begins with the thesis that "all untaught Animals" are motivated only by self-interest, that in "the wild State of Nature" only animals with the "least of Understanding" and the "fewest Appetites to gratify" are "fittest to live peaceably together in great Numbers" (I, 41). In this same "State" Man is the "Species of Animals" least capable of "agreeing long together in Multitudes" without "the Curb of Government." The social evolution of Man is accomplished by "Law-Givers and other Wise Men" who by the "artful Way of Flattery" insinuate "themselves into the Hearts of Men" and begin to "instruct them in the Notions of Honour and Shame." These leaders divide "the whole Species in two Classes," one consisting of "abject, low-minded People," always "hunting after immediate Enjoyment," and the other consisting of "lofty high-spirited Creatures," free from "sordid Selfishness," who esteem "the Improvements of the Mind to be their fairest Possessions" (I, 44). (Mandeville mimics here the patronizing snobbery of the upper classes.) These "first Rudiments of Morality, broach'd by skilful Politicians, to render Men useful to each other as well as tractable," were "contriv'd" so that "the Ambitious might reap the more Benefit from, and govern vast Numbers of them with the greater Ease and Security" (I, 47). It turns out, then, that the "lofty, high-spirited Creatures," "free from sordid Selfishness," have much to gain from the exploitation of the lower class and that "the very worst" of the ruling class "preach up Publick-spiritedness, that they might reap the Fruits of the Labour and Self-denial of others" (I, 48). Rather than defining virtue and vice in terms of an absolute morality based on Christian revelation, Mandeville proceeds to redefine these terms instrumentally according to what is beneficial or injurious to society. Immediately after this utilitarian redefining, Mandeville returns to "Man in his State of Nature":

It shall be objected, that no Society was ever any ways civiliz'd before the major part had agreed upon some Worship or other of an over-ruling Power, and consequently that the Notions of Good and Evil, and the Distinction between *Virtue* and *Vice,* were never the Contrivance of Politicians, but the pure Effect of Religion. Before I answer this Objection, I must repeat what I have said already, that in this *Enquiry into the Origin of Moral Virtue,* I speak neither of *Jews* or *Christians,* but Man in his State of Nature and Ignorance of the true Deity. . . . (I, 49-50)

Since the "Idolatrous Superstitions of all other Nations" were "incapable of exciting Man to Virtue," Mandeville argues that it is "the skilful Management of wary Politicians" that "first put Man upon crossing his Appetites and subduing his dearest Inclinations": "Moral Virtues are the Political Offspring which Flattery begot upon Pride" (I, 51).

But politics is supposed to be a branch of ethics, not vice versa! Mandeville's satirical reversal which reflects the image of a society in which political activities are to be judged by the instrumental needs of society rather than by traditional ethical standards is prepared for by his loaded phrase, "State of Nature," which, I believe, is intentionally derived from Hobbes's famous chapter in *Leviathan,* "Of the Natural Condition of Mankind . . ." (Pt. I, ch. 13). What Mandeville is suggesting is that the dominating ethic of his competitive society is the Hobbist ethic of the marketplace rather than the Christian ethic of the cathedral.

To appreciate fully the significance of this point, C. B. Macpherson's treatment of Hobbes in his *The Political Theory of Possessive Individualism: Hobbes to Locke* (London, Oxford University Press, 1962) becomes of paramount importance. Macpherson believes that the theoretical foundations for the liberal-democratic state stem from seventeenth-century individualism and the political theories of Hobbes and Locke among others which provided the philosophical underpinning for this individualism. The "possessive" quality of this individualism developed from a concept of the individual as essentially a proprietor of his own person or capacities, owing nothing to society for them. The individual is no longer seen as part of a larger social whole, or as an intrinsically moral entity, but as an owner of himself. Society comes to consist of a series of relations of exchanges between proprietors, and political society becomes a calculated device for the protection of the property of proprietors and for the maintenance of an orderly relation of exchange. Macpherson believes that in the past Hobbes's political theory has been studied too narrowly in an analytical philosophical tradition which ignores both Hobbes's historical and cultural context and the unstated assumptions operative in his theory which are provided by a historical frame of reference. In a section entitled "Human Nature and the State of Nature," Macpherson argues persuasively for an interpretation of Hobbes's "Natural Condition of Man" not as literally to be referred to as early primitive man, but as a logical hypothesis about "men whose desires are specifically civilized ... the hypothetical condition in which men as they now are, with natures formed by living in civilized society would necessarily find themselves if there were no common power able to overawe them" (pp. 18-19): "Natural man is civilized man with only the restraint of law removed" (p. 29). What Hobbes has done, according to Macpherson, is to construct a political theory on the model of a "possessive-market society," a society in which the market itself provides the real basis for morality in contrast to traditional society with its basis for morality stemming from Christian revelation and natural law. Men in Hobbes's possessive-market society find themselves "subject to the determination of the market" and this determinism explains "the somewhat inhuman flavour of Hobbes's political obligation" (p. 106). Hobbes's great achievement was to penetrate into "the heart of the problem of obligation in modern progressive societies," even though, as Macpherson wryly notes, "the English possessing class ... did not need Hobbes's full prescription" and had "some reason to be displeased with his portrait of themselves." "Before the end of the century the men of property had come to terms with the more ambiguous, and more agreeable, doctrine of Locke" (p. 106). Though Macpherson's overall treatment of Hobbes appears to be too reductive in order to support a Marxist interpretation, I would plead that his analysis of the ironies of Hobbes's "State of Nature" is sound because he has hit upon the uses of this loaded term for a literary strategy. If political scientists tend to seek only univocal meanings in Hobbes as political scientist, we as literary critics may relish the deliberate plurisignificant meanings in Hobbes as Restoration satirist.[6]

What I am suggesting is that in the 1714 editions of *The Fable* Mandeville was using "State of Nature" in the Hobbist sense. Mandeville's myth or fiction describing how clever politicians govern society by a "Flattery begot upon Pride" reflects the actual expedient ethic of an age governed increasingly by possessive individualism, one which truly needs the "Curb of Government" if men are to restrain themselves. Insofar as the actual

[6] I believe that Mandeville's "State of Nature" is a deliberately loaded phrase used for satirical effects, that Macpherson is the first to show an almost identical usage in Hobbes's use of the term, and that Macpherson's critics have tended to react to Macpherson's interpretation too narrowly in their interpretation of this term. If we admit that Hobbes was satirizing a growing possessive individualism in his society without necessarily providing a justification for it, as Macpherson seems to insist, Macpherson's interpretation of "State of Nature" is still valid. For examples of the spectrum of critical opinion about Macpherson's book see Christopher Hill's review, *Past & Present*, No. 24 (1963), 86-9, and Sir Isaiah Berlin's critique, *Political Quarterly*, 35 (1964), 444-68.

ethic of most men is not a Christian one, but one governed by the market in a mercantile economy, virtue really is "the Political Offspring which Flattery begot upon Pride." Mandeville's genealogy-of-morals parable reflects satirically on his own society. Too many critics have unfortunately read this fiction in a literal sense, partly because Mandeville's contemporary critics deliberately chose to rebut his work by reading it literally rather than as deliberate irony (with the important exception of John Dennis). Quoting Mandeville's insistence that he meant "neither Jews nor Christians, but meer Men in the State of Nature, and Ignorance of the true Deity," Dennis shrewdly observed that it took "very little Discernment" to see "that when he [Mandeville] says Men, he means *Englishmen*, whether they are Christians, or Deists, or Atheists." [7]

Later in "Remark (O)" (1714) Mandeville fuses deliberately "State of Nature" in its Hobbist sense with a theological sense to taunt his readers who are, of course, all in a state of grace: "Thus I have prov'd, that the Real Pleasures of all Men in Nature are worldly and sensual, if we judge from their Practice; I say all Men *in Nature*, because Devout Christians, who alone are to be excepted here, being regenerated, and preternaturally assisted by the Divine Grace, cannot be said to be in Nature. How strange it is, that they should all so unanimously deny it!" (I, 166). The double meaning here is particularly effective in carrying the satiric thrust of the passage. Christian readers living in a state of grace need not fear Mandeville's thesis, but since society assumes that most men are really living their everyday lives as if they were in a fallen "State of Nature" Christians will not find themselves easily able to live in society and still maintain their integrity. By equating the Hobbist "natural condition of man" which reflects a possessive-individualistic market society with the Augustinian view of fallen, unregenerated man in "Remark (O)," Mandeville articulates a highly vexing paradox.

Mandeville's mythical "State of Nature" represents an image of early eighteenth-century London society as it really was. If the Hobbist naturalistic ethic was unacceptable to most Englishmen, John Locke's political theory provided the foundation for a more amiable compromise between the ethic of the marketplace and the traditional ethic of moral authority. Macpherson is again invaluable in his analysis of Locke's compromise. In his rejection of political theories based on paternalism, Locke devised

[7] *Vice and Luxury Publick Mischiefs*: or, *Remarks on a Book intituled, the Fable of the Bees* (London, 1724), p. 30. Dennis interprets Mandeville's usage much as Macpherson has interpreted Hobbes's usage as a logical rather than historical condition. As literary critics, we may see *both* meanings as simultaneously present in Hobbes's and Mandeville's "State of Nature."

a theory of natural right by which men were originally created equal by God and then lost this equality in history. To support this myth of natural right and equality, Locke's "State of Nature" assumes in one sense that "the natural condition of man is eminently rational and peaceable" (Macpherson, p. 245). Locke's optimistic fiction enables him to "base property right on natural right and natural law, and then to remove all the natural law limits from the property right" (Ibid., p. 199). Thereby Locke is able to put men "on their own, and leave them to confront each other in the market without the protections which the old natural law doctrine upheld" (*Ibid.*, p. 245). Macpherson's deduction from this analysis is that Locke conceived "man in general in the image of rational bourgeois man, able to look after himself and morally entitled to do so" (p. 245).

Once Locke had worked out a fiction which would free society from traditional restrictions, he then had to work out an explanation for man's observable inequality. As Macpherson shows, Locke equated this inequality with the difference in men's reasoning powers, and this difference was "not inherent in men, not implanted in them by God or Nature," but rather "socially acquired by virtue of different economic positions" (p. 246). Since men are through this process unequal and possess varying degrees of rationality, a civil society with legal sanctions and a church with spiritual sanctions are necessary to maintain an orderly society. Locke's utilitarian argument for this kind of social order is really focused on what Mandeville terms the "Nature of Society." Macpherson is invaluable in showing how Locke arrives at an ambiguous compromise to accommodate a society based on possessive individualism while defending traditional political institutions. Locke will have it both ways. Unlike Hobbes, according to Macpherson, Locke "refused to reduce all social relations to market relations and all morality to market morality" or to "entirely let go of traditional natural law" (p. 269). On the other hand if Locke "did not read market relations back into the very nature of man, as Hobbes had done," he did read into the nature of society a Hobbist ethic "in the image of market man" (pp. 268-69). This ambiguity in Locke's political theory is the result of a kind of compromise, then, between the necessity for an ethic of economic and political expedience and the necessity for retaining traditional moral sanctions.[8]

---

[8] See John Locke, *Two Treatises of Government,* ed. Peter Laslett, 2nd ed. (Cambridge: Cambridge Univ. Press, 1967), Bk. II, ch. ii, "Of the State of Nature," pp. 287-96. For an essay which seems to me to be directed against Macpherson's interpretation of Locke although Macpherson is never mentioned, see Hans Aarsleff, "The State of Nature and the Nature of Man in Locke," *John Locke: Problems and Per-*

If, as I have suggested, Mandeville's use of paradox is intended to highlight in public consciousness the unstated ambiguities of the compromises in a possessive individualistic society, his paradoxes are indeed the perfect vehicle for his intentions. In his 1714 edition of *The Fable* Mandeville had exploited the satirical possibilities in the Hobbist state of nature. His 1723 addition to *The Fable*, "A Search into the Nature of Society," attacks Shaftesbury and the political compromise of his tutor, John Locke, based on an amiable view of man in a state of nature. It is a logical expansion of his position in "Remark (O)," and to show that man is "sociable beyond other Animals the Moment after he lost Paradise" because of "the Hateful Qualities of Man, his Imperfections and the want of Excellencies which other Creatures are endued with" is to counter the tendency to see society as an extension of the natural goodness of man. The very nature of society itself is intrinsically evil and legislatures should act to harness this society through laws for the public good. In a parody of sermonizing rhapsodies of Man before the Fall, Mandeville alludes to Man "endued with consummate Knowledge the moment he was form'd," "the State of Innocence, in which no Animal or Vegetable upon Earth, nor Mineral under Ground was noxious to him," "wholly wrapt up in sublime Meditations on the Infinity of his Creator" (I, 346). "In such a Golden Age," there is no possible explanation as to why mankind should ever have formed large societies. Only when Man was fallen was there a need for society, and by implication this society by absolute moral standards must be evil although by utilitarian standards absolutely essential for survival. Mandeville's definition of society is that of "a Body Politick, in which Man either subdued by Superiour Force or by Persuasion drawn from his Savage State, is become a Disciplin'd Creature, that can find his own Ends in Labouring for others, and where under one Head or other Form of Government each Member is render'd Subservient to the Whole, and all of them by cunning Management are made to Act as one" (I, 347).

Martin Price has suggested that Mandeville relies on "causal or genetic explanation" as did Hobbes because such explanation "is our stay against confusion in an essentially unknowable world, and its causal nature is the condition of its rationality." [9] But Kaye is surely correct to see Mandeville rejecting such fictions on the genesis of society and believing that

spectives, ed. John W. Yolton (Cambridge Univ. Press, 1969), pp. 99-136. I find, like David Hume, considerable "ambiguity and circumlocution" in Locke in spite of Aarsleff's argument to the contrary.

[9] *The Palace of Wisdom: Studies in Order and Energy From Dryden to Blake* (New York, 1964), p. 114.

civilization is "the result, not of sudden invention, but of a very slow evolution based on man's actual nature" (I, lxiv-lxvi, 46-47, fn. 1). The political-genesis myths of Hobbes and Locke become valuable reductive myths for Mandeville whose real commitment is to an empirical descriptive account of society as it actually is. When Mandeville writes that "no Societies could have sprung from the Amiable Virtues and Loving Qualities of Man," he is attacking those optimistic theories of human nature which seemingly ignored the Fall completely while retaining the Garden of Eden. It is on this point that Macpherson offers an interesting partial explanation for the rise of optimistic theories of human nature in early eighteenth-century thought. Macpherson argues that when Locke chose to depict, unlike Hobbes, an idyllic state of nature in which all men were equal, Locke was conceiving "man in general in the image of rational bourgeois man able to look after himself and morally entitled to do so": "Now when man in general is thus conceived in the image of rational bourgeois man, the natural condition of man is eminently rational and peaceable" (Macpherson, p. 245). If Macpherson is right on this point, and I believe that he is, the rise of optimistic views towards human nature and society in the essays of Addison and Steele and in the ethical theories of Shaftesbury and Hutcheson may be viewed as self-delusionary ideologies which support in all of their affirmative aspects a society committed to possessive individualism while refusing to confront the realities of such individualism in all of its negative aspects. By calling attention to some of the precedents to Mandeville's *The Fable* in Hobbes's *Leviathan* and in Locke's *Two Treatises of Government*, we may develop some genuinely new insights both into the function of Mandeville's satire and into the sociology of competing literary styles.

Mandeville's first satiric target in the 1714 version of *The Fable* was of course not Shaftesbury but Steele: "When the Incomparable Sir *Richard Steele*, in the usual Elegance of his easy Style, dwells on the Praises of his sublime Species, and with all the Embellishments of Rhetoric sets forth the Excellency of Human Nature, it is impossible not to be charm'd with his happy Turns of Thought, and the Politeness of his Expressions" (I, 52-53). Relying on the excessive alliteration of S's and P's and on the burden of meaning being carried vacuously by the adjectives, Mandeville's parody suggests that Steele often substitutes metaphors and analogies for logical exposition and often substitutes for the concrete reality of experience a glib fictitious world too easily gained by the internal coherence of style.

Mandeville's parody of Addison's *The Spectator*, No. 69, may be found, I believe, in his essay "A Search into the Nature of Society" added to the 1723 edition of *The Fable*. The impact of *The Spectator*, No. 69, on eighteenth-century ideology has been discussed by Donald F. Bond who notes that it became for "eighteenth-century Whigs one of the classic expositions of the value of the merchant class to the nation"; and, indeed, Addison's half-comic and half-serious panegyric on the Royal Exchange does seem painfully chauvinistic: "I am wonderfully delighted to see such a Body of Men thriving in their own private Fortunes, and at the same time promoting the Publick Stock; or in other Words, raising Estates for their own Families, by bringing into their Country whatever is wanting, and carrying out of it whatever is superfluous" (*The Spectator*, I, 294).[10] Mandeville, on the other hand, goes to great pains to show both the negative and the positive effects of commerce on the "labouring poor." Whereas Addison tends to rhapsodize over the products which come to England from all over the world, Mandeville dwells on the plight of the human beings who make such commerce possible: ". . . the Losses of Men and Treasure swallow'd up in the Deep, the Tears and Necessities of Widows and Orphans made by the Sea, the Ruin of Merchants and the Consequences, the continual Anxieties that Parents and Wives are in for the Safety of their Children and Husbands, and . . . the many Pangs and Heart-akes that are felt throughout a Trading Nation by Owners and Insurer at every blast of Wind . . ." (I, 361). Whereas Addison celebrated mock-heroically that romanticized image of commerce, "the single Dress of a Woman of Quality," Mandeville countered with a mock-heroic celebration of "Scarlet or crimson Cloth" (I, 356-57). Whereas Addison tends to assume that what is good for private fortunes is good for public well-being, Mandeville examines with considerable glee the conflict between manners and morals involved in an economy of conspicuous consumption:

It is the sensual Courtier that sets no Limits to his Luxury; the Fickle Strumpet that invents new Fashions every Week; the haughty Dutchess that in Equipage, Entertainments, and all her Behaviour would imitate a Princess; the profuse Rake and lavish Heir, that scatter about their Money without Wit or Judgment, buy every thing they see, and either destroy or give it away the next Day, the Covetous and perjur'd Villain that squeez'd an immense Treasure from the Tears of Widows and Orphans, and left the Prodigals the Money to spend: It is these that are the Prey and proper Food of a full grown Leviathan. . . . (I, 355)

---

[10] *The Spectator*, ed. Donald F. Bond (Oxford: Clarendon Press, 1965), I, 296, fn. 2.

F. B. Kaye himself recognized the literary resemblances between Mande-ville's satire and Addison's essay (*The Fable*, I, 357, fn. 1), but the clinching piece of evidence that Mandeville had *The Spectator* in mind was his attack on Addison's rhapsody of England's commercial blessings as a gift from God: Addison exclaims, "Nature seems to have taken a particular Care to disseminate her Blessings among the different Regions of the World, with an Eye to this mutual Intercourse and Traffick among Mankind, that the Natives of the several Parts of the Globe might have a kind of Dependance upon one another, and be united together by their common Interest" (*The Spectator*, I, 294-95). Writing after the South Sea Bubble and refusing to minimize "the necessary Consequence of Foreign Trade, the Corruption of Manners, as well as Plagues, Poxes, and other Diseases, that are brought to us by Shipping" (I, 360), Mande-ville almost certainly refers to Addison when he asks: ". . . would it not be amazing, how a Nation of thinking People should talk of their Ships and Navigation as a peculiar Blessing to them, and placing an uncommon Felicity in having an Infinity of Vessels dispers'd through the wide World, and always some going to and others coming from every part of the Universe?" (I, 361).

It seems to me that Mandeville throughout *The Fable of the Bees* shows a more all-encompassing, genuine sympathy with the laboring poor than Addison ever does. *Spectator*, No. 69, presents an attitude which really does tend to romanticize English commerce as if God were a middle-class merchant. To counter this attitude, Mandeville uses the Hobbist "State of Nature" as a foil with which to attack the delusionary optimism in the Steele-Shaftesbury tradition. To assume that the Chris-tian ethic and the mercantile ethic can be easily unified in an ideological compromise was repugnant to Mandeville. The Financial Revolution is an amoral secular phenomenon, Mandeville seemed to be suggesting, and requires carefully thought-out secular solutions. Within the market-place the Christian ethic has little, if any, place, and one must not pretend that it does. Rather than reacting to the scandal of the South Sea Bubble with jeremiads in the pulpit, Englishmen should follow the lead of the Netherlands and pass good regulations and laws which will hold politi-cians to a strict accounting (*The Fable*, I, 190). But above all, Mande-ville is saying, one must not fall back on a reactionary kind of Luddite Christianity which rejects the modern world or delude oneself with an optimistic "moral" compromise which views the world as made primarily for the affluent middle class.

"Religion is one thing, and Trade is another" (I, 356) is the vexing thesis of "A Search into the Nature of Society." Mandeville brought home to his contemporaries more dramatically than almost any other writer the intimations of a modern world with an economic soul while appearing not to condemn such a world, and for this he was made a scapegoat. Swift, too, brought home the shock of recognition with re-marks in *Gulliver's Travels* to the effect that the "positive, confident, restive temper, which Virtue infused into Man, was a perpetual Clog to public Business" (III, viii) and that the failure of the Brobdingnagians to apply such secrets as the manufacture of gunpowder to affairs of state resulted from their failure to reduce *"Politicks* into a *Science,* as the more acute wits of *Europe* have done" (II, vii). But I would suggest that, unlike Swift, Mandeville is a modern who saw that to cope with the complexities of the modern secular state a political science *was* necessary.

"Charity," "Pity," and the Problem of the Poor

Mandeville's treatment of "State of Nature" and the "Nature of Society" so as to bring out into the open all of the implications of a society in-creasingly governed by the market-place while professing Christian values is based on his primary satiric norm which is defined in *Free Thoughts on Religion, the Church, and National Happiness* (1720): "Whoever would be happy should endeavour to be wise, and as this consists in having a diffusive Knowledge of the real worth of Things, and a Capacity of chusing on all Emergencies what to sound and unbyass'd reason would seem the most eligible, so it is by shaking of all Clogs of Prejudice, and Fetters of human Authority, by thinking freely, that Men can only mount to Wisdom. There is no better way of curing groundless Jealousy and pannick Fears, than by daring to examine and boldly look into the Face of Things" (p. 335). Unlike the genteel liberalism of Addison and Steele which tended to view society in terms of the middle class while un-intentionally patronizing the poor, Mandeville's hard-boiled acceptance of the implications of the Financial Revolution enabled him to see things as they really were and to sympathize with the laboring poor without sentimentalizing over them. The historian Charles Wilson has shown how in the late seventeenth century there developed a particular concern over the relief and employment of the poor and over the relationship of employment to the national welfare as reflected in the balance of trade and how efforts were made to find new alternatives for the relief of the poor in contrast to the passive forms of relief (alms) common in earlier periods.[11] New solutions were necessary because of the flow of population to London from the country as families sought to be nearer to the financial centers and because of the subsequent increase of urban poor, probably from the servant classes and farm workers who followed householders into the city. Organized philanthropy, supported primarily by the merchant and middle classes, was unable to ameliorate the lot of the urban poor to any great extent because of their large numbers. In the ensuing national debate over the problem of the poor which lasted for almost a century one side saw the solution to be through the charity school and the workhouse while the other side, which included Mandeville, saw the solution to be "only through an accelerated rate of economic activity in general" (p. 99). The parallel to our age seems obvious. Now that the most highly industrialized society in the twentieth century has discovered how much institutionalized welfare leaves to be desired and how in such a society as ours jobs, and access to jobs are desperately needed by the poor to sustain a living standard commensurate with human dignity, perhaps Mandeville's "Essay on Charity, and Charity-Schools" will no longer be interpreted as brutally cynical.

Mandeville's essay seems even less cynical if one is fully aware of just how much the charity schools had become a political pawn in Anglican politics. In the second decade of the eighteenth century many of the London charity schools were considered hotbeds of Jacobite sympathizers.[12] They constituted for Mandeville the symbol of the vicious repression of the Societies for the Reformation of Manners and the reactionary dogmatism of the Society for the Promotion of Christian Knowledge which had in the second decade hounded out of the charity-school movement the nonconformists. The hypocritical compromise of the charity schools was their effort to indoctrinate, rather than to educate genuinely, the children of the poor. Worse yet, this attempt to control the poor by indoctrinating their children submerged its intention under the smokescreen of helping to solve the problem of the poor by training their children for suitable jobs. Thus in *Spectator*, No. 294, Steele could plead

---

[11] "The Other Face of Mercantilism," *Trans. Royal Hist. Soc.*, 5th Ser., 9 (1959), 81-101. See also David Owen, *English Philanthropy* (London: Oxford Univ. Press, 1965); and Charles Wilson, *Mercantilism*, Hist. Assoc. Pamph., No. 37 (London, 1958).

[12] See M. G. Jones, *The Charity School Movement: A Study of Eighteenth-Century Puritanism in Action* (Cambridge: Cambridge Univ. Press, 1938), p. 113. This valuable study is essential for any real understanding of Mandeville's "Essay on Charity," but Miss Jones treats the "Essay" apart from *The Fable* and yokes it with the "Cato" attack on charity schools (*The British Journal*, June 15, 1723) as a two-prong Whig attack (p. 123). This is sheer conjecture and requires considerably more support to be accepted as valid.

good-naturedly with his readers to contribute to the charity schools even if for no "other Expectation than that of producing a Race of good and useful Servants, who will have more than a liberal, a religious Education" (III, 49). Steele's concluding sentence is from a charity-school sermon: *"Thus do they* [the students] *become more exalted in Goodness, by being depressed in Fortune, and their Poverty is, in Reality, their Preferment to Heaven"* (III, 50). It was just such an attitude that angered Johnson in his review of Jenyns.

The charity schools through their subscription campaigns offered the middle class the opportunity to placate its conscience, and the charity school sermon or subscription illustrates a particularly egregious form of conspicuous consumption. One such event is described in the 1720 enlarged edition of Stow's *Survey of the Cities of London:* "And here the Charity Children are brought and placed with their Masters and Mistresses, in convenient Seats, where they may be seen decently habited, sitting or standing, joining with the Publick Prayers, responding, singing the Psalms, and sometimes answering their Catechisms; *to the great Delight and Satisfaction of the better sort that see and hear them* [italics mine]" (p. 49). In later editions of Stow's *Survey,* Strype included a description of the annual gathering of London charity children at St. Andrew's Holborn Church (later held at St. Paul's) and which was one source for William Blake's "Holy Thursday" poems. From Mandeville's point of view the propaganda in favor of the charity schools was a well-meaning but totally self-deluding effort that failed to see that the long-range solution to the problem of the poor would have to be political and economic. Mandeville deliberately takes an unpopular stance on the issue of charity schools and the problem of the poor, and if a precedent is to be found in eighteenth century literature to William Blake's poetical indictment of false charity and patronizing pity, it is in Mandeville's "Essay on Charity, and Charity-Schools."

Genuine charity is defined at the beginning of the "Essay on Charity" as the "part of that sincere Love we have for our selves" which is "transferr'd pure and unmix'd to others" (I, 253). Mandeville distinguished between charity and pity: "This Virtue is often counterfeited by a Passion of ours, call'd *Pity* or *Compassion,* which consists in a Fellow-feeling and Condolence for the Misfortunes and Calamities of others: all Mankind are more or less affected with it; but the weakest Minds generally the most" (I, 254). To make his point that the response of pity is universal so that if charity were synonymous with pity even an "Highwayman, an House-Breaker, or a Murderer" would be charitable,

Mandeville presents the extraordinary instance of a man locked in a room being forced to watch a "nasty over-grown Sow" devour a very young child without being able to help the child: "To see her widely open her destructive Jaws, and the poor Lamb beat down with greedy haste; to look on the defenceless Posture of tender Limbs first trampled on, then tore asunder; to see the filthy Snout digging in the yet living Entrails suck up the smoking Blood, and now and then to hear the Crackling of the Bones, and the cruel Animal with savage Pleasure grunt o'er the horrid Banquet; to hear and see all this, What Tortures would it give the Soul beyond Expression!" (I, 255). The comic exuberance of this description which is gleefully concrete – "smoking Blood," "the Crackling of the Bones" – the reversal of man eating animal to animal devouring man, and the concreteness of the immediate situation to counter the abstractions and clichés of organized philanthropy which will be present later in the essay, all conspire to vex the reader of tenderly exquisite – and phony – sensibility. If pity is a universal passion and if charity is merely pity, then such undiscriminating universal charity would be absurd and meaningless. Mandeville asserts that although pity "is the most amiable of all our Passions," no "Pity does more Mischief in the World than what is excited by the Tenderness of Parents, and hinders them from managing their Children as their rational Love to them would require" (I, 260). Mandeville's point is identical with Swift's indictment of "fondness" in Book Four of *Gulliver's Travels*: "They [the Houyhnhnms] have no fondness for their colts or foals, but the care they take in educating them proceedeth entirely from the dictates of *Reason*." "Fondness" meaning foolish affection was meant by Swift to be pejorative in the context of the Houyhnhnms, who try to raise their offspring by rational principles.

Mandeville proceeds next to show how false charity, *i.e.*, pity, is exploited by the professional beggar and then goes on to show how conspicuous charity in the form of the Radcliffe endowment to Oxford is really a clever manifestation of pride. Finally, he reaches his main target, the charity schools, a form of organized philanthropy which promotes "Sloth and Idleness" and which destroys "Industry" (I, 267). After carefully stipulating that he believes in "sufficient Hospitals for Sick and Wounded" and in tender care for "Young Children without Parents, Old Age without Support, and all that are disabled from Working," Mandeville argues that all of the rest of the poor "should be set to Work." This unpopular position is contrary to the "Enthusiastick Passion for Charity-Schools" that has "bewitch'd the generality" so that he who "speaks the least Word against it" it branded "an Uncharitable, Hard-hearted and Inhuman, if not a Wicked, Prophane and Atheistical Wretch" (I, 269). After defining this mock-villain role in the simplistic idiom of a charity-school fanatic, Mandeville proceeds to play the role to the hilt.

The charity schools participated in the social compromise in that the middle class purported not only to teach morals to the aristocracy but to teach morals and manners to the children of the poor. Unintentionally, the London charity schools were molding a small minority of the children of the poor into the narcissistic image of the prospering urban middle class, and there can be no doubt at all that Mandeville spends much of his essay attacking the charity schools as a middle-class phenomenon and as an *urban* phenomenon.[13] When Mandeville maintains that true "Innocence and Honesty" are most generally characteristics of the "poor, silly Country People," "poor" and "silly" mimic the patronizing of country folk by the urban gentility. Mandeville refuses to patronize the laboring poor when he tartly asserts that it "is not Compliments we want" of the "Labourious Poor" but rather "their Work and Assiduity" (I, 270). Furthermore, it will not be the charity schools that will prevent crime through moral education because those poor parents who care about their children will keep their children off the streets at night and will make their children "do something or other that turns to Profit" (I, 270). There is some historical evidence to suggest, as we have noted earlier, that the rapid growth of London and the increase of urban poor was caused by the Financial Revolution and by the need of country gentry to be near the center of eighteenth-century English commerce. The urban middle class's support of charity schools to control crime is a pathetically puny attempt to cope with the symptom rather than the cause. To control the children of the urban poor by educating them just enough – but not too much – to be servants and obsequious clerks is rank hypocrisy. It would remain for Charles Dickens to show how such efforts could backfire in his portrayal of the 'umble Uriah Heep. Mandeville's satire, however, goes directly to the heart of the matter.

If the urban middle class opts for the affluence which is the result of

---

[13] In *The Guardian*, No. 79, 1713, Steele had deplored the fact that "only the middle kind of people" seemed to be concerned with teaching the young or with charity. See also Dorothy Marshall, *English People in the Eighteenth Century* (London, 1956), p. 161. Cultural historians now seem generally agreed that "middle-class" is an attitude of mind rather than a rigidly economically or quantitatively defined category. For a very commonsensical discussion of the use of "class" in historiography see the preface to E. P. Thompson, *The Making of the English Working Class* (Harmondsworth, Middlesex, England: Penguin Books Ltd., 1968), pp. 9-12.

London's rapid growth, then it will have to accept the consequences of the "enormous Crimes" which are the result of density of population: "One of the greatest Inconveniences of such vast over-grown Cities as *London* or *Paris*" is that they harbor "Rogues and Villains as Granaries do Vermin" (I, 272). Just as a sociologist would see the charity schools as an urban phenomenon designed by the middle class to cope with the large masses of children of the urban poor, so Mandeville also sees the growth of crime as stemming from the complexity of urbanization itself: "It is manifest then that many different Causes concur, and several scarce avoidable Evils contribute to the Misfortune of being pester'd with Pilferers, Thieves, and Robbers, which all Countries ever were and ever will be, more or less, in and near considerable Towns, more especial-ly vast and overgrown Cities" (I, 274). Mandeville goes to great pains to show the middle-class origins of the charity school in a kind of mock case-history of how such a school is founded. They are started by not very successful "young Shop-keepers." In contrast, "Men of Worth, who live in Splendor" and "thriving" business men are "seldom seen among" the organizers of the charity schools. Mandeville was to write in 1724 a sarcastic dedication to the "Gentlemen" of the Societies for the Refor-mation of Manners," [14] and he mingles them with the charity-school supporters when he refers to those "diminutive Patriots" who enlist the support of "stanch Churchmen" and "sly Sinners" at meetings where they declaim on "the Misery of the Times occasion'd by Atheism and Profaneness" (I, 279). The underlying motive for many who attend is "Prudentially to increase their Trade and get Acquaintance." The "Governours" of this school once it is organized are "the midling People" (I, 280), and their real motive for serving in such a capacity is for the sheer "Pleasure in Ruling over any thing" – particularly over "the Schoolmaster himself!" (I, 280-81). In a really stunning insight into the structure of his society Mandeville notes that the middle-class supporters of the charity school take particular pleasure in their vicarious ownership of 'Our Parish Church" and 'Our Charity Children" (I, 282): "In all this *there is a Shadow of Property*" [italics mine] that tickles every body that has a Right to make use of the Words, but more especially those who actually contribute and had a great Hand in advancing the pious Work" (I, 282). Here Mandeville himself is looking at the genteel ideology of his own society and observing that it is grounded in possessive individual-ism. Macpherson's thesis could hardly be more effectively vindicated.

When Mandeville follows with a relatively straightforward analysis of

[14] *A Modest Defence of Public Stews* (London, 1724).

how charity schools are a smokescreen which cover up a failure to solve the problem of the poor, there is little ambiguity in what he is saying. But when he writes that charity schools interfere with the market economy by incapacitating the children of the poor for "down right Labour" and that the "Proportion as to Numbers in every Trade finds it self, and is never better kept than when no body meddles or interferes with it" (I, 299-300), we are wrong to infer that Mandeville believed in a laissez-faire economy (a nineteenth-century development).[15] On the contrary Mandeville sees the charity schools as an ill-conceived, unilateral attempt which educates the children of the poor for jobs which are not necessarily in any real demand. Within the context of this essay Mandeville's argument is for continuation of a planned economy – the kind Walpole was running – and, indeed, he later writes that "the Conveniency of the Publick ought ever to be the Publick Care" (I, 319) and that it is "the Business of the Publick to supply the Defects of the Society, and take that in hand first which is most neglected by private Persons" (I, 321). When read within the context of the eighteenth-century debate over the problem of the laboring poor, Mandeville's essay is not cynical. In fact his proposal to solve the problem of the poor by keeping them employed was a radical one as he himself suggests: "The Fearful and Cautious People that are ever Jealous of their Liberty, I know will cry out, that where the Multitudes I speak of *should be kept in constant Pay* [italics mine], Property and Privileges would be precarious" (I, 319).[16]

Mandeville's attack on charity as a form of self-delusion founded on the passion of a pejorative kind of pity brought the economic debate over the problem of the poor into the center of literary consciousness. Fielding's concern with the true meaning of charity, Goldsmith's satire on universal benevolence, and Johnson's refusal to accept the status quo of the poor, all reflect different aspects of the same humanitarian concern. After Mandeville, no serious writer could employ "charity" without testing the meaning of the term in the realm of experience. For Fielding "charity" was a genuine virtue and not a mere empty word, but only empirically in the fictitious world of *Tom Jones* is the term reinvested with its true significance.

15 See Nathan Rosenberg, "Mandeville and Laissez-Faire," *JHI*, 24 (1963), 183-96. The late Jacob Viner rightly insisted that Mandeville, like the other major satirists of the century, accepted the "then-existing economic structure of society." "Satire and Economics in the Augustan Age of Satire," *The Augustan Milieu: Essays presented to Louis A. Landa,* ed. Henry Knight Miller, Eric Rothstein, G. S. Rousseau (Oxford: Clarendon Press, 1970), p. 95.
16 It is this proposal which for me distinguishes Mandeville from Addison and Steele and gives his "Essay on Charity Schools" an almost visionary quality.

The most complex treatment of "Charity" and "Pity" occurs in the poetry of William Blake. Blake found pity in the form of organized, institutionalized charity to be perversely depersonalized, a "Human Abstract," and hence a way for individuals to avoid personal commitment. Jean Hagstrum finds that Blake is "one of the most unrelenting satirists of Pity and Love that England ever produced" and that in "an analysis of social 'virtues' worthy of Bernard Mandeville, Blake perceives that Urizenic pity arises from social poverty, Urizenic mercy from a lack of equal happiness." [17] It is not, I believe, by mere coincidence that Mandeville and Blake are compared. There is every reason to believe that Blake had read Isaac Watts' *Essay on Charity-Schools* (1728) which, as Vivian de Sola Pinto has shown, reflects a "charactersitic dualism of thought" in that Watts sympathizes on the one hand with the children of the poor while defending on the other hand the social structure which assumed the status quo of the poor.[18] Nowhere in eighteenth-century literature is the social compromise with all its limitations so graphically shown as in the concessions which Watts makes to charity school opponents. Watts' original 1727 sermon which was expanded into the 1728 *Essay* was in fact specifically in answer to Mandeville's attack on the charity schools. Both Mandeville and Blake in his "Holy Thursday" poems are indicting the same genteel compromise, and Mandeville's influence en Blake is more complex than one of direct influence. Rather, Watts, forced by Mandeville to state explicitly all of the unstated assumptions behind the charity-school movement, revealed to Blake all of the hypocrisies of these assumptions. Mandeville's "Essay on Charity and Charity-Schools" and Watts' reply to Mandeville form a kind of eminent domain, the reverberations of which form the texture of Blake's poetic analysis of "Charity" and "Pity." Mandeville's clarification of the issues involved in these terms – even if written within the limits of the "single Vision" – must have served as a valuable catalyst to Blake's poetic imagination.

"Honor" – The Usefulness of Christianity in War

Rachel Trickett has shown how honor "had been the ideal of a chivalric military society" and how it was being replaced in the eighteenth century by the ideal of honesty which "epitomized all that was best in a world

---

[17] " 'The Wrath of the Lamb': A Study of William Blake's Conversions," *From Sensibility to Romanticism,* ed. Frederick W. Hilles and Harold Bloom (New York: Oxford Univ. Press, 1965), p. 316; and *William Blake: Poet and Painter* (Chicago: Univ. of Chicago Press, 1964), p. 84.

[18] "Isaac Watts and William Blake," *RES,* 20 (1944), 214-23.

where peace and prosperity in a well-ordered state was the common aim." [19] The attempt to redefine an aristocratic mode of secular manners by integrating it with middle-class morality was one of the professed aims of Richard Steele, and such a social compromise may be traced in his work from *The Christian Hero* to *The Conscious Lovers* (1722). Such a compromise at its worst tended toward the genteel, toward a reduction of complex tensions to a simplistic middle-class solution. Swift's contribution to the reformation of manners, *A Project for the Advancement of Religion and the Reformation of Manners* (1709), need not be interpreted as anything but straightforward, but his method of proceeding towards such a reformation is highly original. Instead of a hypocrisy which allows one to profess Christianity while expediently living by a set of secular values, Swift proposes a hypocrisy whereby nonbelievers both profess *and* practice Christian values. As Claude Rawson observes, whereas "Fielding and Chesterfield both seek to narrow the gap between morals and manners, Swift makes use of a logic which inexorably widens this gap until the whole social basis of the compromise is reduced to nullity. In an absolute morality, there can be no chartable point where gallantry ends and infamy begins." [20]

While Addison and Steele continued to rework honor in genteel terms, Mandeville proceeded to destroy its use in such a sense so that it could not easily be used as a reifying concept. "Remark (C)" with its conclusion that "Good Manners have nothing to do with Virtue or Religion," directly challenges the aims of the *Societies for the Reformation of Manners*. For Mandeville, like Swift, there can be no real compromise between absolute morality and gallantry: "Virtue bids us subdue, but good Breeding only requires we should hide our Appetites" (I, 72). Mandeville's satiric strategy here as elsewhere in his works is to cite illustrations of his shocking paradoxes that are "low" in subject matter. This technique of burlesque which gave his enemies the opportunity to call him "coarse" is a form of proof in its appeal to everyday experience bluntly and concretely described as well as a means of satirizing genteel insipidity which by an implicit censorship of language and content devitalizes literary discourse. Thus Mandeville demonstrates his distinction between virtue and good breeding by a ludicrous contrast between the "fashionable Gentleman" and the "brutish Fellow" who both have violent inclinations to a woman. The "fine Gentleman" by virtue of being "well

[19] *The Honest Muse* (Oxford: Clarendon Press, 1967), p. 118.
[20] "The Character of Swift's Satire," *Swift*, ed. C. J. Rawson, "Focus" series (London: Sphere Books, 1971), p. 44.

bred" arrives at his goal of sexual consummation through the courtship ritual culminating in marriage. If he is "hotter than Goats or Bulls," as soon as the wedding is over he may have at it and "sate and fatigue himself with Joy and Ecstacies of Pleasure" (I, 73). Better yet, he will even have a cheering section in that "all the Women and above Nine in Ten of the Men are of his side" (I, 74). Mandeville's marvelous Rabelaisian exuberance here drives home his point that often polite marriages grounded only on sexual desire, although civilly correct, are merely a form of what Defoe termed "conjugal whoredom."

For Mandeville "Manners and good Breeding" may be merely another means of "flattering the Pride and Selfishness of others, and concealing our own with Judgment and Dexterity" (I, 77), and his habit of asserting such theses absolutely rather than conditionally is another satiric technique which serves to vex the opposition. One can trace throughout the remainder of "Remark (C)" Mandeville's incremental repetition of "well-bred Man" until it becomes a thoroughly pejorative phrase. The undermining of honor continues in "Remark (R)" when Mandeville writes: "Honour in its Figurative Sense is a Chimera without Truth or Being, an Invention of Moralists and Politicians, and signifies a certain Principle of Virtue not related to Religion, found in some Men that keeps 'em close to their Duty and Engagements whatever they be . . ." (I, 198). In this prose remark it is "Man of Honour" that becomes a key pejorative phrase. Mandeville exploits the animal analogy by comparing the aggressive behavior of men of honor to bulls and cooks in heat. Since modern man's real underlying ethic is determined by the pragmatic ethic of his society, Mandeville chooses to redefine honor as a useful social code based upon pride and fear. Though morally wrong, duelling makes men watch their manners! Mandeville knew very well of the campaign by Collier, Steele, and the Societies for the Reformation of Manners against duelling. His comic reversal which makes duelling useful in this reform can only be read satirically as an attack against the genteel compromise between morals and manners: "If every ill-bred Fellow might use what Language he pleas'd, without being called to an Account for it, *all Conversation would be spoil'd*" [italics mine] (I, 219).

The genteel attempt to have the best of both possible worlds on watered-down terms will not do for Mandeville. He insists that "modern honour" be recognized as a purely secular code and that to do otherwise is another form of self-delusion. After writing that the "*only* thing of weight that can be said against modern Honour is, that it is directly opposite to Religion" [italics mine], Mandeville lists the differences:

Religion commands you to leave all Revenge to God, Honour bids you trust your Revenge to no body but your self, even where the Law would do it for you: *Religion plainly forbids Murther, Honour openly justifies it* [italics mine]: Religion bids you not shed Blood upon any account whatever: Honour bids you fight for the least Trifle: Religion is built on Humility, and Honour upon Pride: How to reconcile them must be left to wiser Heads than mine. (I, 221-22)

It should be clear from this passage that Mandeville's defense of duelling is a mock one and that in reality he condemns it as "Murther." Louis Landa has noted the similarity between Mandeville and Swift who was "contemptuous" of the "whole 'Cant of Honour' " and of efforts by Shaftesbury and others to "construct an independent or secular ethics" and to make a distinction "between true and false honour." [21] It is enough that a satirist such as Mandeville demonstrate through his paradoxes the discrepancy between secular manners and Christian morality.

Why then did Mandeville feel compelled to write his last and perhaps most neglected treatise, *An Enquiry into the Origin of Honour, and The Usefulness of Christianity in War* (London, 1732)? I believe that the answer is in Francis Hutcheson's refusal to accept the implications of Mandeville's satire and in fact to reify honor as a kind of moral sense in a work which cited *The Fable of the Bees* as an adversary in the title: *An Inquiry into the Original of our Ideas of Beauty and Virtue; in Two Treatises. In which the Principles of . . . Shaftesbury are . . . defended against . . . the Fable of the Bees* (London, 1725). Hutcheson was later to claim in 1730 that in his *Inquiry* he had provided ample "Proofs and Illustrations of a *moral Sense*, and a *Sense of Honour*." But other than mere repetition and assertion, Hutcheson's primary proof is a circular argument that the "Determination to love *Honour*, presupposes a *Sense* of *moral Virtue*, both in the Persons who confer the Honour, and in him who pursues it" and that we possess "by NATURE, a moral Sense of virtue . . . antecedent to *Honour*" (pp. 225, 231). Hutcheson's treatment of honor explains the opening of the third dialogue in Berkeley's *Alciphron* which deals with honor for several pages even though the dialogue is supposed to be directed towards Shaftesbury. Berkeley clears away the debris on honor created by Shaftesbury's chief disciple before he directs himself to his main target. Alciphron begins the dialogue with a definition of honor as "a noble unpolluted source of virtue, without the least mixture of fear, interest, or superstition" which is to be "found among persons of rank and breeding." When Euphranor asks if "a man of honour

---

[21] Jonathan Swift, *Irish Tracts 1720-1723 and Sermons,* ed. Herbert Davis with Introd. and Notes by Louis Landa (Oxford: Basil Blackwell, 1948), pp. 114-16.

is a warm man, or an enthusiast," Alciphron is reduced to protesting that the "high sense of honour which distinguished the fine gentleman" was a "thing rather to be felt than explained." Unfair as Berkeley may be to both Mandeville and Shaftesbury in *Alciphron*, there can be no doubt that he sees the emphasis on "modern honour" to be pretentiously genteel.

Mandeville's *Origin of Honour* once and for all seeks to discredit the compromise between honor and Christian morality. Mandeville's mock defense of duelling as an aid to manners is now extended to an ironic defense of the "usefulness" of Christianity in fighting a war. As we have shown earlier in *The Fable* Mandeville had reversed the traditional relationship of ethics and politics to show that in the modern world politics and the market govern the ethical behavior of both individuals and nations. Now the pattern of reversal is repeated to claim that politicians use a "Gothic" notion of Christian honor – a contradiction in terms – to encourage soldiers to fight well in battle.

According to Jeremy Collier in his essay "Upon Duelling" duelling was not characteristic of classical civilization nor of primitive Christian culture, but was derived from the Lombards, Saxons, and Normans. This thesis was developed far more elaborately in John Cockburn's *The History and Examination of Duels, Shewing Their Heinous Nature and the Necessity of Suppressing them* (London, 1720), a book owned by Henry Fielding and to which Fielding was probably indebted in his treatment of duelling, war, and the spectrum of Gothic honor in *Tom Jones*. Cockburn identifies the custom of duelling with the Gothic custom of trial by ordeal and with the encouragement of this custom by the Church of Rome. This equation of Gothic honor with Popery forms a large part of Mandeville's *Origin of Honor*. Rather than merely showing the incompatibility between war and Christian virtue, Mandeville argues that by means of army chaplains quoting from the Old Testament rather than the New, Christian doctrine is useful in preparing soldiers to fight courageously in battle. Thus under the banner of "Honour" Christianity in the new society is converted from an end to a means. With this *reductio ad absurdum* Mandeville's final corrosive treatise on honor posed a formidable barrier to any future attempt to fuse honor and Christian value.

It is true that skepticism about honor was pervasive in the eighteenth century and much earlier, Falstaff's speech being a good case in point. But Mandeville's *Fable* and *Origin of Honour* were so vigorously written and so shocking to the age, that every major writer was forced to find the answers to the questions which he put to posterity. It is not within the province of this essay to show, for example, how profoundly Mandeville influenced Fielding. When, however, the Lieutenant in *Tom Jones* exclaims, "I love my religion very well, but I love my honour more" (Bk. VII, ch. xiii), it is hard to see how Fielding could not have been painfully aware of Mandeville's *Origin of Honour*. If *Tom Jones* begins with the question of what is true honor, it ends by scrapping honor altogether and replacing it with Christian goodness. One can make a strong case for one of the differences between *Tom Jones* and *Amelia* being Fielding's increasing awareness that it was a Mandevillian world, and no longer possessing the resilience to transcend that realization in style and artistic choice.[22]

It is here that we confront a complex difficulty in our understanding of Mandeville. To his contemporaries he was "man-devil," a cynical disciple of Hobbes. In answering Mandeville such writers as Fielding and Pope were forced to reinvest stale terms with earned meanings and to clarify their own ideas in significant literary ways. But if my interpretation of Mandeville's satire is valid, we are obligated as twentieth-century readers to see how much in common Mandeville had with some of his illustrious adversaries in attacking the same satiric targets. It seems to me that his contemporaries owed much to Mandeville in his refusal to allow language and experience to be censored and devitalized by the Societies for the Reformation of Manners, by the genteel "Christian Hero" ideology of Addison and Steele, and by the reifying deistic optimism of Shaftesbury and Hutcheson. Mandeville deliberately sought out key phrases that carried the semantic burden of these genteel ideologies and then proceeded to deflate their flatulences by mimicry, low burlesque, and shockingly asserted paradoxes. Insofar as Mandeville put his contemporaries on their mettle by forcing them to redefine, and thus earn the right to use, some of these key-words, his adversary role in the foreground of eighteenth-century English literature is a positive gain. But I should like to hope that ultimately Mandeville's relevance as a perceptive satirist of the genteel compromise and of the contradictions and hypocrisies of our own "liberal" compromise, shared in a common historical heritage, will allow his work to be recognized as a substantial achievement in its own right.

---

[22] For analysis of Mandeville's impact on Fielding's art see Glenn Hatfield, *Henry Fielding and the Language of Irony* (Chicago: Univ. of Chicago Press, 1969) and C. H. K. Bevan, "The Unity of Fielding's *Amelia*," *Renaissance and Modern Studies*, 14 (1970), 90-110. Both of these studies tend to accept a pejorative view of Mandeville even while recognizing his considerable influence as an adversary on Fielding.

MANDEVILLE'S PARADOX

PHILIP PINKUS

Perhaps the real paradox of *The Fable of the Bees* is that Mandeville's
values were orthodox and unexceptionable, and yet as far as his contemporaries were concerned, he wrote like a heretic. Mandeville flaunted
an excess of honesty: he dared to say that the emperor was naked, that
society prospered by means of the very qualities that Swift and his fellow
satirists were condemning. In his *hubris*, he assumed too literally that
special mode of the Augustans which was to look at things as they are,
not as they pretend to be, and for his pains was treated as the Machiavelli of his age. Swift also looked at things as they were. But he was not
content with showing the truth as he saw it, he imposed a judgement.
With all his genius he revealed the iniquity of what he saw, and to that
extent deflects our attention towards the judgement itself and the values
behind it. But Mandeville seems to make no judgement, except spo-
radically, even though the picture he shows is not very different from
Swift's. What Swift presents as horrifying, Mandeville shows as the
foundation of a strong and prosperous society. He does not say that this
is good or evil, he simply demonstrates that the worldly qualities that
Swift condemns, the corruptions inherent in society, provide the fuel that
makes society thrive. If you eliminate the corruption you destroy the
strength and prosperity, as well as those cultural advantages that accompany wealth and leisure. This state of affairs may or may not be
deplorable. Mandeville insists only that it is the way of the world. On
occasion, Mandeville asks if people realize that the price they pay for
their worldly success is the jettisoning of their Christian values, and
raises the question, is prosperity worth it? But this is no judgement. He
leaves such moral questions for the reader to answer. He contents himself with showing the inescapable facts as he sees them. As for the reader,

he is left to wriggle on the *Fable's* paradox, "Private Vices, Publick Benefits."

The reaction of Mandeville's contemporaries was understandably violent. They said he was immoral, a dangerous cynic, that he championed vice, undermined the foundations of society, completely reversed the roles of good and evil, that he was, in short, satanic, and for the cheapest of reasons, merely to create a sensation: he had built his paradox, some insinuated, on chop logic by deliberately equivocal definitions of vice and virtue. It was not easy to avoid detesting Mandeville in his day. All those who believed that moral and religious values are essential to society – almost everyone – must have done so. To draw such immense opposition was no inconsiderable achievement, for what began as a six-penny quarto of doggerel. The first installment of the *Fable*, "The Grumbling Hive" (1705), was twenty-six pages long. Mandeville spent the next twenty-four years of his life elaborating, explaining, justifying, defending that bit of doggerel, making his arguments stronger and stronger until they became virtually impregnable. But it seemed that the more he explained the more he was misunderstood, or at least, the more he was attacked; he may have been understood only too well. Throughout the years there has been surprising agreement that the *Fable* was a reprehensible work, but relatively little agreement about why. Each generation seems to have hurled at the *Fable* its own special prejudices. When a work is so unpleasant to so many for so long, whatever the reason, it becomes a rhetorical phenomenon that deserves attention. Over the years the critical questions have persisted. What manner of work is the *Fable*? What is the nature of its aesthetic and philosophical impact? What contributes to this effect? Such questions have produced a confusion of responses. At the risk of adding to the confusion, I submit that most of the difficulty in understanding the *Fable* arises from a misconception of its genre. If we can determine the nature of the genre, we will have come a long way towards determining the nature of the *Fable*, which is the intention of this paper.

F. B. Kaye puts Mandeville in the tradition of the great Renaissance and seventeenth century sceptics, Montaigne, La Rochefoucauld, Pascal, Fontenelle, and particularly Pierre Bayle, whom he considers Mandeville's "great thought-ancestor." For many of Mandeville's contemporaries, the association with Bayle would have been reason enough for detesting him, for Bayle had sliced his way through more sacred cows than any other man of the period, and had incurred that special wrath reserved for the great inconoclasts of history. Bayle's theories provide a

useful point of departure for understanding Mandeville. According to
F. B. Kaye, Mandeville basic theories are in Bayle:

the general scepticism as to the possibility of discovering absolute truth; the
anti-rationalism, which held that men do not act from principles of reason
or from regard for abstract morality, but from the reigning desires of their
hearts; the corollary opinion that Christianity, despite the lip service paid it,
is little followed in the world . . . the definition of Christianity as ascetic; and
the belief that Christianity thus defined and national greatness are incompatible.[1]

This is a great deal to have in common. But Kaye goes on to describe
other aspects of Bayle's thought, with the assumption that what he says
of Bayle is true of Mandeville. Pierre Bayle, according to Kaye, "spent
his prolific genius demonstrating with gusto the essential discordance
between revealed religion and any appeal to experience. . . . With Bayle
the appeal to experience led to a relativism so extreme as to approach a
thoroughgoing anarchism. . . . On the other hand, Bayle took pains to
impress on his readers that religion demands precisely that finality which
is unattainable from experience." Man's reason, therefore, is antithetical
to human nature (I, xlii-xliii). Kaye's argument reflects the traditional
attitude to Bayle, that he is a thoroughgoing empiricist with a relentlessly
rational mind – insofar as the one is compatible with the other – and
through these twin perspectives all mysteries dissolve away. Religion itself is pushed dangerously close to mere superstition. Since there is no
place for reason in religion, a religious man must abandon his mind to
an act of faith. As for Pierre Bayle's own claim to orthodoxy, it is a mere
pose to hoodwink the authorities. This was the general argument of
scholars like F. B. Kaye over the years. One cannot deny that many of
Mandeville's ideas are similar to Bayle's and that Bayle's notoriety likely
accounted for a great deal of Mandeville's. But does even Bayle deserve
his reputation? Modern scholars [2] tend to look more kindly on Bayle's
claim to orthodoxy. They argue that he had no need to pretend to
orthodox views because his books were written in Holland, which had
complete freedom of the press. Had Bayle intended to attack the Church,
he could have attacked it directly without any fear of reprisal. Nor are
Bayle's ideas necessarily heretical; they can be seen as part of a century-

[1] Bernard Mandeville, *The Fable of the Bees,* 2 vols., ed. F. B. Kaye (Oxford:
Clarendon Press, 1924), Vol. I, p. civ. All references to the *Fable* will be from this
edition.
[2] For example, Karl C. Sandberg, *At the Crossroads of Faith and Reason* (Tucson:
University of Arizona Press, 1966); Richard H. Popkin in his Introduction to Pierre
Bayle, *Historical and Critical Dictionary,* trans. Richard H. Popkin (New York: Bobbs-
Merrill Co., 1965).

long tradition of Christian scepticism that began with Montaigne, though Bayle made these ideas more immediate and provocative. The main concern of this scepticism – in the area of religion, fideism – was to show that our senses and our reason were not to be trusted in the search for truth, especially the highest truth. The sceptic could accept fundamental truths only on faith. By the end of the seventeenth century Christian scepticism seemed to take a new form; it became more polemical, more militant, as the new rationalism and particularly its religious counterpart, deism, became stronger.

Perhaps the sceptical philosophy at this point is better described as anti-rationalism. Bayle was one of the first to adopt this militant attitude; therefore he is not only part of a long tradition that precedes him, but one of the leaders of a tradition that follows him. The anti-rationalist movement included writers like, Swift, William Law (*The Case of Reason*, 1731), Bishop Butler (*The Analogy of Religion*, 1736), and Bishop Berkeley (*Alciphron*, 1732), many of whom felt themselves completely at odds with Bayle's thinking. Yet on several crucial points they all agreed: the Deists' belief that the human reason can reach divine truth is a form of *hubris* – in lifting one's eyes to the stars, says Swift, man's feet may betray him into a ditch; reason unaided by divine grace is an insufficient guide to enable man to live a rational, that is, a virtuous life; man's reason is weak and very fallible, and only by recognizing these limitations can man approach his God. The essential element of anti-rationalism is that man must humble his reason if he is to be truly religious. Bayle's particular emphasis was to analyse intellectual theories to a *reductio ad absurdum* in order to demonstrate the inadequacy of reason to resolve any question. If reason is so inadequate in these secular areas, the argument follows, how fallible it must be as a guide to faith and revelation. Bayle undoubtedly denied the value of reason in religion more thoroughly than did the other anti-rationalists, but it does not follow that he was therefore trying to undermine the basis of religion by making it irrational and ridiculous. He was a member of the French Reformed Church of Rotterdam for most of his life. Bayle's Calvinism is precisely consistent with his theme that man's reason is inadequate to cope with his intellectual endeavours, and that the only certainty he can find is in faith and revelation. Of course, Swift puts more importance on the place of reason in religion, but the difference between him and Bayle is not so great. Both use the argument of the sceptics to attack Deism and rationalism in the name of religion. If some of Mandeville's ideas are similar to Bayle's, therefore, he is in good company.

But Mandeville's emphasis is very different from Bayle's. His main purpose is not to show how ineffectual reason is in the pursuit of truth, nor does he have the Calvinist interest in asserting the powers of grace at the expense of reason, nor is he particulerly concerned with philosophical or religious polemic. He uses some of Bayle's ideas – they are, after all, the common heritage of the period – but as a point of view rather than a judgement. His scepticism is a mode of perception, not an instrument of war; it is the mode of the paradox, and if less offensive than Bayle's, it is hardly less troublesome. Mandeville also has been accused of atheism, and on the same grounds as Bayle, for showing that society functions quite well without reason, without religion and without any of the virtues that religion supports. And Mandeville also insisted that he was religious, though his religion is very different from Bayle's. Repeatedly throughout the *Fable* he makes the point that "in all Societies, great or small, it is the Duty of every Member of it to be good, that Virtue ought to be encourag'd, Vice discountenanc'd. . . ." (I, 229) Mandeville intended this in the Christian sense. In the Dialogues he is more explicit: "It is [Mandeville's] Opinion," says Cleomenes, who speaks for the author, "that there is no solid Principle to go by but the Christian Religion. . . ." (II, 102); and again:

Where the Christian Religion is thoroughly taught, as it should be, it is impossible, that Honesty, Uprightness, or Benevolence should ever be forgot; and no Appearances of those Virtues are to be trusted to, unless they proceed from that Motive; for without the Belief of another World, a Man is under no Obligation for his Sincerity in this: His very Oath is no Tye upon him.
(II, 314) [3]

These are orthodox views of the established church, and there seems to be no reason for Mandeville to proclaim them if his intention was to undermine religion. For such a purpose, the law was no more obstacle to Mandeville than to Bayle. Nor does there seem to be any rhetorical purpose in pretending to be Christian if he wanted to attack it. On the contrary, Mandeville's rhetoric makes sense only if his religious protestations are sincere: the power of his paradox, the entire thrust of the *Fable*, depends on his orthodoxy, as I shall try to demonstrate.

[3] How different is this from Swift's conclusion in "The Testimony of Conscience"? It plainly appears that unless Men are guided by the Advice and Judgment of a Conscience founded on [the Christian] Religion, they can give no Security that they will be either good Subjects, faithful Servants of the Publick, or honest in their Mutual Dealings.
The Works of the Reverend Dr. Jonathan Swift, 20 vols. (Dublin: George Faulkner, 1772), Vol. 8, p. 302.

Professor Chiasson [4] provides a compelling argument for Mandeville's orthodoxy in the *Fable*, even if he does miss the point of how he uses it. He links him with Hooker, putting him within the Christian humanist tradition which asserts that ultimately there is no conflict between faith and reason or between revealed and natural truth; that despite the Fall, man is not entirely restricted to revelation for his knowledge of God and for the substance of his moral duties. That is, the sceptical aspects of Mandeville's thought are put within the mainstream of Anglican theology. There are many passages one might quote to illustrate that reason and revelation are not in conflict in the *Fable*.[5] Mandeville attains a balance between them that is consistent with Anglican doctrine. On the one hand he rejects Deism because its pride in human reason makes it seem sufficient without God. On the other hand he rejects Calvinism because it abandons reason altogether in the reach for salvation. "I would not be a Believer, and cease to be a rational Creature," Mandeville said. Yet, "we are convinc'd, that human Understanding is limited" (II, 315). Mandeville is equally orthodox in his balancing of reason and the passions, as we see in his conception of sin. "All Passions and Instincts in general," Mandeville says, "were given to all Animals for some wise End, tending to the preservation and Happiness either of themselves or their Species: It is our Duty to hinder them from being detrimental or offensive to any Part of the Society; but why should we be ashamed of having them?" (II, 91) But the Passions must be controlled by reason: "It is not in feeling the Passions, or in being affected with the Frailties of Nature, that Vice consists; but in indulging and obeying the Call of them, contrary to the Dictates of Reason" (II, 7). Man is free to choose

---

[4] Elias J. Chiasson, "Bernard Mandeville: A Reappraisal," *Philological Quarterly*, 49 (1970), 489-520.

[5] The following are cited from Professor Chiasson's article:

The Exercise of [Men's] highest Faculty, will infallibly lead [them] to the certain Knowledge of an infinite and eternal Being; whose Power and Wisdom will always appear the greater, and more stupendious to them, the more they themselves advance in Knowledge and Penetration;   (II, 208)

A Man must be pretty far advanced in the Art of thinking justly, and reasoning consequentially, before he can, from his own Light, and without being taught, be sensible of his Obligations to God. The less a Man knows, and the more shallow his Understanding is, the less he is capable either of enlarging his Prospect of Things, or drawing Consequences from the little which he does know;   (II, 211)

When I cannot comprehend what my Reason assures me must necessarily exist, there is no Axiom or Demonstration clearer to me, than that the Fault lies in my want of Capacity, the Shallowness of my Understanding. From the little we know of the Sun and Stars . . . and what we are more nearly acquainted with, the gross, visible Parts in the Structure of Animals . . . it is demonstrable that they are the Effects of an intelligent Cause, and the Contrivance of a Being infinite in Wisdom as well as Power.   (II, 311)

between good and evil; it is his reason that distinguishes between them –
in Milton's phrase, reason is but choosing. "Those, who act from a Principle of Virtue take always Reason for their Guide, and combat without
exception every Passion, that hinders them from their Duty!" (II, 119)
To the degree that reason plays a part in combating evil, Mandeville
sees man as not totally depraved but capable of acts of goodness. Professor Chiasson argues that Mandeville's description of Christian man as
"regenerated and preternaturally assisted by the Divine Grace" (I, 166),
puts him in the tradition of Hooker who also sees grace as *regenerative*
(*Polity*, V, lxii, 13).[6]

I have been trying to show that Mandeville's views are consistent with
orthodox Anglicanism, and that even his similarities with Pierre Bayle
do not diminish his orthodoxy. I am not suggesting that the *Fable* is
therefore more agreeable or less provocative. On the contrary, Mandeville's orthodoxy makes the *Fable* all the more disturbing. His values, I
have suggested, are similar to Swift's. They are within the same tradition
of Anglican theology; they have the same conception of man's fallen
nature and the same attitude about the place of reason in revelation. I
have suggested also that even the picture of society that Mandeville
presents resembles Swift's. In *Gulliver's Travels* Swift shows that man's
nature is fundamentally Yahoo: at least, the Yahoo is Swift's satiric
vision of man's essence. Man uses his reason only to transform his Yahoo
qualities into something more sophisticated and more cruel, giving him a
capacity for destruction equal to the viciousness of his intent. What
emerges is man's society, built by the ingenious manipulation of man's
Yahoo nature by his God-given reason. For Swift, the forms of civilized
behaviour tend to conceal the Yahoo within. Of course, there are obvious
differences between Swift's view of life and Mandeville's. But if, for a
moment, we dwell on the similarities, we see Mandeville in a new perspective. Three main aspects of Swift's satiric vision in the *Travels* are
that man's nature is essentially Yahoo; that he uses his reason to extend
his Yahoo qualities into society; that society itself serves as a cloak for
man's Yahoo nature. Mandeville also speaks of society as a structure that
conceals man's dark passions:

Ashamed of the many Frailties they feel within, all Men endeavour to hide
themselves, their Ugly Nakedness, from each other, and wrapping up the
true Motives of their Hearts in the Specious Cloke of Sociableness, and their

---

[6] Professor Chiasson reminds us that Calvin sees grace as mere cloaking of sin.
Ibid., p. 498.

Concern for the publick Good, they are in hopes of concealing their filthy
Appetites and the Deformity of their Desires.

(I, 234-235)

He describes man's passions as bestial, in fact, worse than the beasts', as
we see in the fable of the lion and the merchant:

But if a Man had a real Value for his kind [the lion is speaking], how is it
possible that often Ten Thousand of them, and sometimes Ten times as
many, should be destroy'd in few Hours for the Caprice of two? ... The
Gods have appointed us to live upon the Waste and Spoil of other Animals,
and as long as we can meet with dead ones, we never hunt after the Living.
'Tis only Man, mischievous Man, that can make Death a Sport.

(I, 177-8)

"No wild Beasts are more fatal to our Species," Mandeville says later
(II, 238), "than often we are to one another." Yet out of these bestial
appetites man builds his society, shaped by the politician's ingenuity:

Hunger, Thirst and Nakedness are the first Tyrants that force us to stir:
afterwards, our Pride, Sloth, Sensuality and Fickleness are the great Patrons
that promote all Arts and Sciences, Trades, Handicrafts and Callings; while
the great Taskmasters, Necessity, Avarice, Envy, and Ambition ... keep the
Members of the Society to their Labour.

(I 366)

Many passages in the *Fable* describe an ugly, cruel world driven by vicious appetites, manipulated for political reasons into an efficient society,
in effect, the same society that Swift describes, and covered over by the
same cloak of respectability, agreeably fashionable. It is "a most beautiful
Superstructure ... upon a rotten and despicable Foundation" (II, 64).

The difference between Swift and Mandeville is expressed by the
difference between the genres that they use. Swift is writing satire. The
Yahoo society he describes is evil, and he lashes out at the horror of it.
But Mandeville, I have suggested, is not writing satire. The focus of the
Fable is not on the evil of this society, which is an essential requirement
for satire, but on the paradox, on the fact that from this evil comes
pleasure, prosperity and what we call civilization. The difference in
emphasis is fundamental. It is as if Swift had described a rich and happy
society run by Yahoos pretending to be Houyhnhnms, and invited us not
to judge the Yahoos but to observe that they are necessary if society is to
thrive, and that this is the way the world is. In the *Travels* Swift tears
away at the civilized pretense of society to expose the Yahoo within. In
the *Fable* Mandeville shows how the Yahoo within creates the only
civilization we know.

The problem of whether or not the *Fable* is satire is obviously a matter of definition and in most literary terms there is always the danger of making one's definitions so restrictive as to be meaningless. Mandeville himself makes several references to satire in the *Fable*. Cleomenes says ironically that he has "a strong Aversion to Satyr," (II 43) but this is hardly more than a rhetorical flourish to shake Horatio out of his complacency. More typical is the reference to the *castrati* where Cleomenes talks of Mandeville's "Design being Satyr" (II, 105). Here and elsewhere Mandeville refers to certain passages in the *Fable* which are undeniably satiric, rather than to the whole. I have not found a single instance in which Mandeville asserts that the genre of the *Fable* is satire. Another argument advanced is that over the years the *Fable* generally has been considered satire and therefore usage makes it satire. Definitions, after all, are descriptive rather than prescriptive, and it does seem pedantic to argue against usage. But we are concerned about the genre of the *Fable* not because it is neat and tidy to label works of art but because in the Augustan period in particular the genre prescribes the rules of composition, the aesthetic expectations, to some degree even the content of the piece; more than in any other period to know the genre is to understand the work. In this instance the argument from usage begs the question because it still does not determine the generic qualities that Mandeville tried to attain. For this we must examine the work itself, applying simple criteria and making them as flexible as possible.

If the *Fable* is indeed satire, then what is being satirized? It is certainly not man's innate viciousness, the kind of satire against mankind as we have in *Gulliver's Travels*, because Mandeville states explicitly that out of vice emerges public benefit, and he intends you to believe him. His entire paradox revolves around the empirical fact that man's vice does indeed build his civilization:

> Thus Vice nurs'd with Ingenuity,
> Which join'd with Time and Industry,
> Had carry'd Life's Conveniencies,
> It's real Pleasures, Comforts, Ease,
> To such a Height, the very Poor
> Liv'd better than the Rich before,
> And nothing could be added more.
>
> (I, 26)

Nor is the satire directed against the prosperous hive, that is, showing that the prosperity Mandeville describes is meretricious, concealing an evil that cannot be borne. The prosperity is real, the very poor do live better than the rich before. However, there are isolated passages that appear to satirize a false prosperity, such as the attack on the gin trade:

The vast Number of the Shops I speak of throughout the City and Suburbs, are an astonishing Evidence of the many Seducers, that in a Lawful Occupation are accessary to the Introduction and Increase of all the Sloth, Sottishness, Want and Misery, which the Abuse of Strong Waters is the immediate Cause of, to lift above Mediocrity perhaps half a score Men that deal in the same Commodity. . . .

The short-sighted Vulgar in the Chain of Causes seldom can see further than one Link; but those who can enlarge their View, and will give themselves the Leisure of gazing on the Prospect of concatenated Events, may, in a hundred Places, see *Good* spring up and pullulate from *Evil*, as naturally as Chickens do from Eggs. . . . Should no Spirits be distill'd from [malt], the Publick Treasure would prodigiously suffer on that Head.

On the other hand, a "sharp-sighted good-humour'd Man" [7] interested in defending the gin trade would argue

That the stupid Indolence in the most wretched Condition occasion'd by those composing Draughts, was a Blessing to Thousands, for that certainly those were the happiest, who felt the least Pain. As to Diseases, he would say, that, as [gin] caused some, so it cured others, and that if the Excess in those Liquors had been sudden Death to some few, the Habit of drinking them daily prolong'd the lives of many, whom once it agreed with; that for the Loss sustain'd from the insignificant Quarrels it created at home, we were overpaid in the Advantage we receiv'd from it abroad, by upholding the Courage of Soldiers, and animating the Sailors to the Combat. . . .

If I should ever urge him, that to have here and there one great Distiller, was a poor equivalent for the vile Means, the certain Want, and lasting Misery of so many thousand Wretches . . . he would answer, that of this I could be no Judge, because I don't know what vast Benefit they might afterwards be of to the Commonwealth.

(I, 91 ff.)

At first glance, this passage seems like the satire of Swift's *Modest Proposal*, applying the values of the economic projector to human beings, assessing their worth according to how profitable they are to society, in monetary terms. It seems to evoke the same bone-chilling irony. But the epigraph of "Remark (G)," from which this passage comes, is this:

The worst of all the Multitude
Did something for the Common Good.

[7] By giving this argument to a dramatic character, the "sharpsighted good-humour'd Man," Mandeville seems to divorce himself from this position, until we realize that the speaker's values are consistent with the whole of "Remark (G)" and, in fact, with the whole of Mandeville's paradox.

And if Mandeville is serious about his paradox – insofar as one can be serious about any paradox – then he must be serious about his epigraph, the truth of which he attempts to prove in the "Remark" that follows. The illustration of the gin sellers is just one of a number in this section that makes the point that even the worst does something for the common good. What the gin sellers do is evil, and Mandeville minces no words in showing it, which creates an ambivalent effect that tends to obscure the paradox. By giving the main argument in this passage to the "good-humour'd Man," a *persona* – to use the present critical jargon – Mandeville is able to thrust satirically at the paradox itself at the same time as he maintains it. The gin sellers are an appalling evil and it is corrosively ironic that society is so built that they contribute to the common good, yet the fact is that they do. But Mandeville does not dwell on the evil of the gin sellers and he quickly leads us back to the paradox itself, *a fortiori*: even out of this comes good. That is, even here, perhaps the most likely example of satire against the economic values that lead to prosperity, the satire is only secondary. Mandeville does not explore and extend the viciousness of the vice, as he would if he were writing satire. The main focus is on the paradox itself.

There is one other possible target for the satire in the *Fable*, hypocrisy. In his Preface to the Dialogues (II, 18) Mandeville describes Cleomenes, in effect, Mandeville's spokesman, as a man who "took uncommon Pains to search into human Nature, and left no Stone unturn'd, to detect the Pride and Hypocrisy of it. . . ." This is how Mandeville sees himself. It does not follow that this principle informs the *Fable*, though detecting pride and hypocrisy is clearly an important part of the work. Mandeville specifically intends the *Fable* to break through the enormous web of pretence that society calls virtue and describe men as "they really are" (Introduction, I, 39). He distinguishes between virtue and good breeding: "a Man need not conquer his Passions, it is sufficient that he conceals them. Virtue bids us subdue, but good Breeding only requires we should hide our Appetites" (I, 72). Clergymen are "made of the same Mould, and have the same corrupt Nature with other Men, born with the same Infirmities, subject to the same Passions, and liable to the same Temptations, and therefore if they are diligent in their Calling, and can but abstain from Murder, Adultery, Swearing, Drunkenness, and other Hainous Vices, their lives are called unblemish'd, and their Reputations unspotted" (I, 155). The whole of the *Fable* shows the discrepancy between virtue and good breeding, religion and honour, private sin and social decorum, individual and public behaviour. Society is one great hypocrisy. Yet man's hypocrisy is not satirized, and this is the point of the paradox. Given the society that Mandeville describes, impelled by lusts, manipulated by flattery, "it is impossible we could be sociable Creatures without Hypocrisy" (I, 349). "It is impossible that Man, mere fallen Man, should act with any other View but to please himself while he has the Use of his Organs" (I, 348). Yet:

the World every where, in Compliment to itself, desires to be counted really virtuous, so barefac'd Vices, and all Trespasses committed in Sight of it, are heinous and unpardonable . . . a Violation of the Laws of Decency, and plainly Shews a Want of Respect and Neglect of Duty, which every Body is supposed to owe to the Publick.

(II, 13)

The Power and Sagacity . . . of the Politician in civilizing the Society, has been no where more conspicuous, than in the happy Contrivance of playing our Passions against one another. By flattering our Pride and still increasing the good Opinion we have of ourselves on the one hand, and inspiring us on the other with a superlative Dread and mortal Aversion against Shame, the Artful Moralists have taught us chearfully to encounter ourselves, and if not subdue, at least so to conceal and disguise our darling Passion, Lust, that we scarce know it when we meet with it in our own Breasts.

(I, 145)

We conceal and disguise our lusts so that we can pretend we are nobler than other animals, and however ridiculous this may be, our pride requires it, and pride is the handle which the politician manipulates to civilize society. It is important, Mandeville argues, that we be aware of the role that pride and hypocrisy play in our lives, and the *Fable* provides this awareness in no uncertain terms. But essentially what we become aware of is that pride and hypocrisy are necessary. There is no sustained developing image showing the evil of hypocrisy which satire requires. It is not shown as evil at all but as essential, perhaps the most essential of the vices that contribute to the public good.

If, then, it is not man's vice that the *Fable* satirizes, if it is not his economic values, if it is not his hypocrisy, then we are back where we started from. What is being satirized in the *Fable*? Except for a few satiric thrusts, the answer, I suggest, is nothing. Where there are no satiric targets there can be no satire. Where there are no sustained judgements imposed, no developing movement showing climatically that some aspect of man and society are evil, there can be no satire. Every satiric passage in the *Fable* is subordinated to the paradox that private vices make public benefits. That is, even where Mandeville shows that something is evil, he does so not to explore the nature of the evil but to demonstrate that out of this comes civilization. This is not satire but paradox. Now the paradox may very well be satiric, as it is in *A Tale of a Tub* where the hack author argues that "modern" works are immortal, by asserting the basic principle of modernism that Monday's works are superseded by Tuesday's. Swift uses the paradox to show the absurdity of "modernism." But in the *Fable* the paradox is used for its own sake, not to show how ridiculous or evil the subject is. In short, if we can assign a genre to the *Fable*, it is simply a paradox, with no other purpose but to show the paradoxical nature of "private vices, publick benefits." This seems, perhaps, a simple-minded way of taking Mandeville at his word. The fact is that the *Fable* revolves around the paradox. The paradox is the beginning and end of the work, and its entire point.

I do not mean to suggest that the *Fable of the Bees* is a unified work conforming to a predetermined generic structure. The manner of its composition precludes this. Perhaps it is safer here to avoid using the term *genre* altogether and fall back on that convenient catchall, *mode*, indicating a predominant attitude, a guiding principle, which informs every aspect of the work regardless of its structure, imposing certain characteristics as traditionally determined as the genre's. The paradox is in the classical tradition of rhetoric and was very popular in the Renaissance.[8] Its logical tricks and equivocations, its sudden surprises, its sharp reversals, gave the Renaissance an opportunity to indulge its taste for exuberant word play and quibbles. The paradox takes many forms, such as the riddles of Zeno, the mock encomium (*The Praise of Folly*), but with few exceptions, its distinguishing feature is a surprising inversion or reversal involving some logical conundrum. Usually there is no logical structure or narrative sequence, but a series of digressions, surprises, inversions, sustained by the basic contradiction of the paradox itself, the logical impasse, and all dissolving into one dominant irony. At its best, Miss Colie explains,[9] the paradox requires an exquisite control, a delicate touch, so that the linguistic acrobatics, the reversals, appear effortless. We see this in *A Tale of a Tub* and in *The Praise of Folly*. The *Fable* does not possess the verbal acrobatics and playful exuberance that Miss Colie requires for a successful paradox. Nor is it Mandeville's intention. The paradoxical style was no longer fashionable in the Augustan period: Swift's use of it in the *Tale* was ironic, an example of Grub Street writing. Yet there is still something of this quality in the *Fable*, a few mercurial shifts of emphasis, as in the gin trade argument and the com-

---

[8] Cf. Rosalie L. Colie, *Paradoxia Epidemica* (Princeton University Press, 1966).
[9] *Ibid.,* p. 13 ff.

ment on hypocrisy in clergymen, where we suddenly lose ourselves in a subtle ambivalence. But mainly it is the teasing, witty thrust of that outrageous phrase, "Private Vices, Publick Benefits," that captures the spirit of the paradoxical mode, and this phrase is the substance of the *Fable*. It sets the tone for the entire work. For the sake of this phrase Mandeville was prepared to withstand charges of equivocation and sensation-mongering, because the phrase was necessary to create the proper aesthetic effect that the paradox requires – stupefaction. If Mandeville's touch is not light, as the paradox demands, it is sharp and penetrating. Having set the tone of his paradox, Mandeville builds it in as clear and direct and compelling a way as he can. Every addition to the *Fable*, however discursive and piecemeal, adds to the clarity.

Yet there is a certain vagueness in Mandeville's definition of vice, as Johnson charged, though it is no more vague than Erasmus' use of the term, *folly*, in *The Praise of Folly*. A certain amount of vagueness seems to be necessary in the central terms of the paradox in order to bring about the reversal. The only requirement is that out of this some deeper truth should emerge. Since Mandeville's conception of vice is one of the areas his critics have seized on, however, we should examine it further. To begin with, it is *vice*, not *evil*, on which Mandeville builds his paradox, presumably because it has more secular associations. Mandeville distinguishes between private and public morality. The focus of the paradox is society, not society as it should be, but society as it is, given the fact that man is a creature of original sin. The "Publick Benefits" are seen in relation to public, that is, social, morality. The vice is an expression of individual, that is, private morality, but within the paradox it has a second meaning, a utilitarian one. Mandeville goes to great lengths to show that he is not encouraging vice, but neither is he urging a return to virtue. He is merely showing that vice is the paradoxical source of our prosperity. It is a secular perspective. We have assumed that we live in a Christian society, that our operative values are determined by the Christian religion, but this is precisely what does not happen, the *Fable* demonstrates. The Christian religion and the Christian way of life are irrelevant to the building of a prosperous society. Here is the centre of the paradox, and Mandeville's conception of vice should be seen within this framework. Mandeville, we have seen, defines vice in terms that are consistent with orthodox Anglicanism: it is "indulging the Passions contrary to the dictates of Reason" (II, 7). Those "who act from a Principle of Virtue take always Reason for their Guide," (II, 119), and by Reason Mandeville means a reason rooted in religion. In this context, to insist that self-

denial is the basis of virtue is to recognize man's burden of sin and the need
for restraint from within, both rational and religious. Mandeville's position,
I have argued, is very similar to Swift's. Swift also rejected Shaftesbury's
creed that the uncontrolled passions may lead to goodness. For both
Swift and Mandeville, indulging the passions means abandoning moral
principles and all restraints except those of expediency. It means that
everything is permitted that society will allow, and society requires only
that you conceal your worst excesses. In such a society, virtue is a clog.
Swift demonstrates this precise point in Book III of *Gulliver's Travels*. As
for vice, that is, indulging one's passions without restraint, it may be unchristian, but it is the basis of our prosperity – and this is Mandeville's
paradox, an emphasis which separates him from Swift. In its broad out-
line, therefore, the paradox is clear enough, and we may assume, then,
so are the terms on which it is based.

Essentially, the paradox emerges from Mandeville's distinction between
private and public morality:

> It is certain that the fewer Desires a Man has and the less he covets, the
> more easy he is to himself; the more active he is to supply his own Wants,
> and the less he requires to be waited upon, the more he will be beloved and
> the less trouble he is in a Family; the more he loves Peace and Concord,
> the more Charity he has for his Neighbour, and the more he shines in real
> Virtue, there is no doubt but that in proportion he is acceptable to God and
> Man. But let us be Just, what Benefit can these things be of, or what earthly
> Good can they do, to promote the Wealth, the Glory and the worldly Great-
> ness of Nations?
>
> (I, 355)

A man must pursue his own salvation, he must be virtuous in the full
Christian sense of the word. Yet what good are the Christian virtues for
building a thriving society?

> I lay down as a first Principle, that in all Societies, great or small, it is the
> Duty of every member of it to be good, that Virtue ought to be encourage'd,
> Vice discountenanc'd, the laws obey'd, and the Transgressors punish'd....
> I never said, nor imagin'd that Man could not be virtuous as well in a rich
> and mighty Kingdom, as in the most pitiful Commonwealth; but I own it is
> my Sense that no Society can be rais'd into such a rich and mighty Kingdom,
> or so rais'd, subsist in their Wealth and Power for any considerable time,
> without the Vices of Man.
>
> (I, 229)

Repeatedly throughout the *Fable* Mandeville asserts his belief in Christian virtue while pointing out how useless it is in sustaining a "rich and
mighty Kingdom." A virtue like frugality, for example, which the

Church had preached for centuries in its campaign against usury and capitalist enterprise, is a mean and starving virtue for a "rich and mighty Kingdom." It may make a man a good Christian but it makes a poor politician (I-104). To make a kingdom mighty we turn from private to public morality, from the old religion to the new economics which Swift satirizes in *A Modest Proposal*, and the new economics has no use for frugality.

As men we have souls and spiritual needs, yet we are social animals, and our inclinations impel us to live in society and submit to social standards that are antipathetic to Christian ones. We cannot escape the old virtues, but as social beings we can pay only lip service to them:

> The generality of Wise Men that have liv'd ever since to this Day, agree with the Stoicks in the most material Points; as that there can be no true Felicity in what depends on Things perishable; that Peace within is the greatest Blessing, and no Conquest like that of our Passions; that Knowledge, Temperance, Fortitude, Humility, and other Embellishments of the kind are the most valuable acquisitions; that no Man can be happy but he that is good; and that the Virtuous are only capable of enjoying *real Pleasures*.
>
> (I, 151)

To which Mandeville comments:

> I don't call things Pleasures which Man say are best, but such as they seem to be most pleased with; how can I believe that a Man's chief Delight is in the Embellishments of the Mind, when I see him ever employ'd about and daily pursue the Pleasures that are contrary to them? ... The real Pleasures of all Men in Nature are worldly and sensual, if we judge from their Practice.
>
> (I, 151)

As social beings we live in a secular world, creatures of appetite, manipulated by politicians for economic ends. "How necessary our Appetites and Passions are for the welfare of all Trades and Handicrafts has been sufficiently prov'd throughout the Book, and that they are our bad Qualities, or at least produce them, no Body denies" (I, 344). Even the avarice that leads to the gin trade, with all its attendant miseries, we have shown, provides "a considerable part of the National Revenue" (I, 91). Given the values of an economic society, "Religion is one thing and Trade is another," and Trade is "the greatest Friend to the Society" (I, 356). In this society we still talk of ethics, but we mean utilitarian ethics. We talk of virtue, but we mean the social virtues:

> The Reason why there are so few Men of real Virtue, and so many of real Honour, is, because all the Recompence a Man has of a virtuous Action, is

the Pleasure of doing it, which most People reckon but poor Pay; but the Self-denial a Man of Honour submits to in the Appetite, is immediately rewarded by the Satisfaction he receives from another, and what he abates of his avarice, or any other Passion, is doubly repaid to his Pride: Besides, Honour gives large Grains of Allowance, and Virtue none. . . . A Man of Honour must never change his Religion for Interest, but he may be as Debauch'd as he pleases, and never practise any. He must make no Attempts upon his Friend's Wife, daughter, Sister, or any body that is trusted to his Care, but he may lie with all the World besides.

(I, 222-3)

That is, the custom, the fashion of the moment, determine the operative virtues of society, and if these social virtues are not openly defied, within broad limits a man may abandon himself to his passions. Honour is "an Invention of Moralists and Politicians, and signifies a certain Principle of Virtue not related to Religion" (I, 198). Shame, its opposite, is society's evil. These are the rewards and punishments that politicians use to manipulate our passions. They have a greater hold on us than their spiritual counterparts. As social creatures, we evidently believe that paradise in this world is happier far than that of the next. We have chosen prosperity in the here and now, indulging our passions, presumably at the risk of our eternal souls. But the choice is almost theoretical. However much we desire individual salvation, we want our society prosperous. As individuals we may choose to follow the Christian life, but if the citizens of an entire country did so, there would be economic disaster and the quality of civilization would diminish accordingly – for it is wealth that creates the audience and the leisure necessary for the arts to flourish. Therefore as responsible citizens we seem obliged to contribute to the prosperity of our society. But it is at the expense of our individual salvation. Mandeville himself does not put it in these bald terms, but the logic of the argument dictates this conclusion. It would seem as if some cruel joke of cosmic proportions has been played on man.

The main metaphor of the *Fable* is the *hive*. It is the image of an efficiently organized society of creatures without souls, whose entire reason for being can be considered only in relation to their community. They may delight in gathering together the nectar from the flowers and in feeling the warm sun on their wings, but their joy is subsidiary to the function they serve, which is to contribute to the hive. In a sense they have no existence apart from their hive. Man, of course, does have a soul, and he does have an individual existence. As an individual he may reject society's values and declare that his own individual salvation comes before obedience to the community. But if he does so he is likely to be pilloried as a Daniel Ellsberg. In general, to the degree that man is a social animal, he lives by the social virtues, measures his value in social terms which, we have seen, are inimical to the Christian values we pretend to. The result is a prosperous hive.

The paradox gets even more complicated. The kind of society that Mandeville describes, however crass it may be, however utilitarian and economic its values, clearly does much good not merely for society in the abstract, but for the people within it. If we take the pragmatic view we readily accept Mandeville's point that "Pride and Vanity have built more Hospitals than all the Virtues together" (I, 261). A virtuous man who abandons all wordly interest, excels in probity, temperance and austerity of life, "and ever trod in the strictest Path of Virtue" (I, 264 f.), would likely die poor and leave nothing as a monument to himself except his own good name, which probably would die with his nearest relations. But "a rich Miser, who is thoroughly selfish, and . . . has nothing else to do than to defraud his Relations, and leave his Estate to some famous University," or some hospital, can buy his immortality. Regardless of the motive and the character of the donor, society is the richer for this gift: "let the Money and the Motive of the Donor be what they will, he that receives the Benefit is the Gainer." Can we not proceed further, Mandeville infers, and conclude that this rich and corrupt man, whose entire life was built on fraud and deceit, is more of a benefactor to society than the man who is virtuous but poor? His contribution to society is far greater, and he likely will be remembered long after the poor but virtuous man is forgotten. And is this not just? By contributing to a university the rich miser likely has helped increase the sum of human learning; by contributing to a hospital he likely has helped comfort the sick; while the poor but virtuous man has achieved little more than his own individual salvation. A man must, indeed, be virtuous. But we might logically conclude that in a secular world, that is, in society as we know it, what price virtue if vice, indeed, is more beneficial? At this point the distinctions between good and evil begin to blur. Our values are turned upside down, and the Christian humanist tradition that the Augustans idealized is shown to be not only irrelevant but an impediment.

Under the circumstances it is not difficult to understand why Mandeville was unpopular in his day. In moral terms, he was shooting Niagara. The Augustan satirists recognized the precariousness of their civilization. Beneath its surface, they show in works like *The Dunciad* and *Gulliver's Travels*, are the powers of darkness ready to erupt at any moment. They felt that the Millennium of Anti-Christ was approaching. Then along comes Mandeville to show that the forces of darkness are not only at hand but are the basis of all that we pretend is civilization. Without them, this fine Augustan edifice would be a barbarous waste land. By asserting that man's civilization has its source and inspiration in his Yahoo instincts, Mandeville has proclaimed as here and now the precise horror that the satirists have fought with all their strength to avoid and has shown that, as far as society is concerned, it does not appear to be so horrible after all. It works. The Yahoos and the Dunces have created an admirable hive where people live prosperously and the arts flourish: it is the world we live in. If that is so, and Mandeville seems to make his conclusions inescapable, then where is that great rational structure we call Augustan civilization? What we are shown is not particularly rational, nor particularly religious, nor particularly moral; the only operative virtues are utilitarian, not Christian; the only guide is the politician's, not God's. Yet Mandeville does not give us even the satisfaction of condemning this society. The satirist provides a direction, if only by inference. Mandeville leaves us with his paradox, offering no resolution, no counsel, proclaiming the true religion only to demonstrate the mystery of our confused being.

SELECTED BIBLIOGRAPHY

I. THE MANDEVILLE CANON

Thirty years after the publication of F. B. Kaye's sumptuous edition of *The Fable of the Bees* (2 vols., Oxford, 1924: reprinted 1957), his edition remains the most important single work on Mandeville in our century. Kaye (I, xxx-xxxi) regarded the following works as authentic:

Bernardi à Mandeville de Medicina Oratio Scholastica.   Rotterdam, 1685
Disputatio Philosophica de Brutorum Operationibus.   Leyden, 1689
Disputatio Medica Inauguralis de Chylosi Vitiata.   Leyden, 1691
Some Fables after the Easie and Familiar Method of Monsieur de la Fontaine.   1703
Æsop Dress'd or a Collection of Fables Writ in Familiar Verse.   1704
Typhon: or the Wars between the Gods and Giants: a Burlesque Poem in Imitation of the Comical Mons. Scarron.   1704
The Grumbling Hive: or, Knaves Turn'd Honest.   1705
The Virgin Unmask'd: or, Female Dialogues betwixt an Elderly Maiden Lady, and her Niece.   1709
A Treatise of the Hypondriack and Hysterick Passions.   1711
Wishes to a Godson, with Other Miscellany Poems.   1712
The Fable of the Bees.   1714
Free Thoughts on Religion, the Church, and National Happiness.   1720
A Modest Defence of Publick Stews.   1724
An Enquiry into the Causes of the Frequent Executions at Tyburn.   1725
Letters published in the *British Journal*, April 24 and May 1, 1725.
The Fable of the Bees. Part II.   1729
An Enquiry into the Origin of Honour, and the Usefulness of Christianity in War.   1732
A Letter to Dion, Occasion'd by his Book Call'd Alciphron.   1732

Since 1924 these attributions have been added to the Mandeville canon: (1) a 26-line poem, "In Authorem de usu Interno Cantharidum Scribentem," prefixed to *Tutus Cantharidum in Medicinâ Usus Internus* by John Greenfield, M.D., second edition, London, 1703 (see the entry for H. Gordon Ward, below). (2) The 32 Lucinda-Artesia papers which appeared in *The Female Tatler* between November 2,

1709 and March 31, 1710 (see the entries by Paul Bunyan Anderson and Gordon Vichert, below).

Among the doubtful works listed by Kaye, only *The Mischiefs that ought justly to be apprehended from a Whig-Government* (1714) appears to be a defensible attribution. These remain doubtful:

The Planter's Charity.   1704

A Sermon Preach'd at Colchester ... By the Reverend C. Schrevelius ... Translated into English by B.M. M.D.   1708

Two letters to the *St. James Journal,* April 20, 1723 and May 11, 1723.

Remarks upon Two Late Presentments of the Grand-Jury ... wherein are shewn, the Folly ... of Mens Persecuting One Another for Difference of Opinion in Matters of Religion.... By John Wickliffe.   1729

Other attempts to attribute various works to Mandeville have been rejected by Kaye and Vichert, in articles listed below.

II. SECONDARY WORKS, including introductions to editions and to reprints of Mandeville's works since 1924.

Anderson, Paul Bunyan. "Bernard Mandeville on Gin." *PMLA,* 54 (1939), 775-84.

—. "Splendor out of Scandal: The Lucinda-Artesia Papers in *The Female Tatler.*" *Philological Quarterly,* 15 (1936), 286-300.

Arata, Fidia. "*Le api*" *di B. de Mandeville.* Torino, 1953.

Burton, Jean. "Mandeville: A Post-Augustan Pessimist." *Dalhousie Review,* 8 (1928), 189-96.

Chalk, Alfred F. "Mandeville's *Fable of the Bees*: A Reappraisal." *The Southern Economic Journal,* 33 (1966), 1-16.

Chiasson, Elias J. "Bernard Mandeville: A Reappraisal." *Philological Quarterly,* 49 (1970), 489-519.

Colman, John. "Bernard Mandeville and the Reality of Virtue." *Philosophy,* 47, no. 180 (1972), 125-39.

Cook, Richard I. "Introduction" to *A Modest Defence of Publick Stews* (1724), by Bernard Mandeville. (Augustan Reprint Society, No. 162). Los Angeles, 1973.

—. *Bernard Mandeville.* Twayne's English Authors Series. New York, 1974.

Deckelmann, Wilhelm. *Untersuchungen zur Bienenfabel Mandevilles und zu ihrer Entstehungsgeschichte im Hinblick auf die Bienenfabelthese.* Hamburg, 1933.

de Labriolle-Rutherford, M. R. "L'Évolution de la notion du luxe depuis Mandeville jusqu'à la Révolution," *Studies in Voltaire and the Eighteenth Century,* 26 (1963), 1025-36.

Dobrée, Bonamy. *English Literature in the Early Eighteenth Century.* Vol. 7 of The Oxford History of English Literature. London, 1959. Pp. 266-71.

—. "Mandeville's Fable of the Bees." *Variety of Ways: Discussions of Six Authors.* Oxford, 1932. Pp. 100-118.

Edwards, Thomas R., Jr. "Mandeville's Moral Prose." *ELH*, 31 (1964), 195-212.

Fichter, J. H., S. J. "Root of Economic Liberalism: Bernard Mandeville, 1670-1733." *Roots of Change*. New York, 1939.

Garin, E. "Bernardo de Mandeville." *Civiltà Moderna* (1934), 70-91.

—. "Lettera aperta sul Mandeville." *Studi Senesi*, 65 (1953), 578.

Garman, Douglas, Introduction to *The Fable of the Bees*. London, 1934.

Goldsmith, M. M. "Introduction" to Mandeville's *An Enquiry into the Origin of Honour and the Usefulness of Christianity in War*. London, 1971.

Goretti, Maria. "Ancora la Bienenfabel Kontroverse?" *Studi Senesi*, 65 (1953), 350-66.

—. "Bernardo de Mandeville nella storia del pensiero giuridico-etico inglese." *Studi Senesi*, 64 (1952), 77-143.

—. *Il Paradosso Mandeville: Saggio sulla "Favola delle Api" col testo inglese a fronte e bibliographia*. Firenze, 1958.

Grégoire, F. *Bernard de Mandeville et la "Fable des Abeilles."* Nancy, 1947.

Harth, Phillip. "Introduction" to *The Fable of the Bees*. Harmondsworth, 1970.

—. "The Satiric Purpose of *The Fable of the Bees*." *Eighteenth Century Studies*, 2 (1969), 321-40.

Harder, J. H. "The Authorship of *A Modest Defence of Public Stews, etc.*" *Neophilologus*, 18 (1933), 200-03. (Rebutted by R. S. Crane in *Philological Quarterly*, 13 [1934], 122-23).

Hayek, F. A. "Dr. Bernard Mandeville." Lecture on a Master Mind. *Proceedings of the British Academy*, 52 (1966), 125-41.

Hind, George. "Mandeville's *Fable of the Bees* as Menippean Satire." *Genre*, 1 (1968), 307-15.

Hübner, Walther. "Mandevilles Bienenfabel und die Begründung der praktischen Zweckethik in der englischen Aufklärung. Ein Beitrag zur Genealogie des englischen Geistes." In *Grundformen der englischen Geistesgeschichte*, ed. Paul Meissner. Stuttgart and Berlin, 1941. Pp. 275-331.

Jones, Harry L. "Holberg on Mandeville's *Fable of the Bees*." *CLA Journal*, 4 (1960), 116-25.

Jones, M. G. *The Charity School Movement: A Study of Eighteenth Century Puritanism in Action*. Cambridge, 1938.

Kaye, F. B. "The Influence of Bernard Mandeville." *Studies in Philology*, 19 (1922), 83-108. Reprinted in *Studies in the Literature of the Augustan Age: Essays Collected in Honor of Arthur E. Case*, ed. R. C. Boys. Ann Arbor, 1952. Pp. 150-75.

—. "Mandeville on the Origin of Language." *Modern Language Notes*, 39 (1924), 136-42.

—. "The Mandeville Canon: A Supplement." *Notes & Queries*, Vol. 146, No. 44 (May 3, 1924), 317-21.

—. "A Bibliographical Survey of the Writings of Bernard Mandeville." *Journal of English and Germanic Philology*, 20 (1921), 419-67.

Kramnick, Isaac. *Bolingbroke and His Circle*. New Haven, 1969. See pp. 201-04, "Bernard Mandeville: Philosopher of Avarice."

Lamprecht, Sterling P. "*The Fable of the Bees.*" *Journal of Philosophy,* 22 (1926), 561-79.

Lecler, Joseph. "Libéralisme économique et libre pensée au xviiiᵉ siècle. Mandeville et La Fable des Abeilles." *Études,* No. 230 (March 5, 1937), 624-45.

Lloyd, James Hendrie. "Dr. Bernard Mandeville and his 'Fable of the Bees.' " *American Medical History,* 8 (1926), 265-69.

Lovejoy, Arthur O. *Reflections on Human Nature.* Baltimore, 1961.

Maxwell, J. C. "Ethics and Politics in Mandeville." *Philosophy,* 26 (1951), 242-52.

Miner, Earl R. "Dr. Johnson, Mandeville, and 'Publick Benefits.' " *Huntington Library Quarterly,* 21 (1958), 159-66.

Morize, André. *L'Apologie du Luxe au XVIIIᵉ siècle et 'Le Mondain' de Voltaire.* Paris, 1909.

Novak, Maximillian E. *Economics and the Fiction of Daniel Defoe.* Berkeley, 1962.

Noxon, James. "Dr. Mandeville: 'A Thinking Man.' " In *The Varied Pattern: Studies in the 18th Century,* ed. Peter Hughes and David Williams. Toronto, 1971. Pp. 233-52.

Olscamp, Paul J. *The Moral Philosophy of George Berkeley.* (International Archives of the History of Ideas, No. 33.) The Hague, 1970. See Chapter VII, "Berkeley and Mandeville."

Primer, Irwin. "A Bibliographical Note on Bernard Mandeville's 'Free Thoughts.' " *Notes and Queries,* (May, 1969), 187-88.

—. "Introduction" to *The Fable of the Bees.* New York, 1962.

Price, Martin. *To the Palace of Wisdom: Studies in Order and Energy from Dryden to Blake.* New York, 1964. See Chapter IV, "Mandeville: Order as Art."

Rogers, A. K. "The Ethics of Mandeville." *International Journal of Ethics,* 36 (1925), 1-17.

Rosenberg, Nathan. "Mandeville and Laissez-Faire." *Journal of the History of Ideas,* 24 (1963), 183-96.

Rousseau, G. S. "Bernard Mandeville and the First Earl of Macclesfield." *Notes and Queries,* 18 (1971), 335.

Saccenti, Mario. "Illuministi inglesi: il paradosso Mandeville." *Convivium,* 29 (1961), 92-4.

Schneider, Louis. "Mandeville as Forerunner of Modern Sociology." *Journal of the History of the Behavioral Sciences,* 6 (1970), 219-30.

Scott-Taggart, M. S. "Mandeville: Cynic or Fool?" *Philosophical Quarterly,* 16 (1966), 221-32.

Shea, John S. "Introduction" to *Aesop Dress'd; or a Collection of Fables Writ in Familiar Verse* by Bernard Mandeville. (Augustan Reprint Society, No. 120.) Los Angeles, 1966.

Skarsten, A. K. "Nature in Mandeville." *Journal of English and Germanic Philology,* 53 (1954), 562-68.

Smith, LeRoy W. "Fielding and Mandeville: The 'War Against Virtue.' " *Criticism,* 3 (1961), 7-15.

Spengler, Joseph J. "Veblen and Mandeville Contrasted." *Zeitschrift des*

Instituts für Weltwirtschaft, 82 (1959), 35-65.

Talluri, B. "Cinquant'anni di critica intorno al pensiero di Bernardo de Mandeville." *Studi Senesi,* 63 (1951), 322-38.

—. "I limiti e le risorse speculative nel pensiero politico e morale di B. de Mandeville." *Studi Senesi,* 62 (1951), 95-111.

Vichert, Gordon S. "Bernard Mandeville and *A Dissertation upon Drunkenness.*" *Notes & Queries,* N.S. 11 (1964), 288-92.

—. "Some Recent Mandeville Attributions." *Philological Quarterly,* 45 (1966), 459-63.

—. "The Theory of Conspicuous Consumption in the 18th Century." In *The Varied Pattern: Studies in the 18th Century,* ed. Peter Hughes and David Williams. Toronto, 1971. Pp. 253-67.

Viner, Jacob. "Introduction" to *A Letter to Dion* (1732) by Bernard Mandeville. (Augustan Reprint Society, No. 41.) Los Angeles, 1953.

Wade, Ira O. *Studies on Voltaire: With Some Unpublished Papers of Mme du Châtelet.* Princeton, 1947.

Ward, H. Gordon. "An Unnoted Poem by Mandeville." *Review of English Studies,* 8 (1931), 73-6.

Willey, Basil. *The Eighteenth Century Background: Studies on the Idea of Nature in the Thought of the Period.* London, 1940; reprinted Boston, 1961.

Young, James Dean. "Mandeville: A Popularizer of Hobbes." *Modern Language Notes,* 74 (1959), 10-13.

Zirker, Malvin R. "Introduction" to *An Enquiry into the Causes of the Frequent Executions at Tyburn* (1725) by Bernard Mandeville. (Augustan Reprint Society, No. 105), Los Angeles, 1964.

CONTRIBUTORS

ROBERT ADOLPH, Associate Professor of English at York University, Toronto; author of *The Rise of Modern Prose Style* (M.I.T. Press, 1968); co-editor, *Canadian Review of American Studies*.

A. OWEN ALDRIDGE, Professor of Comparative Literature, University of Illinois; editor of *Comparative Literature Studies*; author of numerous articles and of books on Shaftesbury, Franklin, Jonathan Edwards and Paine; a biography, *Voltaire and the Century of Light* (Princeton) is in press.

RICHARD I. COOK, Professor of English at Kent State University; author of *Jonathan Swift as a Tory Pamphleteer* (U. of Washington Press, 1967); his book-length study of Mandeville has been published by Twayne, 1974.

HARRY T. DICKINSON, Reader in History, University of Edinburgh; author of *Bolingbroke* (Constable, 1970), *Walpole and the Whig Supremacy* (English Universities Press, 1973), *The Correspondence of Sir James Clavering* (Surtees Society, 1967), *Politics and Literature in the 18th Century* (Dent, 1974), and numerous articles in learned journals; Fellow of the Royal Historical Society.

J. A. W. GUNN, Professor in the Department of Political Studies, Queen's University, Ontario; author of *Politics and the Public Interest in the Seventeenth Century* (U. of Toronto Press, 1969), *Factions No More* (Frank Cass, 1972), and of articles in learned journals.

ROBERT H. HOPKINS, Professor of English, University of California at Davis; a founding editor of *Eighteenth-Century Studies* and author of scholarly articles and a book, *The True Genius of Oliver Goldsmith* (The Johns Hopkins University Press, 1969).

MALCOLM R. JACK, completed a dissertation on Mandeville at the London School of Economics is an author of articles and has been employed in the House of Commons.

E. D. JAMES, University Lecturer in French, St. John's College, Cambridge; author of articles on literature and religion in the period of French classicism, and of a book, *Pierre Nicole* (Nijhoff, 1972).

JOHN ROBERT MOORE, until his recent death, Distinguished Professor of Literature Emeritus at Indiana University; one of the world's foremost authorities on Defoe and bibliographer of Defoe; author of many articles and books on this subject.

PHILIP PINKUS, Professor of English, University of British Columbia; author of articles on Swift and Augustan satire; editor of *Jonathan Swift: A Selection of his Works* (Macmillan, 1965) and *Grub Street Stripped Bare* (Constable, 1968).

IRWIN PRIMER, Professor of English, Rutgers University, Newark; author of articles on Mandeville, Erasmus Darwin and Godwin; edited selections from *The Fable of the Bees* (Capricorn paperback, 1962).

W. A. SPECK, Reader in History, University of Newcastle upon Tyne; author of *Tory and Whig: the Struggle in the Constituencies,* 1701-1715 (Macmillan and Co., Ltd., 1970), and other studies in eighteenth-century political and social history.

G. S. ROUSSEAU, Associate Professor of English, U.C.L.A., an editor of the Iowa Edition of the writings of Smollett; co-author (with Marjorie Hope Nicolson) of *"This Long Disease my Life": Alexander Pope and the Sciences* (Princeton U. Press, 1968) and author of numerous studies in Augustan literature.

GORDON S. VICHERT, formerly Assistant Professor of English at McMaster University and now Secretary of the New Democratic Party, Ontario; author of articles and a dissertation on Mandeville (University of London, 1964).

INDEX

Names and subjects in the Selected Bibliography are not indexed. For any entry, page numbers printed in italics indicate a more significant discussion.

220   INDEX

Congreve, William: *Incognita*, 6
Constantine, Emperor, 47
courage (fortitude, bravery), 55, 120, 164
Courtines, Leo P., 134n
Craftsman, The, 91
Crane, R. S., 23n
Croll, Morris, 167
Cullen, Dr. William, 18n

Davenant, Charles, 122
Deckelmann, H., 43n, 103n
Defoe, Daniel, 67–8, 76–7, *119–25*, 158, 189;
  Giving Alms No Charity, 30; *Moll Flanders*,
  3; *Review of the Affairs of France*, 75n;
  Robinson Crusoe, viii–ix, xi
deism, 52, 137, 138, 145, 192, 196, 198
Dennis, John, 170, 174
Descartes, René (Cartesian), 49–50, 151
Dickens, Charles, 184
Dickson, P. G. M., 169
Diodorus Siculus, 132
Dissenters, 45, 77, 84–5, 87, 90, 109, 120
divine grace, 60, 64–5, 104, 174, 196–7, 199
Du Châtelet, Emilie, 142–3, 146, 153–4

Edwards, Thomas R., 80n, 137n
Ellsberg, Daniel, 210
empiricism, empirical, 35, 42, 177
envy, 71, 83, 159, 166, 200
Epicurean, 57–8
Erasmus, Desiderius: *The Praise of Folly*,
  205–6
Esprit, Jacques, 54n, 106, 156
evil, 60, 64, 102, 104
experience, vs. reason, 15n; 186, 192, 195

Feltham, Owen, 109n
Fiddes, Richard, 170
fideism, 48, 52, 196; *see also* skepticism
Fielding, Henry, x, 186, 188, 191, 192
Financial Revolution, 180, 184; *The Grumb-
  ling Hive* as a defense of, 169
flattery, 50, 55, 171–4
Fletcher, Andrew, 133n
Fontenelle, Bernard le Bovier de, 194
Foxon, D. F., [1]–2
France (government, society), 74–5, 84, 88
Francis of Sales, Saint, 53
free will and predestination, 48–9, 104
Frye, Northrop, viii *n*, 161
functionalism, 98, 117

Garman, Douglas, 121
Gassendi, Pierre, 50
George I, King of England, 89
Gibson, Edmund, Bishop of London, 61
Glock, J. P., 99
Glorious Revolution, 73–4, 78, 81, 114;
  Revolution Settlement, 85, 87, 95
God, 34, 44–8, 52, 69–70, 86, 102, 104–8,
  116–18, 150, 152, 156, 157, 164, 171, 175,
  179, 196, 198

Goldsmith, M. M., 40, 41n, 42, 43n, 93n
Goldsmith, Oliver, 186
Goldwater, Barry, 158
Gordon, Thomas, ix *n*, 94, 133n
Grampp, William D., 101n, 115n
Grean, Stanley, 117n
Greene, Donald, 127n
Greenleaf, W. H., 99n
Gregory the Great, Pope, 132–3

Hagstrum, Jean, 187
Halifax, George Savile, Marquis of, 3
Haller, Albrecht von, 156
happiness, 27, 61–2, 115, 160, 162, 166, 180,
  198
Harder, J. H., 23n
Harrington, James, 100; *Oceana*, 108, 132,
  133n
Harth, Phillip, xi, 57–8, 80n
Hatfield, Glenn, 192n
Hayek, F. A., xii–xiii, 80n, 97n
Helvétius, Claude Adrien, ix, 143
Herodotus, 132
Highmore, Dr., 17
Hill, Christopher, 173n
Hill, Sir John, 13, 14n, 17n
Hind, George, viii *n*, 166n
Hoadly, Benjamin, Bishop of Winchester, 77
Hobbes, Thomas (Hobbesian), 11, 53–4, 63,
  78, 131, 172–7, 179
Holbach, Paul Henri Thiry, Baron d', xi
Holland, the Dutch Republic, x, 12n, 72–5,
  81, 89, 119, 167; Shaftesbury and Bayle in,
  134; Leyden, ix, 11; Rotterdam, 44, 196
Holmes, Geoffrey, 81n
Honour, 53–5, 114, 129, 159, 164, 171, *187–
  92*, 203; definition of, 209
Hooker, Richard, 198–9
Horace, 166
human nature: *see* nature of man
Hume, David, xii, 18n, 176n
Hutcheson, Francis, 170, 190, 192
hypocrisy, 26, 33, 37, 55–9, 64–5, 67, 160,
  162, 170, 188, 192, 203–4, 206

immortality of the soul, 49, 50, 51, 150
individualism, 99, 101, 104, 109, 110, 112,
  114–16; possessive, 172–3, 185
irony, [vii], [1], 9, 25, 31, 162, 173–4, 191,
  201, 203, 205

James II, King of England, 66, 77
James, E. D., 137n, 138n
Jansenism, 43n, 47, 57, 63–4
Jauncy, J. (bookseller), 135
Jenyns, Soame, 182
Johnson, Samuel, x, 12, 182, 186, 206;
  Rasselas, 5
Jones, M. G., 181n
Julian, Emperor, 132
Juvenal, 161, 166